SOMEONE LIKE YOU

SANDY BARKER

Boldwood

First published in Great Britain in 2024 by Boldwood Books Ltd.

Copyright © Sandy Barker, 2024

Cover Design by Alexandra Allden

Cover Images: Shutterstock

Every effort has been made to obtain the necessary permissions with reference to copyright material, both illustrative and quoted. We apologise for any omissions in this respect and will be pleased to make the appropriate acknowledgements in any future edition.

A CIP catalogue record for this book is available from the British Library.

Paperback ISBN 978-1-80549-878-0

Large Print ISBN 978-1-80549-879-7

Hardback ISBN 978-1-80549-877-3

Ebook ISBN 978-1-80549-880-3

Kindle ISBN 978-1-80549-881-0

Audio CD ISBN 978-1-80549-872-8

MP3 CD ISBN 978-1-80549-873-5

Digital audio download ISBN 978-1-80549-875-9

This book is printed on certified sustainable paper. Boldwood Books is dedicated to putting sustainability at the heart of our business. For more information please visit https://www.boldwoodbooks.com/about-us/sustainability/

Boldwood Books Ltd, 23 Bowerdean Street, London, SW6 3TN

www.boldwoodbooks.com

For Ben
Thank you for the life we've made, which surpasses all my dreams.
Here's to many more adventures together...

PROLOGUE
SEVERAL MONTHS AGO

'And the winner of *Britain's Best Bakers: Festive Baking Spectacular*, taking home the coveted trophy and fifty thousand pounds is... Rafferty Delaney!'

Raff hadn't expected to win.

Even as, week by week, the judges had praised everything from his gingerbread house to his rugelach with homemade blackberry jam to his marzipan nativity scene, which had earned him a Grant Bakefield high-five, it hadn't seemed real. He was a marketing director who 'baked sometimes at the weekend'. What was he doing standing outside Britain's most famous barn accepting a trophy and an oversized bank cheque from Dame Vicky Harrington?

His fellow competitors, people he'd become friendly with over the past couple of months, gathered around him, slapping him on the back and kissing him on the cheek, offering their congratulations. He looked over at his finale bake, a three-tier, Christmas-themed wedding cake, seeing it through fresh eyes. It really was spectacular, and he swelled with pride.

Grinning, he turned to the audience, looking for his invited guests.

His best friend, Gaby, was in the front row, clapping her hands above her head and woohoo-ing loudly, and next to Gaby, his Aunt CiCi beamed at him proudly. But where was Winnie? She was supposed to be sitting with Gaby and Aunt CiCi, but her seat was empty. He cast his eyes about – maybe she'd come to join him on the small stage – but he couldn't see her.

A camera on a huge crane swung back from the stage, capturing the final shot from the season that would begin airing in three months' time, and the director yelled, 'Cut. And that's a wrap, everyone!'

Raff stepped down from the stage, awkwardly carrying the trophy and the cheque, and headed towards Gaby and his aunt.

'I am so proud of you!' Gaby said, her North-American twang lingering on the 'O' of 'so'. 'I knew you'd win!' She threw her arms around his neck and hugged him tightly, but with both hands full, he couldn't return it.

'Bravo, my boy,' said Aunt CiCi, her eyes glistening with unshed tears. 'I'll have you working at Baked to Perfection before you know it.'

Raff laughed nervously and dipped his chin modestly. 'We'll see, Aunty. Um, have you seen Winnie?' he asked them, scanning the small crowd. Maybe she'd gone to the loo. If so, the timing was rubbish, but she could hardly be blamed for nature calling.

'Actually, no,' said Gaby with a pained expression. 'She didn't show up.'

'Oh,' he said. 'Something must have happened.' He set down the trophy and the cheque on an empty chair, then fished his phone out of his front trouser pocket and turned it on. There was a message from Winnie:

Sorry but I can't do this any more

He blinked at the screen, his brain taking a moment to divine the meaning of those eight words.

'Raff? Is everything okay?' Gaby asked.

He held up the phone so she could read it.

'What? She's breaking up with you via text?' she shrieked.

Raff cringed and looked around, hoping Gaby hadn't drawn attention to them.

'She never,' said his aunt, leaning closer to read his phone. She gasped and the two women exchanged a weighty look.

'Sorry, Raff,' Gaby said, reaching up and rubbing his arm in commiseration.

'I don't understand,' he said, staring at the ground. 'Do you really think she'd... And *today*? I should... Should I message her?' he asked, lifting his gaze to meet Gaby's eye.

'No, hun,' she replied, grasping his arm. 'It's pretty clear from her absence on one of the biggest days of your life that she means it. Don't reply. She doesn't deserve it. She doesn't deserve *you*.'

'What do you mean, she doesn't deserve me? I thought you liked Winnie.'

'I...' Gaby expelled a sigh, then glanced at Aunt CiCi, who nodded her agreement. 'I've never liked her,' she said to him.

'Nor me,' said Aunt CiCi. 'I've never thought she was good enough for you.'

'Oh.'

It was all he could think to say, because what else was there when your closest friend and the aunt who raised you didn't like the woman you'd intended to propose to that night?

1

GABY

'Gaby, it's back on!' CiCi calls out from the living room.

Attempting to hurry, I twist the cork so forcefully that frothy wine cascades over the rim, spilling everywhere. 'Shit.' I look around for something to clean up the mess and try tearing a sheet from a roll of paper towels one-handed. Only it isn't a one-handed task and now I've unrolled enough to sop up a mid-sized murder scene.

'What *are* you doing?' asks Raff.

'Help!' I wail.

I am hands-down the clumsiest person I know – mini disasters like this one are par for the course – but they're about to announce Raff as the winner, so no time for my typical ha-ha-I'm-such-a-hot-mess brand of self-deprecation.

With a soft chuckle, Raff helps by tearing off a couple of sheets.

'Thanks,' I say, mopping up wine from the counter, my hands, and finally the bottle. I deposit the soggy paper towels in the trash, then catch sight of the shitty job Raff's done of winding up the extra sheets. When she sees that, CiCi will emit a sigh so loud, my parents will hear her back in Seattle.

'Gaby! Raff! They're about to announce the winner!' yells our best friend, Freya.

'Coming!' we reply in unison.

'Are you ready?' I ask him.

'Mixed feelings,' he replies, his lips wrenching into a wry smile.

'It might not be that noticeable.'

'A confused me looking for my absent girlfriend while the camera's zoomed in on my face? Yes, you're probably right.'

'Will you two please hurry up?!' Freya yells again – and Freya rarely raises her voice.

'After you,' I say.

Reluctantly, Raff heads back to the living room and I follow. While he folds himself onto the floor in front of the huge modular sofa, I zip around and top up everyone's glasses then take my seat next to Freya. She claps her hands under her chin with excitement.

It's corny, all of us pretending we don't know who wins, but the impending absent-Winnie drama aside, this is also fun. And even though CiCi and I were there on the day of filming, we weren't allowed inside the barn, so getting to see how Raff made his winning cake has been incredible.

'You are proper sweating, you are,' says Raff's Uncle Devin, his eyes fixed on the TV version of Raff.

'Well, yes, because they filmed in the middle of August during a *heatwave*, but we still had to wear festive jumpers!'

'Shh, this is it,' says CiCi.

We fall silent, the rest of us leaning closer to the TV while Raff gnaws on a thumbnail in my periphery.

'And the winner of *Britain's Best Bakers: Festive Baking Spectacular*, taking home the coveted trophy and fifty thousand pounds is... Rafferty Delaney!' says the host, a moderately funny, middle-aged comedian who dyes his hair black.

We whoop and cheer as if we're genuinely surprised and Raff's cheeks flood with colour, a wide grin spreading across his face.

'All right, all right, no autographs, please,' he says, holding up his hands, pretending to fend off the hoards.

Onscreen, Raff receives one of those giant novelty cheques and a gaudy trophy, then he's swamped by his fellow contestants. Only, as he's the tallest person onstage and (literally) head and shoulders above everyone else, it's painfully obvious the moment he clocks Winnie's absence from the crowd. His eyes narrow in confusion as he scans the small crowd, then his face falls, switching from elation to disappointment in an instant. The moment passes quickly enough, a back slap from a short, stocky man restoring the smile to his face.

I catch Freya's eye and jerk my head towards the kitchen. She nods, and as the theme song plays and the credits roll, we sneak off, leaving Freya's boyfriend, Freddie, rapid-firing questions at Raff.

'That was brutal,' Freya whispers when we're out of earshot.

'I told you.'

'I never liked Winnie,' she says with a scowl.

'No kidding?' I say sarcastically. 'You've never said anything.'

We lock eyes, holding each other's gaze, then chuckle. Freya is the nicest person I've ever met and for her not to like someone *and* admit it is a huge deal.

'I can't *believe* he was going to propose to her after only six months. And can you imagine having her as a pseudo sister-in-law for the rest of our lives?' she asks. 'Christmases, birthdays, holidays...'

'God no. It was bad enough hanging out with her.'

'Or *not* hanging out, as it were,' retorts Freya. Winnie didn't exactly like socialising with us. Throughout their entire relationship, Raff and I rarely got together outside of work.

'What are you two gossiping about?' CiCi enters carrying a picked-over platter of antipasto.

'Nothing,' I reply.

'Winnie,' Freya replies immediately after. If Freya were a Viking in a former life – a possibility considering her heritage – she'd be 'Freya the Benevolent and Guileless', as she's a stalwart of kindness and honesty.

'Horse-faced cow,' CiCi mutters under her breath, but still loud enough for us to hear.

'CiCi! That's not very nice. It's not her fault she looks like that,' scolds Freya. As I said – kind, but also honest.

CiCi chuckles. 'Fine, that wasn't the nicest thing to say. But ending things with our Raff the way she did – and by bloody text message! *Surely* I'm entitled to call her a cow after that?'

'Hmm – fair, I suppose,' Freya concedes.

'And you disliked her as much as I did,' adds CiCi, wagging her finger at Freya.

'Also fair,' says Freya.

'Okay, so none of us could stand her – are we all in agreement?' I ask, eliciting self-aware laughter from them both.

I've lived in England eight years, and I love it, but I still don't understand the convoluted way people express themselves here – all that understatement and politeness. CiCi is one of the few English people I know who tells it like it is – maybe the only one.

'Agreed,' says CiCi, 'and if I ever see that little trollop again, I'll—'

'Okay, okay...' I interject before she starts plotting revenge on Winnie. She may be sixty-something and only five-two, but *I* wouldn't cross her.

'Actually, I've been thinking...' says Freya. She trails off like usual, leaving her thought incomplete and us hanging.

'About?' I prod.

'Matching Raff,' she replies in a conspiratorial whisper.

Ah, of course. Freya is a professional matchmaker, Raff is our closest friend, and he's been moping about ever since Winnie ended their relationship. I should have seen this coming.

And it's not a *terrible* idea.

'But you've been a matchmaker for years. Why now?' asks CiCi, eyeing Freya curiously.

'Because of *that*,' Freya whispers, her arm extended towards the living room. 'Raff was putting on a brave face just now, but you could tell it still hurts – the breakup.'

'Hmm,' CiCi murmurs, a concerned frown nestling on her face.

'And think about it,' Freya continues. 'Normally, Raff would start seeing someone new within a week – maybe two – but it's been *ages*.'

'Yeah,' I say. 'Three months – give or take.'

'Exactly. He's obviously still devastated by what Winnie did and if I can help in any way, then...' She trails off again, looking between me and CiCi.

'I take your point, but are you allowed to do that?' CiCi asks. 'Match one of your closest friends?'

She edges closer, her eyes on Freya as she fixes the messy paper towels. I *knew* she wouldn't be able to let that slide. Her kitchen looks like something out of *House and Garden* – even *after* hosting a celebratory gathering for Raff. Fitting, I guess, for one of the UK's most successful bakers.

'Well, no,' Freya responds, 'but I could refer him to a colleague. Do you remember Poppy?' she asks me.

'Oh, yeah, the Aussie gal. I like her – she's cool.'

'I can ask her,' Freya says. 'It'll depend on her case load, of course. We'd also have to get approval from Saskia and Paloma,' she says, referring to the agency's founders and her bosses, 'but don't forget I get a gratis referral each year.'

Oh, I haven't forgotten. I've known about Freya's annual freebie since she left the marketing firm where we met and became a matchmaker. It was one of the first things she told me about her new job because she wanted to match *me*. I declined so vehemently – I'm strictly a casual dater – that she never offered again.

'What would that entail, Freya?' CiCi asks. 'Do you just set Raff up on lots of dates and see how it goes?'

'Er, not exactly...'

While Freya always maintains client confidentiality by anonymising identifying details, she'll sometimes spill about her juicier cases to me and Raff. It's been fun to get a peek into such a fascinating field. There's also a lot of cross-over between match-making and marketing: primarily, gaining an understanding of what people want – even if it's different to what they *say* they want – then giving it to them.

If I had *any* interest in HEAs, as Freya calls them – or 'happily ever afters' to us mere mortals – then I'd leap at the chance to work for the Ever After Agency. It sounds like a blast.

But I am not what you would call 'a romantic'.

CiCi prompts Freya to expound upon 'not exactly' and Freya explains how matching Raff might work – essentially, building a comprehensive profile of Raff, then vetting and ranking potentials matches, and *then* the part where he's set up on dates.

'The first two steps are the most time-consuming,' she says, 'but the more thorough we are in the planning stages, the more chance of success.'

'Chance of success for what?' asks Raff, who has somehow snuck up on us.

Our open-mouthed heads turn in sync as if we're those clowns at the carnival – the ones with the pivoting heads you throw balls into.

'We were...' I start.

'Oh, nothing,' says CiCi, waving him off.

'Finding you a match,' Freya replies.

'Oh, for god's sake,' I mutter. Sometimes I wish she had at least a *scrap* of guile.

Raff splutters out a nervous laugh. 'Uh, no thanks,' he says, looking at me then CiCi to share the joke.

Only it's not a joke, which becomes apparent almost immediately and the smile falls from his face. He clears his throat. 'Seriously?' he asks Freya. 'That's what you were talking about? As if I'm some sort of desperate charity case?'

'No!' we all chorus.

'And you know my clients are anything but desperate charity cases,' Freya asserts, but Raff seems unconvinced.

'What's all this then?' asks Devin, entering the kitchen. He sets a decimated bowl of chips on the counter, and I fish for crumbs – there's just enough for a mouthful.

'Apparently, they're in here conspiring to find me a girlfriend,' Raff replies, his hands placed indignantly on his hips. He looks ridiculous.

'Okay, drama queen,' I say, my hand over my mouth. I swallow the chips. 'We're not *conspiring*.'

'We only want you to be happy, love,' CiCi chimes in.

'And to be with someone who deserves you,' says Freya. 'Because you're *wonderful*, Raff.'

'Yes, you're the thinking person's crumpet,' adds Devin with a devilish grin.

This portrayal of Raff started doing the rounds on social media the week after episode one aired. The show's producers leapt on it – and who could blame them? It's a *genius* marketing angle. And so, Raff, with his strawberry-blond curls, wide-set green eyes, and crooked smile, has become something of a heartthrob across Britain, particularly amongst straight women and gay men.

'Oh god,' Raff groans.

He breaks into a reluctant smile, shaking his head as the rest of us chuckle.

'That's a good point, love,' CiCi says to Devin. She turns to Raff. 'No need for a matchmaker when half of Britain's banging down your door, is there?'

'It's hardly— There was that *one* time,' Raff retorts with a reluctant smile.

He's talking about an incident at Tesco where someone recognised him in the fresh produce department, and he ended up signing autographs and taking selfies for twenty minutes. I'm positive he wishes he hadn't told us about that.

'Why are you all laughing? This isn't funny!' Raff insists, only it *is* funny and he knows it, which is why he starts laughing too.

'Have we moved the party in here, then?' Freddie asks as he enters.

'Sorry, Freddie, we didn't mean to forget about you,' Freya replies. He appears to take her comment in stride even though it's mildly insulting. 'We're talking about Raff's love life.'

'Can we not? *Please?*' whines Raff, setting off another chorus of chuckles at his expense. Freddie pats him on the shoulder the way men do to show solidarity, and Raff must see this as an in for getting Freddie onside.

'Did you know your girlfriend has this ludicrous idea about matching me?' he asks.

'Well, she is a top-notch matchmaker and you are "sans girlfriend",' Freddie replies, making air quotes. 'So why not?'

Raff's shoulders slump a full inch. '*Et tu, Brute?*' he asks, but Freddie only shrugs. 'So, let me get this straight,' says Raff, addressing all of us. 'I've just been named Britain's Best Baker—'

'Well, you were three months ago,' interjects Devin, but Raff silences him with a scowl. 'Sorry,' says Devin, shooting CiCi a look that says, 'Oops'.

'As I was saying, I've just been named Britain's Best Baker *on the telly*,' Raff says, pointedly clarifying that it's now public knowledge, 'and all you lot can talk about is that I'm single. Not successful or accomplished, not perfectly happy, thank you very much. But *single*.'

'Oh, love,' says CiCi. 'Of course, we know how successful you are – *and* happy,' she adds.

But what's left unspoken is that everyone in this room – except maybe Freddie – knows that Raff is only truly happy when he's in love – or *believes* he is. Including Raff.

'How about this?' he says, turning to Freya, a defiant glint in his eyes. 'Go ahead and match me.'

'Really?' she asks, surprised.

'Really. If I'm such a miserable, lonely git—'

'Hey, you're none of things,' I say vehemently. CiCi and Freya also protest but he talks over us.

'Wait, where was I? Oh yes, a miserable, lonely git,' he says again, the tone of self-deprecating humour ebbing from his voice. '*And* if you're so convinced that you can save me from my misery,' he says to Freya, 'then how can I say no?'

'Seriously?'

'Sure, why not?' Raff replies sarcastically, throwing his arms out wide.

This conversation is stupid *and* it's upsetting Raff. We need to shut it down.

I catch Freya's eye and lift my hand to draw it across my neck – the universal sign for 'STOP!' – but her eyes have taken on an excited glow. *Crap!* She's taken Raff at his word, but it's obvious he's only saying yes to shut us up. He doesn't mean it.

'Only I don't want to know anything about it. I don't even want to know it's happening,' he adds, his voice strained.

'Know it's...? Wait...' says Freya, her head tilted. 'How do you mean?'

'Yeah,' I throw in, now curious. 'How can Freya match you without you knowing?'

'I don't know. I'll leave that to the professionals to figure out. But I'm not going on any more bloody dates. I'm done with dates!' he declares.

'To be absolutely clear,' says Freya, that gleam still in her eyes, 'as long as I avoid setting you up on dates, you'll let me match you?'

Raff expels a sigh. 'Freya, if you're positive you can find me a match without me having to go on any dates, then be my guest. I honestly don't care.'

Freya emits a high-pitched, excited peep. Yup, she definitely thinks he's serious. I'll need to intervene before she starts lining up eligible women in the driveway.

'Right,' says CiCi, draping a dish towel over one shoulder, 'have we sufficiently celebrated your crowning as Britain's Best Baker?' she asks Raff.

'As in, this is your polite way of asking us to leave?' he responds.

'Exactly.'

And just like that, the topic of Raff's love life is closed, and we're being ousted. Gotta love a hostess who essentially says, 'I love you, but please get out of my house.' I wish I could be as forthright as CiCi. If she taught lessons, I'd sign up in a heartbeat.

As always, our offers to help clean up are met with pursed lips and a knitted brow from CiCi and a friendly, 'No, thanks, we'll manage,' from Devin.

Freya and Freddie leave first to walk to the train station a quarter mile away. But as I'm a total wuss when it comes to walking through a torrential downpour, I'm springing for an Uber back to

Kingston. Although, it's not that far – CiCi and Devin only live in Weybridge – and Raff will split it with me; his apartment is only a few streets away from mine.

I tell Raff when the app says our driver is three minutes away and we head to the foyer to say our goodbyes.

Stooping to land a kiss on CiCi's cheek, he says, 'Thanks again, Aunt CiCi. It really was lovely.'

'You're welcome, love,' she replies. 'And let's talk next week, yes? You've been dodging me for far too long.' She flashes a smile that takes the edge off her wagging finger.

Raff straightens to his full height. 'Yes, yes, all right,' he replies with trepidation. Something's up but I'll ask about it later.

When the car arrives, we dash from the front door to the driveway, getting drenched in mere seconds. I slide into the backseat first, then Raff climbs in, slamming the door behind him. The driver confirms that I'm Gaby and as we back out of the driveway, I ask, 'What's going on with CiCi? What have you been dodging?'

He sighs. 'Aunt CiCi wants me to come work at Baked to Perfection.'

'What, like part-time? How would you even fit that in?' I ask with a laugh.

'No, not part-time. She wants me to leave my job. She wants us to be partners.'

'Partners— Wait, *what*?'

2

GABY

'Are you considering it?' I ask, and our eyes meet across the backseat.

'You know how you can be completely oblivious to what you want until it's presented to you and then you realise it's all you've ever wanted but you're terrified of taking the leap?'

'Not really,' I respond with a slight smile.

'Well, it's like that,' he says.

'So, you want to do it, but you're scared?'

'In a nutshell, yes.'

'Happy to be a sounding board if you like,' I offer.

'Maybe later?' he replies.

'Sure,' I say, faking a supportive smile even though my stomach is in knots.

Raff is not only one of my two best friends, he's also my work husband. If he leaves to partner with CiCi, it will be far worse than when Freya left to become a matchmaker.

I'll be on my own.

Well, not *technically* on my own. Global Reach is a multi-national marketing firm with thousands of employees across the world. I'll still be part of a team, but Raff is my (professional) soft place to land, a necessity when the work is fast-paced and always high stakes. For the most part, it's interesting, and on any given day, I enjoy what I do, but it can also be overwhelming at times.

That's why I'm grateful to Raff and Freya for 'adopting' me.

Eight years ago, when I transferred from the Seattle office to London, I knew no one. Not a soul. And, as luck would have it, I joined a team that included Raff and Freya, who were already a firm duo, and from week one, we became a tightknit trio.

I imagine they took pity on me – poor, helpless waif. And rightly so. I was mid-twenties, far from home, living in a city ten times the size of the one I'd left behind, and *American*. The culture shock was so extreme, it knocked me sideways.

Seattle and London may both be famous for their rainfall, but that's where the similarities end. Where Seattle is low-key and chill, London is fast-paced and... well, the opposite of chill. Moving here was the steepest learning curve of my life and there is no way I would have made it through my first year without Raff and Freya patiently teaching me the ins and outs of London life.

And professional life. No showing up to work in Central London in jeans and a T-shirt – even on non-client-facing days. Oh, the horror! On the Monday of my second week, Freya caught up to me right as I was about to walk into the building. 'You *cannot* wear that to work,' she said, steering me away from the revolving doors.

We called in late – both blaming the trains, even though I'd taken the underground – sorry, the *Tube*. Then she led me to the nearest Marks & Spencer where I bought a cheap suit and an even cheaper blouse. I had decent work clothes back at my accommodation but, according to Freya, this would be faster.

When we arrived at work thirty minutes late, our manager gave us the side-eye but said nothing. I made sure never to be late again and to always dress for business.

I was so sad when Freya left to work at the Ever After Agency. Even though we still hung out socially, her absence was a gaping hole in my work life. Raff felt it too. I'm guessing that's why we ended up even closer than ever, and he evolved from colleague/friend to work husband.

I need to spitball an idea: Raff's my guy. I need to complain about Janine (an extremely annoying colleague in another team): Raff lends a friendly ear. I need another set of eyes on a presentation that's missing something: Raff takes it to the next level.

He's also a half-decent gossip, but I'm positive that's only to humour me.

I watch his profile as he gazes out the rain-splattered window, his jawline tense. I can't imagine being torn between two professions – especially when they're polar opposites. Raff may be a marketing whizz but he's also an incredible baker. I couldn't say how many times I've shown up at his apartment and sat down to the best pie I've ever had or the most chocolaty cake or perfectly baked macarons...

But no matter how hard it would be on me if we didn't work together, baking is Raff's passion and if he wants to partner with CiCi, then I will support him 100 per cent.

'It sounds like an incred—'

'I think I want to—'

'Go ahead,' I tell him.

He grins at me. 'I think I want to do it. It scares the bejeezus out of me but...' He shrugs, baring his teeth – his oh-my-god-what-am-I-doing? face.

'*But* you'll regret it if you don't.'

'Yes, I think I would. You know I was properly pissed off when Aunt CiCi entered me in *Britain's Best Bakers* behind my back...'

'*No way!*' I quip, pretending to be incredulous.

When the producers called out of the blue, asking Raff to come in for an audition, he was baffled. When he put two and two together and got CiCi, baffled turned into furious. I was there when he confronted her – it wasn't pretty.

'All right, I *may* have overreacted.'

'Mmm.'

'But, of course, she was right.'

'Mm-hmm.'

Ever since I've known him, Raff has wanted to be on that show, only if any of us told him to apply, he balked. CiCi did what she had to do to nudge him over the line.

'And now you've got an opportunity to make baking your career,' I add.

'Yes. And if nothing else, it will help keep my mind off losing Winnie. Can't mope about feeling sorry for myself if I'm starting a new venture.'

'Right,' I agree, unsure of what else to say. I *could* go with, 'Hey, Raff, maybe don't make a major life decision because your (boring, snobbish) girlfriend dumped you.' I'm sure he'd *love* that.

And the mention of Winnie sends me back to Freya's idea.

If Raff was pissed at his aunt for applying to a TV show on his behalf – a show he'd dreamt of being on for *years* – how pissed will he be if Freya attempts to match him?

I really need to talk Freya out of it.

* * *

I didn't talk Freya out if it. Instead, it's late afternoon on Monday and I'm at Freya's agency for an 'informal chat' with her colleague, Poppy.

I've been to the Ever After Agency several times over the years – mostly to meet Freya after work. It's a modern, open-plan office that occupies the top floor of a building overlooking the Thames in

Richmond. We're in one of the meeting rooms, which has a view of the river, and Poppy is leaning against the windowsill listening intently to Freya.

I've hung out with Poppy before – so has Raff – and she's an easy-going, affable gal who comes out with the most hilarious Australian expressions. She once said yes to a glass of wine because her throat was 'drier than a dead dingo's donger'. I'm sure I'll remember that for the rest of my life.

And she's married to the best-looking guy I've ever seen (and I'm not exaggerating). His name is Tristan and they were matched through the agency – there was an inheritance and he needed to get married in a month or something. Anyway, they're one of those couples they write romcoms about – madly in love, only have eyes for each other... If I *were* a romantic, their relationship would be #couplegoals.

'So, what do you think?' Freya asks Poppy when she finishes outlining her plan. Since Saturday afternoon at CiCi and Devin's, it has grown legs, arms, and a torso, including an absurd suggestion that we wear disguises to spy on Raff.

Poppy looks to me, wearing a curious expression. 'I'm more interested in what *you* think,' she says.

'Oh, I...' I look over at Freya, who nods at me enthusiastically. Only if I answer honestly, she's not going to like what I have to say.

'Any reservations?' Poppy adds. 'From your reaction, it seems like you weren't across some of the details till now.'

Poppy is also super sharp. Freya once told me her ability to read people is second to none at the agency – something to do with her being a psychologist before she became a matchmaker.

'Reservations, uh... yes,' I reply, and she nods in understanding. Her eyes dart towards Freya then back to me, telegraphing that I need to speak up.

She's right and with a sigh, I turn to Freya. 'Hun, I'm sorry, but this is insane.' She visibly deflates. 'Well-intentioned, absolutely,' I hurry to add, 'and I'm with you on the whole Raff-deserves-better thing...' To Poppy, I say, 'It's impossible to exaggerate how much we disliked Winnie.'

'Uh, I'd say Freya made that pretty clear,' Poppy says, her mouth twitching at the corners.

'But, even so,' I say to Freya, 'you've got us running around London in disguise, spying on Raff... If he caught us...' Now I'm doing a Freya and leaving my thoughts half unsaid.

'But he deserves to be happy,' she insists.

'Totally, without question. It's just... what if he gets pissed at us for interfering in his love life?'

'But he said to go ahead,' she replies earnestly.

'He was kidding, Frey!'

She frowns. Nope, that's a pout. My best friend is pouting like a little kid.

'Can I step in here?' asks Poppy.

'Fine,' Freya replies tersely. This obviously isn't how she saw the conversation going.

'*Please*,' I say, hoping Poppy will be the voice of reason.

'I've met Raff a few times, but it's not like I've ever quizzed him on his philosophy of love – those were social occasions. Still, from everything I've heard – including today – he does seem like a true romantic, someone who loves love.'

'Meaning?' I ask.

'Meaning that from my limited perspective, I'd say Raff longs to be in a relationship – so much so, he'll settle for one that isn't right for him.'

'*None* of them have been right for him,' Freya mumbles.

'That only gives more weight to my theory,' states Poppy. 'How did he meet Winnie?' she asks us.

'Flutter,' we reply together.

'He's been on other dating apps,' I add, 'but he said the women on Flutter were more interested in relationships than... well, *sex*.'

Poppy nods. 'That's our experience too. Quite a few of our potential matches come from Flutter – and a couple of other apps that focus more on love than casual dating or hookups,' she says, revealing a facet of matchmaking I hadn't considered before – where the matches come from.

Freya catches my eye. She knows I use those apps – the casual dating ones, not the ones solely for hookups – but I trust her not to mention it to Poppy. Some things are sacrosanct between best friends.

'Anyway,' Poppy continues, 'taking everything I know into consideration, including Raff being on Flutter *and* planning to propose to Winnie only six months after they started dating... I'd say there's a strong chance he wants to find real, lasting love.'

'Wait – what are you saying?' I ask her.

'I'm saying that I can see Freya's point.'

'Hah!' Freya exclaims, being uncharacteristically smug.

'Rude!' I exclaim back.

'Agreed, Frey, and calm the farm,' says Poppy, busting out one of her Australianisms. 'You may have made your point, but there are a *lot* of other considerations. Mostly, that I'm not wholly convinced this is a good idea.'

Oh, thank god.

'Why?' asks Freya.

'*Because* matching someone who doesn't want to be matched – that's setting us up for a fall – *all* of us, especially Raff. He could get hurt, Frey, and if this blows up in our faces, it could ruin your friendship.'

Two-four-six-eight, who do we appreciate? P-O-P-P-Y! Poppy! She really *is* the voice of reason. Now we just need Freya to listen.

'But you'll consider it?' Freya asks, hopeful.

'I'll consider it. But to say yes, I'll need to be convinced Raff is on board – even subconsciously.'

I hadn't thought of that – Raff wanting Freya to match him, but not realising it.

'And if we are doing this,' she continues, 'I *definitely* won't have you traipsing around London in disguise. This isn't *Mission Impossible* and you're not Tom Cruise.'

'Hah!' I say to Freya, and we both crack up, her with a self-deprecating eye roll.

'So, what now?' she asks Poppy excitedly, getting ahead of herself again.

'Now I figure out how to be sure – about Raff's true aim,' Poppy replies.

'I could just ask him,' says Freya.

'No,' Poppy and I reply together.

Freya looks between us. 'Why not?'

'Do you want to take this one?' Poppy asks me.

I turn to Freya, quickly assembling my argument. I've *got* to get through to her.

'Because of what you said at CiCi and Devin's – about Raff still being devastated by the breakup. Think about it, Frey. For years now, we've seen Raff go from one relationship to the next looking for "the one". Then there was Winnie – and yes, she was a piece of work and totally wrong for him – but he clearly loved her enough to propose. It might be too soon to be matching him with someone else.'

She gives me one of her I'm-not-sure-I-agree frowns.

'Besides,' I add hurriedly, 'he's recently come off this win, he's about to change careers... Maybe Raff doesn't want his true love sprung on him in the middle of everything else that's going on.'

Freya's still frowning, but her head bobs in a short, sharp nod as if she's finally getting it.

I turn to Poppy. 'Look, everything you've said today... it makes a lot of sense. Even though Raff *was* kidding when he said to go ahead—'

'He wasn't k—'

'Let me finish, Frey.'

'Fine,' she replies gloomily.

'Even though I'm positive about that, there's something *you* said earlier, Poppy – about him wanting this subconsciously – and I see how that could be true.'

'Wait – so, you're saying yes?' Freya asks me, perking up. 'You'll help?'

'*If* this is happening, I'll help,' I say. I'm still reluctant, but it would be worse if this plan went ahead and I wasn't involved.

Freya misses the hesitancy in my voice and grins at me.

'So, anything you need right now – from us, I mean?' I ask Poppy.

Freya springs out of her chair, bellowing, 'Be right back,' as she shoots out the door.

Poppy chuckles. 'I can't say I've ever seen her this excited about a case,' she says.

'Me neither – or anything else for that matter. Freya's usually the subdued, introverted one in our group.'

'I'll do my best to keep her in check. This could all be moot, though. She still needs Saskia and Paloma to sign off. And if they do, there will be strict parameters around Freya's involvement.'

'Okay.' I don't tell Poppy that I'm half-rooting for their bosses to say no, putting an end to this thing entirely.

'Got it,' says Freya, bursting back into the meeting room. She holds up a fat stack of paper.

'What in god's name is that?' I ask.

'That,' says Poppy, 'is your homework.'

'Huh?'

'The client questionnaire,' replies Freya. 'Because Raff wants us to go ahead without his input' – I don't correct her that this 'fact' is still in dispute – 'we'll need to complete it for him.'

'Wonderful,' I say sarcastically.

'Um, Frey? Maybe wait till you've got the go-ahead?' Poppy suggests, and I could kiss her. Any reprieve from this insanity is welcomed.

Predictably, Freya pouts again. 'All right. But as soon as they say yes, we're getting to work,' she tells me. 'Between the two of us, we should be able to answer most questions. And if we get stuck, we can call CiCi.'

Poppy looks at me quizzically.

'His aunt,' I tell her.

'Ahh, right. Okay, I'm off like a bucket of prawns in the hot sun – I've got a hubby, friends, and a kitty waiting at home for me. Freya, keep me posted and, Gaby, I'll see you soon.'

'Thanks, Poppy. See you.'

'Bye,' says Freya, throwing her arms around Poppy's neck. 'You're the best!' Poppy returns the hug, then leaves.

'How many pages is that thing?' I ask Freya.

'Only fifty-eight,' she replies matter-of-factly.

'Terrific,' I mutter.

3

POPPY

'I'm here, I'm here, I'm here!' I call out as I enter our flat. Staying after work to talk to Freya and her bestie, Gaby, has made me later than I'd hoped.

I kick off my heels, dump my handbag on the hallstand, and shrug out of my coat and hang it up. When I whip around, I discover *my* bestie, Shaz, her girlfriend, Lauren, and my husband all watching me with amusement.

'Hi, lovelies,' I say, breaking into a wide smile. I duck around the breakfast bar and plant a kiss on Shaz's cheek, then Lauren's. I ruffle the fur on Saffron's head, and she leaps from Lauren's lap to the floor in protest.

'Little minx,' I say under my breath. Our cat is madly in love with Tristan, will suck up to anyone who visits, including Tristan's ice queen of a mother, but she barely tolerates me – the person who loves her most.

'Hi, darling,' says Tristan, coming around from the kitchen. Even wearing an 'I love Tasmania' apron – a gift from Mum and Dad last Christmas – he looks handsome. He lands a soft, lingering kiss on my lips and any residual stress from my workday washes away.

My job is incredible, but helping people achieve their HEAs comes with the hefty weight of responsibility. I cherish my down-time, especially when I get to spend it with people – and a certain feline – I love.

I climb onto the stool next to Shaz, and Tristan, who's now back in the kitchen, slides a glass of white wine across the countertop – he knows me so well. I blow him a kiss and he winks back. I take a sip – it's my new fave, a Soave from northern Italy.

'Client meeting run late?' asks Shaz.

'Sort of. You know Freya?'

She and Lauren nod – they've met Freya and her boyfriend, Freddie, a few times.

'She wants me to match one of her best friends.'

'Ooh, is it Gaby?' asks Lauren. ''Cause she is...' She waggles her eyebrows suggestively.

'Hey! I'm right here,' says Shaz, feigning indignation.

'You think she's hot as well,' Lauren quips back, and Shaz concedes with a shrug.

Gaby *is* very attractive. She has a heart-shaped face, huge brown eyes, an upturned button nose, and full lips, and wears her wavy, chocolate-brown-with-caramel-highlights hair in a shoulder-length bob. She once told me that she inherited her frame – petite and compact with slim hips and lean, muscular limbs – from her mother. But I also know from Freya that she maintains it by working out a few times a week. She's just not one of those people who talks non-stop about how much they exercise.

'It's not Gaby,' I tell them. 'It's Raff.'

'He's the bloke who just won *Britain's Best Bakers*,' Tristan says over his shoulder as he stirs a giant pot on the stove. From the aroma, it's goulash – perfect for a wintery night. 'He deserved to win.'

BBB, as we call it, is one of the few TV shows Tristan watches avidly. I encourage this near obsession for selfish reasons, as the baking challenges frequently inspire him to try new dishes. (Tristan's the home chef in our family, whereas my kitchen-based abilities end with pouring cereal into a bowl and adding milk.)

'Oh, yeah, I know who he is,' says Shaz. She taps on her phone and brings up the *BBB* Instagram account, then shows us a post about Raff's win.

Lauren reaches over to scroll through the comments. 'Looks like you've got at least three hundred takers here, Poppy.'

'Yeah, he's become a bit of a pseudo-celeb-slash-heartthrob over the past few months,' I reply.

'Do people still say that, Poppy? Heartthrob?' Lauren teases.

I shrug. 'Better than "stud muffin",' I reply.

'Oh hell, yes.'

'Ha-ha!' barks Shaz, who's still reading the comments. 'Listen to this one: "Rafferty Delaney is the hottest thing since sliced bread".' The three of us groan at the terrible joke.

The topic of Raff now exhausted, Shaz goes back to the story she was telling Tristan when I arrived home about their weekend away to the Cotswolds. For some reason, they were shocked by how cold it was – imagine cold weather in November! – and spent the entire weekend snuggled up inside the B&B (the poor things).

I only half listen as I sip my wine, happily observing how they are together, especially how contented Shaz is. This relationship is a far cry from the shitshow that made her want to leave Melbourne and start a new life here in London – with me in tow, also heartbroken. *And* any of the shitshows since.

Although, it wasn't all smooth sailing for Shaz and Lauren, and

I did my part to help Shaz admit her feelings by playing agony aunt and devil's advocate in equal measures.

But this is one aspect of being a matchmaker I've struggled with. Just because I'm a professional matchmaker doesn't mean I need to steward the relationships of all the people I love – even peripherally.

Which brings me back to Freya and her plan for helping Raff. If Saskia and Paloma agree to let me take the case, how much is Freya going to want to interfere? There's drawing a professional line in the sand and there's reality. I know Freya, and I doubt she'll be side-lined without peeking over my shoulder and giving her two cents' worth.

'*Poppy?*'

'What, sorry?' I say, my attention snapping back to the flat.

'You were off with the fairies,' says Shaz.

'Yeah, sorry – already noodling on the case.'

'Everything okay?' she asks.

'Can I ask you guys something?' They both reply yes. 'If you were single and your best friend was a matchmaker—'

'My best friend is a matchmaker.'

'Yes, thank you, Captain Obvious – I'm trying to set up a hypothetical here.'

Tristan joins us and tops up our wine glasses.

'Thanks, babe. Right, so hypothetical... And, Tris, you answer as well. So, you're single and your best friend is a matchmaker and they tell you they want to match you and you say, "Go ahead, as long as I don't know it's happening," but your *other* best friend thinks you're only saying that to shut down the conversation, and *they* try and convince the matchmaker to leave it, but the match-maker is adamant that you meant it when you said to go ahead and—'

'Can you go back to the part where my best friend's a match-

maker?' asks Shaz, and I can't tell if she's being obstreperous or if
she's genuinely confused.

'I'm with Shaz, darling. I'm completely lost,' says Tristan.

'I think I get it,' says Lauren. 'Raff told Freya to go ahead with
the matchmaking, but Gaby's convinced he didn't mean it.'

'Yes – *that*,' I reply.

I'm typically more discreet about my cases, only discussing
them with my friends after anonymising the details. But everyone
here knows everyone I'm talking about – or at least knows of them
– so I may as well get their take on things.

'Why don't you ask him?' asks Tristan.

'No, we're not doing that.'

'Why not? You know him. Couldn't you reach out and say,
"Hello, do you actually want to be matchmade, or were you just
humouring Freya?"'

'Is that the right word? Matchmade?' asks Lauren. 'It sounds
strange, doesn't it?' she says to Shaz.

'First: yes, that is technically correct, but we just say "matched",
and second...' I say, turning to Tristan, 'I'm not asking him outright
– because, well... *reasons* – but you have given me an idea. Maybe I
can get Greta to interview Raff for *Nouveau Life*.'

Greta is a former client and the managing editor of *Nouveau
Life*, the online magazine where I posed as an advice columnist
during her case. The writing gig didn't pan out – they had to pull
the column before it was published and even if they hadn't, it turns
out I'm a terrible writer – but Greta and I have stayed close.

'Love it,' Shaz declares. 'Then you can find out what he really
wants without asking him explicitly.'

'Yeah, that's what I'm thinking.'

'Will she go for it, do you think?' Tristan asks.

'I can't see why not. Raff's recently won a major competition
show – the *Christmas* edition, which would be a perfect fit for the

December issue. Plus, thousands of people up and down Britain think he's hot, so he brings a ready-made readership. She's also convinced she owes me a favour.'

She doesn't – it was my job to help Greta achieve her HEA, but she brings it up every time I see her.

'Ooh, I'm too excited now. I'm going to give her a call,' I say, slipping off my stool. 'How long till dinner?' I ask Tristan.

'Ten or fifteen minutes.'

'Perfect.'

I head into the study/guest room – or if you ask Saffron, *her* room – to call Greta.

* * *

The next morning, I'm sipping my tea – poured from a perfectly brewed pot-for-one – when Freya drops a fat sheaf of paper on my desk, startling me.

'Oh my god, Freya,' I chide, reaching for a tissue to mop up the tea I've spilt.

'Sorry, Poppy, but look!' In true Freya fashion, she's bouncing on her toes, her fingertips pressed against her lips as her gaze lands on the client questionnaire.

'You finished already?' I ask, picking it up and flicking through. 'Wasn't Gaby supposed to help?'

She flaps a hand dismissively. 'Oh, once I got going I couldn't stop. There are a few blanks – I have no idea about his first pet or how old he was when he learnt to drive – but I'll call CiCi later and ask.'

I stop flicking and set the questionnaire on my desk. This is exactly what I was worried about – we're less than a day in, Freya still hasn't got approval from our bosses, and she's already proceeding at a rate of knots.

'Frey, I reckon we should take this a little slower.'

'How do you mean?' she asks. The bouncing stops and her gleeful demeanour disappears in an instant.

I've worked with Freya for years and I've never seen her this invested in a case. If it *is* approved, I'm going to need to build a metaphorical fortress around it.

'I mean, there are a few more steps before we start assembling a list of potentials.' She blinks at me as if I'm speaking gobbledygook. 'The sign-off?'

'Oh, that'll be fine. I'm talking to Saskia and Paloma after the staff meeting.'

She *really* doesn't understand.

'*And* we'll want Gaby's input on the questionnaire – get both of your perspectives to help round out Raff's client profile.'

'Okay,' she says, her large, round eyes staring at me, unblinking.

'*And* the big one, Frey – I still need to determine if Raff wants to be matched.'

She visibly deflates.

'But hey, I want to run something run past you,' I say, hoping this will wipe that frown off her face.

If I *am* going to match Raff, I'll need to strike a balance between looping Freya in where possible and maintaining necessary boundaries, and sharing my idea for the *Nouveau Life* interview is a start.

'Thoughts?' I ask after I've outlined my idea.

She smiles. 'I love it – very clever. And an interview will give you additional insight into who Raff is. That can only help when assembling potential matches.'

'Exactly.'

'Only...' She frowns again.

'What is it?'

'Well, Raff knows you're my colleague, right? Won't he be suspicious if you're the one who sets up the interview with *Nouveau Life*?'

'I worried about that too at first, but I've found a way to throw him off the scent,' I reply. That is, if Gaby agrees to help me, something I don't mention.

Freya appraises me with admiration. 'Of course you have – you're a true master of the ruse.'

I know she meant it as a compliment, but I'm taken aback. I've only had a few cases that have necessitated subterfuge, and I find it just as challenging as maintaining boundaries with my loved ones – if not more.

4

GABY

'How am I supposed to do that?' I ask Poppy. She's called, hoping I'll convince Raff to agree to an interview with *Nouveau Life*.

'Well, you could—'

'You don't understand, Poppy,' I say, talking over her. 'Raff *hates* publicity. It's bad enough he has radio interviews every night this week, but those are part of his contract with the show – he's obligated. How am I supposed to convince him to do an interview with a huge online magazine? Tell him it'll be fun?' I ask with a sarcastic laugh.

'I understand it could be tricky,' she says, obviously trying to placate me. 'But you said Raff is planning on joining his aunt's company, which also happens to be the biggest chain of bakeries in the UK. Appearing in *Nouveau Life* would be great publicity for Baked to Perfection. Couldn't you put it to him like that?'

'Hmm, maybe...' I say, noncommittally.

'Look, Gaby, I'll be honest, other than asking him point blank if wants to be matched, this is the best chance we have at figuring this out. Unless... *Should* we just ask him?'

'No!' Oops, I hadn't intended to answer so vehemently.

Poppy chuckles. 'Okay then.'

'Sorry, it's just... ever since we met on Monday, I've been thinking about it. And I'm pretty sure that if I went to Raff now and said, "Hey, there's, like, this huge plan to find your perfect match – do you really want that?" he'd say no. Because I'm not sure Raff knows what he truly wants.' I cough out a derisive laugh. 'I mean, do any of us?'

Oh shit. Why did I say that? And to *Poppy*. Now she's probably analysing me.

'Okay, so, what I'm hearing,' she says, sounding exactly like a psychologist, 'is that you agree the interview is the way to go.'

'Yeah, I guess I am.' Then something comes to me – a way to put an end to this, once and for all. 'Hey?'

'Yeah?'

'What are the chances of getting Freya to drop this whole thing?'

She laughs and despite myself, I join in.

'Ah... Yeah, no,' she replies. 'I reckon we've got Buckley's – sorry, that means no chance.'

'Yeah, you're right. At least if Raff does the interview, there's still hope. Maybe it'll reveal that he's *not* looking for love – even subconsciously – and we can shut this down.'

'Possibly...'

God, is it only Thursday? It's only been five days since we were all at CiCi's celebrating Raff's win, but it's feels like *weeks*. Probably because of the constant texts from Freya, most of them nagging me to finish my version of that (stupid) questionnaire. How is knowing Raff's favourite colour supposed to help him find love?

Love...

He really is happiest when he's in love. And don't I want my best friend to be happy?

'Gaby, you still there?' Crap, I've been in my head so long, Poppy thinks the call has dropped.

'I'm here – sorry, just thinking.'

'You don't need to give me an answer right away – we have a bit of time.'

'Thanks. I appreciate that, but I'll do it.'

'Really? That's great. Thanks, Gaby.'

'But I can't promise anything,' I add hastily. 'Raff's his own person.'

'I completely understand. I know you'll do your best.'

'So, let's say I'm successful; when's this interview?'

* * *

'I'm more nervous than I was the first day of filming *Britain's Best Bakers*,' says Raff, and I reach over and pat him reassuringly on the knee.

Ordinarily, we'd be heading into work, as it's Monday morning, but a town car picked us up at Raff's place and we're on our way to *Nouveau* instead.

Our boss, Claire, was surprisingly amenable to giving Raff time off for this interview – and for me to accompany him to 'keep an eye on things'. But it must be good for her to hitch the firm's wagon to Raff's rising star, especially as it's well known he's a marketing director at Global Reach.

Of course, she has no idea he's leaving.

'Do I look all right?' He fidgets with the hem of his bright-red acrylic Christmas sweater. If he wore it to the Rivera family's Ugly Christmas Sweater Party, he'd probably win first prize, but I'm not telling him that. He's nervous enough.

'Super festive,' I say reassuringly. 'And don't worry, I'll be there the whole time. I'm sure it'll be great.'

'Thanks for coming with me,' says Raff, sending a nervous smile my way.

'Sure.' I don't add that it's the least I could do when I'm the one who talked him into it. 'Consider me your personal marketing manager. We're launching a new brand, and it just happens to be you.'

'Ugh,' he groans. 'You know I hate being the centre of attention.' *I sure do.* 'At least those bloody radio interviews are behind me.'

'Seriously, it'll be fine. I checked out Greta Davies, and she's considered one of the best in the biz. And apparently, she's super sweet.' According to Poppy, anyway, but I omit that part.

'Hmm,' he murmurs, clearly unconvinced.

The cab pulls up outside a stylish building on the Strand, one with a seamless blend of the original architecture and modern updates. It's a stark contrast to the glass and steel behemoth Raff and I work in. Though the Shard *is* a cool building and I love that part of London, especially as it's teeming with great options for after-work drinks.

'Ready?' I ask.

'Nope, but let's go.'

He opens the door, unfurling his tall frame onto the sidewalk, and I follow him out the kerbside door.

The receptionist on the ground floor gives us visitor passes and directions to a third-floor conference room. When we arrive, we're greeted by an attractive, petite, curvy woman with wavy red hair worn in an up-do.

'Hello, Greta Davies, lovely to meet you, Rafferty.' They shake hands. 'And you must be Gaby.'

'Hi. Thanks for letting me tag along.'

'Oh, no problem at all. A lot of interviewees bring along someone from their team.'

She must be referring to actual celebrities who have actual teams. Raff and I exchange an amused glance.

'Let's sit, shall we,' says Greta, and we do, taking the three chairs at one end of an enormous conference table.

'Can I just say right off the bat, I'm a *huge* fan,' she says effusively. '*Such* a well-deserved win. That wedding cake – *spectacular*.'

Raff breaks into a grin, his anxiousness melting away in an instant. *Nicely done, Greta*, I think. It's a skill being able to set a stranger at ease – and so quickly. Clearly, he's in good hands.

'Thank you,' he replies to the compliment. 'Just something I'd been working on for a while. But you never really know until the day if it's going to come together.'

He's being modest – he spent *hours* designing and practising that cake – but maybe that will come up during the interview: Raff's dedication to his artistry.

'Right, so let's get you down to hair and makeup, then off to wardrobe,' she says.

'Wait, did you say "makeup"?' he asks.

'Yes – for the photoshoot.'

I knew they'd be taking a photo to publish with the article, but a full *photoshoot*? Then it hits me – this is *Nouveau*, not a local paper – of course there's a photoshoot.

Greta must clock the panicked look on Raff's face. 'I assure you, the makeup's very natural – only a little touch-up for the cameras so you don't look washed out.'

'Okay,' he says, shooting me a look that says, 'Please help me'. All I can do is shrug. Neither of us are rookies in this area, but it was a rookie mistake on both our parts not to have thought about this before.

'And the fashion editor has pulled some great looks for you,' she continues, throwing fuel on the make-Raff-as-uncomfortable-as-possible fire.

'Oh, I thought...' He looks down at his Christmas sweater. 'So, *you're* going to dress me?'

'Absolutely,' Greta replies. 'Our fashion editor – Luca – he's very excited to get his hands on you. Oh, I didn't mean *physically*... We always behave respectfully here at *Nouveau*—'

I stifle a laugh – Greta is unintentionally *very* funny.

'Sorry, I meant that Luca usually styles *fashion* shoots – mostly women and non-binary models – so when he got wind *you* were coming in – a *man* – he insisted on styling you himself. Not that he's — he's not... What I meant to say is that ordinarily one of his fashion assistants would do it. Er... *style* you.'

This gal's hilarious. It's taking all my self-control not to laugh. Raff, however, looks like he's about to hightail it out of here.

'You okay?' I ask him.

'It's just... Now I feel a bit silly showing up in this,' he says, tugging at the sweater.

'Oh, that's probably my fault,' Greta replies. 'I obviously wasn't clear when we spoke on the phone.'

I'm positive she's being gracious. When I showed up at Raff's apartment this morning and he opened the door wearing that (dumb) sweater, I grilled him, trying to figure out exactly what he'd been told. None of what he relayed included the words 'dress in an ugly Christmas sweater'.

Greta checks the time on her phone. 'Oh, we'd better be getting going.'

'Do I really have to wear makeup for the photo?' Raff asks me quietly as we trail behind Greta.

'Yep,' Greta says over her shoulder – the gal's got great hearing, I'll give her that. 'And it's not *a* photo, Rafferty. We'll be including a full photo series with the article.'

'Oh dear god, what have I got myself in for?' he mutters under his breath. When I look up, the small amount of colour in his already pale face drains away.

'It'll be fine,' I whisper.

'Easy for you to say,' he retorts, which is only fair.

* * *

'It seems to be going well,' says Greta.

Raff is on set having his photo taken and we're watching from the back of the studio.

'Yeah, for sure. Raff looks... I don't know – *different*,' I say, regarding him closely as he follows the photographer's directions. 'Like him but elevated, you know.'

'I told you, Luca's a virtuoso when it comes to styling.'

Luca was super enthusiastic about styling a guy, like Greta said he would be, but he also knows his stuff, making the most of Raff's height, broad shoulders, and slim hips. He's dressed Raff in a pair of fitted dark-wash jeans, a crimson dress shirt with the sleeves rolled up – a subtle nod to Christmas, Luca said – and a pair of black leather lace-ups.

This outfit is a *huge* step up from the boxy suits Raff wears to work – god knows how many times Freya and I have nagged him about buying suits that fit – or the baggy jeans and oversized T-shirts and sweaters he favours on the weekends.

Though, I'm one to talk.

I'm the marketing manager for several high-end brands, but I'm hardly a *fashionista*. Early on, I recognised I wouldn't compete with fashion designers and models – and I didn't want to – so I adopted a style that both suits me and fits in with my colleagues and clients. Mostly, I wear tailored suits I procure cheaply and have altered, zhuzhed-up with graphic T-shirts on non-client-facing days and silk blouses on the days I need to impress.

I look back at the set, noting that hair and makeup also nailed it. The hair stylist defined Raff's curls with product, pushing them off his face in a style reminiscent of Henry Cavill – totally off-brand for Raff, who's content to let his curls flop onto his forehead unfettered. That's fine for an angsty teen, but Raff's a thirty-two-year-old man.

And once the photographer – a Dutch guy named Jan – started directing Raff into poses, he visibly started to relax. I'm sure Jan is getting some great shots. If I were overseeing this shoot on behalf of a client, I'd be thrilled – they've gone all out.

And I'm so proud of Raff. This sort of thing is *way* outside his comfort zone, yet here he is being agreeable and in many ways, brave.

When I first brought up the interview, he said no so many times in a row, I lost count after five. But we talked it through and eventually, he sighed and said, 'I'm about to make a major life change and if I can't face the little fears, how will I face that one?' Then he agreed to the interview.

And that right there is the definition of bravery – being afraid but forging ahead anyway.

'So,' Greta whispers, leaning in closer, 'Poppy says you're in the know.'

'In the know?'

She nods. 'About the *favour*.' She loads the word 'favour' with meaning, only I have no idea what that meaning is.

'You've lost me.'

She purses her lips, then guides me by the elbow into a darker corner of the studio.

'You see, Rafferty's win is a hot topic, so saying yes to the interview was a no-brainer – it's a huge coup for *Nouveau Life*. And I'll be asking him all sorts of questions to help flesh out his biography for

Poppy. But you know about the other thing, right? The favour? Poppy says you've been looped in.'

As confusion mars her pretty face, I finally understand what she's talking about: the main objective for the interview.

'Yeah, totally. Sorry, the *favour*.' I shake my head at myself and she sighs with relief. 'So, how are you planning to bring it up?' I whisper.

'I won't come right out with it, of course – too jarring. I'll be framing the question under the guise of exploring Rafferty's "sex symbol" status.'

I laugh loudly, then clap a hand over my mouth. When I glance at the set, both Jan and Raff are looking my way. 'Sorry,' I call out, and they resume the photoshoot.

'It's associating the words "sex symbol" with Raff,' I tell her quietly. 'And it's not only me – Raff thinks it's ridiculous.'

'Even so, he has become one.'

'Right.'

I glance at the set again, seeing Raff through this additional lens. He *is* handsome – even though I've never thought of him that way – but I'd say it's his personality that makes him most attractive. He's just a decent, kind, and often funny guy.

There were countless times on the baking show when he would stop working on his own creation to help someone who was having a hard time. And *so* many tears on that show – you would have thought it was a show about dating, not baking – but Raff was always there to give a hug and some words of encouragement.

I'm now determined to do whatever I can to help him find someone who's worthy of him.

'You're staying for the interview, right?' Greta asks me.

'Hell, yeah. I wouldn't miss it for the world.'

5

GABY

Because of my role at Global Reach, this isn't the first time I've sat in on an interview. But this is the first time I've sat in on an interview with someone I know, especially as well as I know Raff.

Unfortunately, the ease he displayed during the photoshoot has vanished and even though Greta has been lobbing him softballs, such as asking about his favourite recipes, he's fidgeting like a middle-schooler who's been called to the principal's office.

Still, Greta is a pro, navigating the interview perfectly, and it's not long before Raff's shoulders begin to drop a quarter inch at a time.

'And I understand that it was your Aunt CiCi who taught you how to bake?' she asks, something that was made public when the show started airing.

'That's right. My father was a diplomat – he's retired now – but he and my mother lived overseas for my entire childhood – they still do, actually. I lived with them for the first few years, but once it was time for me to start prep, I went to live with Aunt CiCi and her husband, Devin. They couldn't have any children of their own –

even though they wanted them – so they offered me a stable home, which allowed me to go to school in Surrey, rather than hopping about from country to country and school to school every time my parents were posted somewhere new. It worked out well for everyone,' he adds, and I catch the slight waver in his voice.

Because Raff *loves* CiCi and Devin – more than he loves his parents, he once shared with me – but it's still got to hurt knowing your parents thought it was more convenient for you to live with someone else – *for your entire childhood.*

'Anyway, some of my earliest memories are of Aunt CiCi in the kitchen, me standing on a chair at her side and proudly taking on small tasks like cracking an egg or stirring the batter. And I always volunteered to lick the bowl,' he adds with a smile.

'Until I was about twelve, she operated a small baking business from home, specialising in scones. She'd bake them in her kitchen while I was at school and sell to friends and friends of friends, and eventually to local cafés and shops. And after an unexpected windfall – an unearthed art treasure that my uncle sold through Sotheby's – they were able to open a proper shop on Weybridge High Street.

'And, as Devin was an accountant specialising in small businesses, he became her unofficial business manager. When her shop took off, with people coming from miles around to buy her scones, he joined her fulltime and twenty years on, Baked to Perfection is one of the largest bakery companies in England.'

'That's quite the success story,' says Greta.

'It is – a testament to hard work, determination, and following one's passion.'

'Let's explore that avenue for a moment,' she says. 'So, you grew up baking at your aunt's side... At what stage did baking become *your* passion?'

'I can't remember a time when I didn't love it. Even after Aunt

CiCi opened her shop and didn't have as much time to teach me, I baked. I watched baking shows on the telly, I borrowed cookbooks from the library... I was always trying new recipes. I was that one pupil who couldn't wait for Food Technology.' He laughs to himself.

'But rather than becoming a pastry chef, you went into marketing. Why was that?' she asks, posing the first hefty question of the interview.

'Ahh, yes,' he replies, flicking his eyes in my direction. This is something we've talked about *many* times. Raff may be terrific at his job, but he has never really loved it, not the way I do.

'Off the record?' he asks Greta, his eyes filled with trepidation.

'Sure,' she replies with an understanding head tilt.

'I chose it after my parents got wind of my initial plan. I'd decided to forgo the expected university course in commerce or law and study to become a pastry chef. As soon as they heard, they wasted no time in coming straight back to England from Switzerland, sitting me down, and forbidding me from – as they put it – "throwing my life away to bake cakes".' He wiggles his fingers to make the air quotes.

Greta inhales sharply. 'They *forbade* you?'

'Yes.'

'I'm so sorry to hear that,' she commiserates, and I can tell she's being genuine.

'Yes, well, it was to be expected, I suppose,' Raff replies, his tone a mix of resignation and resentment.

'So, if you were supposed to go into commerce or law, how did you end up in marketing?'

'It was as far into the humanities as I could get them to agree to and still cover my university fees. Even now, my father believes I do little more than attend parties for wankers. Again, those are his words, not mine.'

'I suspected as much,' she says, and they share a wry smile. 'So, back to following your passion. Is there any chance you'll ever pursue a career as a pastry chef?'

Raff's eyes dart towards me again, and I nod encouragingly. I told him on the way here that this topic might come up, advising him to be truthful. Even though his decision isn't public knowledge yet – he hasn't even told Claire – the article won't come out until December, so he has time to inform everyone who needs to know.

'Actually, yes,' he says with a proud smile, his whole countenance shifting. 'Aunt CiCi has asked if I'll join her at Baked to Perfection. She wants to branch out into specialty cakes with me at the helm of the new division.'

'Wow, that sounds like a dream come true,' Greta replies.

'Winning *Britain's Best Bakers* was a dream come true. This would be... I don't know – beyond my wildest dreams, I suppose. Actually, she's been asking for some time – it's only now, off the back of my win, that it feels... well, *possible*.' Raff's face suddenly contorts into a frown.

'Is something wrong?' Greta asks.

'Just thinking about telling my parents...'

'Ah,' says Greta.

Raff shakes his head as if he's trying to dislodge the thought.

'You know, it might not be that bad,' I say, interrupting, and they both look at me. 'Maybe they'll be supportive.'

'Hah!' Raff laughs sardonically.

'Okay, but even if they aren't... this is your dream we're taking about. So what if they don't approve?'

'Easy for you to say; you haven't met them. You'd be singing a very different tune if you'd witnessed firsthand how terrifying they can be – especially my father,' he says.

'How about we get Gina over from Seattle to mediate?' I jokingly suggest. 'She can kill them with kindness – maybe hug 'em to death.'

My mom's always telling people, 'I'm a hugger,' right as she captures them in a bear hug. There's no escaping Gina's special brand of affection. As I'd hoped, Raff laughs and the tension in his shoulders falls away.

'Gina is Gaby's mum,' he explains to Greta. 'She believes that hugs are the panacea for any malady – even the absence of parental love.'

'She may be onto something,' Greta replies. 'We published an article a few months ago that explored the healing properties of physical affection – particularly for emotional distress and trauma.'

'Please don't tell my mom that. She'll get T-shirts made,' I quip.

We share a laugh, then Greta checks her notepad. 'Right,' she says. 'How about I ask my last couple of questions, then we can wrap up?'

Raff and I exchange a look and his relief is palpable. 'We're nearly done – hooray!' he says with his eyes.

'Sounds good,' he replies, flashing her a smile. Only, unlike me, Raff doesn't know that Greta's about to get to the crux of the interview and that smile is about to vanish.

'So,' she says, 'you've been touted as something of a sex symbol since *Britain's Best Bakers* aired...'

Not surprisingly, Raff groans, his cheeks flushing from embarrassment. 'Do we really have to talk about that? Can't we go back to something simpler, like my strained relationship with my parents?' he asks, his tone ripe with sarcasm.

Greta regards him thoughtfully. 'We can skip it, but I'm sure many of your fans will be curious about that aspect of your life.'

He huffs out a long sigh. 'I suppose so,' he says, his gaze dropping to the floor. 'Go on, then.'

'Are you dating anyone at the moment?'

She already knows the answer – Poppy will have told her – but it's a decent segue.

'No,' he replies, his voice strained. 'I'm single.'

'So, are you looking for love?' she asks gently.

But despite her gentle tone, everything about Raff tenses up and he sucks in a shallow breath through his teeth. Then it's like the moment a key slots into place and turns, and the lock springs open.

Raff's taut expression softens and a knowing smile of acquiescence tugs at the corners of his mouth. 'I think those who know me well would say I'm *always* looking for love,' he tells her.

I'm in awe at how deftly Greta has navigated this part of the interview. Moments ago, I was positive Raff would clam up entirely. Now he's spilling about his love life.

'Isn't that right, Gaby?' he asks, fixing me with a knowing look.

'I... Umm...'

He laughs. 'Oh, come on, you and Freya are always teasing me about it. Freya's our best friend,' he explains to Greta.

'I wouldn't say we're *always* teasing you,' I retort.

He stares at me, feigning incredulousness. 'Only after every breakup *and* whenever I start dating someone new.'

'Oh,' I say, trying to recall anything specific I've said along those lines.

'Admittedly, Freya's the main culprit, but you *have* teased me before, Gaby – many times. "You're such a hopeless romantic, Raff." Does that ring a bell?'

'Yeah, okay. I have said that,' I admit, now regretting the implied judgement of my words.

'And there's the chat thread.'

'The chat thre— What do you mean?' I ask, baffled.

He looks at Greta. 'We have a group chat, you see – the three of us. Only Freya and Gaby *also* have a chat thread that's just the two of them – one they don't think I know about. Last week, they got the two threads mixed up.'

My eyes widen, a sickening feeling settling into my stomach.

'Wait, what...' I reach for my satchel and take out my phone while Raff and Greta look on. I open the chat thread – the one with all three of us – and scroll up. There it is, an exchange between me and Freya about Raff, concluding with this from Freya:

> You know I'm right. Raff's only truly happy when he's in love. And not with someone like Winnie *vomiting face emoji*

'Oh, fuck.'

Raff chuckles. 'See?'

'Why didn't you say anything? How hard is it to type out, "Hey, guys, wrong chat thread!"?'

He shrugs, his laughter dying down. 'Look, even before those messages, I knew. You think I blindly lurch from relationship to relationship, seeking love.'

'I do not. Not *blindly* – more like *hopefully*.'

'You're splitting hairs,' he retorts, and we're both quiet for a moment.

I note that Greta allows us to talk – not interrupting our conversation, but observing it. If it's a tactic, then kudos to her, as she's gaining quite a lot of insight simply by being quiet.

'Wait,' I say, something occurring to me. 'Why *haven't* you dated anyone new since Winnie?'

He shrugs. 'Well, when a woman ends your relationship the day you'd planned to propose to her, you start wondering if you're just rubbish at choosing who to love. And when your closest friends confirm it in a chat thread...'

'Raff, I'm so sorry. We totally fucked that up, but it comes from a place of love, I promise.'

'I know. That's why I didn't say anything.' He looks over at Greta. 'You should probably know that Freya is a matchmaker, *and* she wants a crack at matching me.' He chuckles good-naturedly, shaking his head.

Greta and I exchange a look and I catch the excitement in her eyes. Raff has unwittingly circled back to the one question we need a definitive answer to.

'And is that something you'd be open to?' she asks evenly.

This is it – the moment that will determine if we're going ahead or calling this whole thing off.

Raff looks her straight in the eye and says, 'Well, she can't be any worse at it than I've been...' He gives a half-hearted shrug. 'So, why not?'

OH MY GOD!

Raff *does* want to fall in love – with the right person this time – and he's willing to let Freya (well, Poppy) match him.

Greta smiles, then drops her eyes to her notes and scans the page. 'You know, I think we have enough here to leave out your romantic status,' she says, following Poppy's 'script' to the letter. 'Especially if I shift the focus to your upcoming career change.'

'Really?' Raff asks. 'But just before, you said... Sorry, I'm confused.'

'That's my fault. I know what I said, but I've changed my mind. We don't need it.'

'Oh, thank you,' says Raff with a relieved sigh. 'I really hadn't intended to be so... well, *open* about all that. In hindsight, it was a bit daft of me.'

He's right. If this were any other interview and he *was* my client, I would have stepped in and shut down that line of questioning.

'And it will certainly make my life a lot easier if all and sundry aren't showing up at my doorstep to court me,' he says with a laugh, 'especially in light of what else is going on in my life.'

'I completely understand,' she replies, smiling warmly.

With that, Greta wraps up the interview, and we have our big, fat green light.

* * *

'You did great,' I tell Raff on the ride home.

'Until I told her how pathetic I am – Rafferty the Lovelorn,' he says ruefully.

I look across at him. 'You're not— Why do you do that?'

'Do what?'

'Put yourself down like that.'

He shrugs, his eyes fixed out the front window. 'Habit, I suppose.'

I wish there was a way to make him see himself the way others do. Not the sex-symbol stuff – that's just media hype and the masses romanticising celebrity – but how *we* see him, the people who know and love him.

I also wish I knew how to express all that, but I'm not eloquent when it comes to this stuff. I can design a multi-layered, multi-faceted marketing campaign, right down to the press release, but expressing *emotions*? Somehow that chip in my brain never got activated.

I huff with frustration. 'Well, quit it, okay?' It's lacking, but at least I've said something.

He looks across at me, amused. 'Quit it? As in "go cold turkey"? I know that can work wonders for smokers but I'm not sure about self-deprecation. I'll have to run that past my support group at the next meeting.'

I try my best to stifle my laughter. 'I'm being *serious*, Raff,' I chide.

'I can tell by the smirk and the way your torso is shaking.'

I release the snigger and backhand him in the chest. He can

always defuse a tense moment with a well-crafted quip, something I both admire and envy.

'Dork,' I say, shaking my head at him.

His reply is a self-satisfied grin, then we both go back to watching out the front window as we zip through inner London traffic towards the Shard.

6

POPPY

This morning, I'm presenting Raff's case at the staff meeting for the first time.

Freya, who's seated next to me, bounces in her chair with anticipation. She's far more excited about Raff's case than her own, matching a thrice-divorced woman with husband number four.

'Poppy, are you ready to present your new case?' asks Paloma, our head of client relations.

'Yes,' I reply. 'Our client is Rafferty Delaney, but his friends and family call him Raff.' Freya emits a high-pitched 'eep' and I send a silencing look in her direction.

'Sorry,' she whispers.

I press a button on a remote and Raff's face appears on the screen at the far end of the conference room. I flick another look Freya's way, but she stays quiet.

'Wait, isn't he the bloke who just won *Britain's Best Bakers*?' asks fellow agent, George.

'The one and the same.'

George swivels towards Freya. 'And isn't he also one of your closest friends?'

'George, astute observations as always,' says Paloma, 'but perhaps you could allow Poppy to continue?'

'Right, yes, sorry.'

'So, with thanks to George for the spoilers...' I say to my colleagues. As well as Freya, George, Saskia, and Paloma, there's another agent, Nasrin, our senior agent, Ursula, and Mia, our tech expert.

'...Raff is a referral from Freya and he was recently crowned *Britain's Best Baker*. He is also a serial monogamist who genuinely wants to find his match – as long as he isn't aware of our efforts. So, we'll be needing your—'

'Sorry,' says George, interrupting again. 'What does that mean – him not being aware of our efforts?'

'He says we're allowed to match him, but he won't go on any dates,' Freya explains matter-of-factly.

Across the table, Nasrin barks out a laugh. 'Good luck with that then. What are you suggesting? Swapping out his personal trainer for a potential match?'

'He doesn't have a personal trainer,' Freya replies earnestly.

'It was an *example*, Freya,' says Nasrin.

'Ursula,' I say, getting this discussion back on track, 'you're the most experienced here. You must have had cases that called for less conventional measures.'

Ursula has been a matchmaker for longer than many of us have been alive. Though the exact number of years is unknown – just like her true age. Let's just say that her immobile face is a testament to her love of cosmetic surgery and the only clues to her age are that her husband is in his early seventies and she occasionally references matchmaking in the nineties when everything was analogue and she used an actual Rolodex.

'I recall a case in 2005,' she begins, 'in which the client engaged me for their friend and wanted the match to seem natural...

random... *happenstance*, if you will. So, I designed a series of meet cutes, and each potential was given a time and location, as well as a photograph of the client and a script outlining how they could "meet by accident".'

'Oh, that sounds *perfect*,' Freya says prematurely.

'And it was successful?' asks George, voicing my exact concern.

'Oh, yes, absolutely,' replies Ursula. 'She met her match on her Sunday morning run. He literally bumped into her as she rounded a corner on the woodlands trail, and that was that – a successful match.'

'Does your boy run, Freya?' asks Nasrin, a teasing edge to her voice.

'No, he's not a runner. But maybe—'

'Freya,' I say, cutting her off, 'Nas was only teasing. We don't have to set up a running-around-the-park meet cute.'

'Oh, of course.'

'So, we appear to have a strategy,' says Paloma, who likes to keep our staff meetings moving along. 'Ursula, will you be Poppy's second on this one?'

'I'd be happy to.'

'What?' says Freya, talking over Ursula. 'But I thought I would...' She trails off as she often does, but her meaning is clear. She wanted to be my lieutenant on this case, something I was worried about.

'You're a little too close to this one, Freya,' Saskia chimes in diplomatically.

'And Ursula has experience with the strategy,' Paloma adds.

'I *designed* the strategy,' says Ursula, her lips quivering almost imperceptibly. This is the Ursula equivalent of peevish lip-pursing.

'Apologies, Ursula,' Paloma says contritely. 'You're absolutely right.'

Ursula's longstanding reputation as one of the top matchmakers in the UK has earned her a status that belies the agency's official hierarchy. Paloma may be a co-founder of the Ever After Agency, but Ursula is the undisputed Queen of Matchmaking, and she benevolently nods her acceptance of the apology.

'That's all, everyone,' says Paloma, closing the meeting.

I get up from the table, but Freya remains seated, her face contorted with disappointment. I sit back down and wait for the others to file out.

'Are you okay?' I ask.

'Hardly,' she replies gloomily. 'Why didn't you speak up? You know I'm far better positioned to be your second on this case than Ursula is.'

I *don't* know that. Actually, I'm positive she isn't, but I need to tread lightly here. Freya is my closest colleague at the agency – and a friend. I would never want to hurt her feelings or make her feel like I'm usurping her in any way. I know what this case means to her.

'Look, we'd need Ursula to approve the list of potentials anyway. With her helping to *assemble* that list, we'll be one step ahead. That means we can start matching Raff sooner. Right?'

I totally pulled that out of my bum – what a load of hooey! This will shave off half a day – *max*. From the way her frown deepens, Freya is also unconvinced, so I try another tactic.

'Frey,' I say as gently as possible, 'you had to know that you wouldn't be assigned to this case, even as my second.'

I regard her closely, witnessing the thoughts playing behind her eyes and the moment she concedes.

'You're right,' she says, and I couldn't be more relieved. I reach over and give her forearm a squeeze. 'But, Poppy, how are you going to pull off these "chance encounters" if I'm not part of the case – not even peripherally?'

How did I miss that key factor when Ursula's strategy seemed like a perfect solution only minutes ago?

'I know,' says Freya, answering her own question. 'Gaby can help.'

'That's a great idea but will she be up for it?' I ask.

Gaby may have got Raff to agree to the *Nouveau Life* interview, but what if she's still hesitant about finding him a match?

'Of course! She said she'd help if I got approval from Saskia and Paloma, remember?' Freya replies, her bright optimism re-igniting. It's something I admire about Freya – how resilient she is – but until I know for sure that Gaby's onboard, I'll hold off on celebrating.

'And Poppy,' says Freya, suddenly serious again, 'even though I'm not your second, you'll keep me in the loop, right?'

With that pleading look in her eye, how can I say anything but yes?

'Of course.'

She smiles brightly, throwing her arms around my neck and hugging me tightly.

* * *

As seems to be happening with more frequency lately, I arrive home from work to find our friends sitting at the breakfast bar sipping beverages while Tristan cooks dinner. This time, it's Tristan's best friend, Ravi, and his wife, Jacinda.

'There you are,' says Jacinda, sliding off her stool.

'Hello, darling,' says Tristan. 'I'll come and welcome you properly after I finish the polenta.' Polenta, as I've learnt since marrying a man who cooks, requires constant stirring or it gets lumpy.

'Hi,' I say to Jacinda, accepting a cheek kiss. 'Hi, Rav,' I say with a wave.

He sends me a warm smile. 'Hiya.'

I shrug out of my coat and hang it up. 'Are you two early or am I late?' I ask, checking the clock on the stove. It's barely gone six.

'We're early,' they both reply, but neither offers an explanation.

'Oh, a Chardy,' I say, spying the open bottle of wine on the counter. I slip past Tristan, sneaking a cheeky bum pat, and get myself a glass from one of the overhead cupboards. 'Who's having a top-up?' I ask.

'Yes, please,' replies my husband, sliding his glass towards me, and I top up his wine.

'Rav? Jass?' I ask, turning around. Only Ravi's having a whisky and Jacinda's drinking— Wait... I meet her eyes. 'Is that water?'

'Yes,' she replies, both hands encircling the glass.

I hold up the bottle. 'Did you want a glass? It's from Burgundy.'

'No, thank you.'

'Okay,' I say brightly, even though it's highly unusual for Jacinda to decline a glass of wine. I suspect I know *why* she's not drinking, but it's something that should come from them, rather than me asking outright.

I put the bottle in the fridge and when I turn back around, they're having a hushed, but intense conversation, making my suspicions mount. To give the illusion of privacy, even though I can make out most of what they're saying, I go and stand beside Tristan and watch him stir the polenta. He flashes me a wink and I blow him a kiss, wondering if he's listening in to our friends' conversation like I am.

'I want to tell them, Rav. I'm practically bursting with it,' Jacinda whispers.

'All right,' Ravi replies softly.

'So, we have some news...' Jacinda begins, raising her voice.

'You *do*?' I ask, spinning around.

Jacinda starts laughing. 'Poppy, you are the *worst* actor. You already know what I'm going to say, don't you?'

'I *may* have figured it out.'

'Figured out what?' asks Tristan, looking over his shoulder.

Jacinda shares a look with Ravi, who beams at her. 'It's early days,' she says, turning back to me, 'and we're not supposed to be telling people yet, but you're not *people*, you're family, so... We're having a baby!'

As the words land, tears spring to my eyes. I'm going to be an aunty! There's going to be a little person in the world who calls me 'Aunty Poppy'!

I run around to Jacinda and throw my arms around her. 'I am so happy for you!'

'Ahem! It wasn't an immaculate conception, you know.'

'Ravi, that's crass,' chides Jacinda as I let her go.

'Congratulations,' I say, giving him a hug. 'Now you'll have a *reason* to tell dad jokes.'

'Oi,' he replies, making me laugh.

'See? I already find you funnier.'

He shakes his head at me, his mouth stretching into a reluctant grin.

'Congratulations,' says Tristan, having left his post. He hugs Jacinda, then shakes hands with Ravi.

'Tris, what about the polenta?' asks Jacinda, eyeing the pot on the stove.

'I've turned off the hob. Your news trumps smooth polenta, Jacinda,' he says with a grin. 'And we can do better than this for a celebratory drink,' he says, taking her water glass. He heads back into the kitchen. 'How about a round of mocktails so we can toast your good news?'

'I won't say no to that,' replies Jacinda, beaming.

I stand between Jacinda and Ravi, hooking my arm over their

shoulders. 'So, when is Baby Sharma due?' I ask, looking between them.

'The beginning of summer,' Ravi replies.

'Oh, a Cancer!' I declare, and Ravi groans, his eyes rolling dramatically.

'Ravi thinks astrology is a load of rubbish,' Jacinda tells me.

'Yes, I'm married to a sceptic as well,' I reply, shooting an amused look at Tristan.

'Because it *is* a load of rubbish!' he calls over his shoulder.

'Are you going to find out the baby's sex before they're born?' I ask, ignoring Tristan. I scoot around Jacinda and slide onto the stool next to hers.

'We're not sure,' Ravi replies.

'We don't care either way, of course,' says Jacinda. 'We just want a healthy child.'

'And we'd happily wait till the baby's born...'

'We would, but my mum's another story,' Jacinda interjects. 'She'll want to know as soon as possible if she's finally getting a granddaughter.'

'Ahh, there *are* a lot of boys in your family,' I say. Jacinda has three older brothers, and they all have sons – one of them has *three*.

'Precisely.'

'Well, whoever Baby Sharma is, they will be so, *so* loved.'

'Thanks, Poppy,' says Jacinda, covering my hand with hers.

'And here we are,' says Tristan, bearing a pitcher filled with a colourful concoction and a tray with four glasses. 'Shall we sit on the sofas?'

'Good idea,' says Ravi, climbing off his stool and stretching his arms overhead.

We make our way to the two facing sofas and get comfy. Tristan smacks a kiss onto my cheek – a delayed 'welcome home' – then pours from the pitcher and hands out the mocktails. When we all have one, he raises his. 'To our dear friends, Ravi and Jacinda, and their soon-to-be addition to the family.'

'To us,' says Ravi. He leans in and kisses Jacinda tenderly – an extremely unusual display of affection for the Sharmas.

'To us,' she says quietly, and they lock eyes as they sip.

I look away, feeling as if I'm intruding on an intimate moment.

'Blimey, that's good, Tris,' says Jacinda. 'You sure there's no booze in that?'

'A total virgin,' he replies.

'Unlike my wife.'

Tristan and I exchange a look, then crack up.

'Ravi!' Jacinda pretends to be outraged but she soon starts sniggering with the rest of us.

A baby in the family... How lovely.

I look across at my husband, feeling sudden and intense longing. We talked about having children before we got married – and both of us want at least one child – but since that first discussion, we haven't really discussed it again. And I'm thirty-seven now.

Maybe it's time to revisit the topic.

Maybe it's time to have a baby.

7

GABY

Here's something I never thought I'd be doing: checking out every woman who comes within five feet of us while we're out at brunch. Is *she* one of Poppy's clandestine matches? How about *her*?

'Gabs?' says Freya, poking me.

'What? Sorry, I uh...' She and Raff are watching me. 'What were you saying?' I ask.

Raff frowns and he and Freya exchange a look. 'I'm just popping to the loo,' says Raff, standing. He drops his napkin onto the table and makes his way to the back of Fortunella Café, one of our favourite haunts.

'You're behaving very oddly,' says Freya when he's out of earshot.

'I know, I'm sorry – but I'm distracted.'

'Yes, clearly. But by what?'

I lean in closer and whisper, 'By pretty much every woman in here.'

She sits back in her chair and regards me curiously. 'Something you want to tell me?' she asks. 'Are you attracted to women now?'

'What? No, I mean because of Raff... His, you know...' I'm doing a Freya again and not finishing my sentences.

'*Oh!*' she exclaims, and several people nearby look our way. I shush her and she starts giggling. 'Poppy hasn't even *started* yet.'

'Really?' This surprises me, but maybe matchmaking moves a lot slower than I realised.

'Well, she *has*,' Freya continues, now sounding frustrated, 'but it's early days. She and Ursula are still vetting potential matches. It'll be some time before... you know...'

'Ursula?' I ask. 'Why is she working with Poppy? I thought *you* would be.'

'Yes, so did I,' she replies, obviously disappointed.

'So, what happened? I mean, I know Poppy has to take the lead but surely—'

Freya shoots a panicked look across the table. 'Later. Raff's coming back,' she whispers, looking past me to the rear of the café.

'Sorry I took so long – there was a queue. Right,' he says, taking a seat, 'where was I?'

I look to Freya because I have no idea how to answer that.

'You were telling us about how the partnership would work – logistically,' she says.

'Right, yes.'

'It's generous that CiCi and Devin only expect a nominal buy-in to join the business,' Freya adds, feeding me a lifeline.

'True,' he replies.

'That must be a big plus in the take-the-offer column?' I ask, finding my way back into the conversation.

Raff sets his knife and fork on his empty plate and leans back in his chair. 'It is – absolutely. *Almost* enough to counter how my parents will react.'

Freya places her hand on top of his. 'Your parents have *never* approved of your job. How is this any different?'

Raff scowls, his hurt unmistakable.

'Perhaps a different way to reframe it,' I say, switching to marketing mode, 'is that by following your passion and making this career change, you can finally be free from the weight of their expectations.'

'How so?' he asks, his interest clearly piqued.

Freya props her chin on her hand and looks at me expectantly.

Great. Now I need to spin what seemed like a simple statement into a tangible reason for sloughing off his parents' disappointment.

My thoughts immediately go to my mom and dad. Gina has always been my biggest champion, instilling in me since I was a little girl that I could be anything and do anything, as long as I worked hard and never gave up. That was her only stipulation – not the weight of parental expectation, but that I develop a strong work ethic, determination, and grit.

My dad was less vocal but equally as supportive, willing to let my mom be my head cheerleader, but he was always there to help me dust myself off and get up and try again – literally and figuratively.

Even when I decided to move to London after my college boyfriend of six years (Eric, rhymes with Pencil Dick – kinda) left me for his co-worker of three months, they supported me. They were heartbroken I would be so far away, but they didn't make my decision any harder than it already was.

And there's the rub. Raff has never experienced that level of support from his parents. Well, screw them! And that's exactly what I need to say.

'*Gaby?*' prods Freya. I must have been pondering far longer than I realised.

'Raff,' I say, looking him in the eye, 'screw your parents. Seriously, just screw 'em.'

He blinks twice, then stares at me wide-eyed. 'I beg your pardon?'

'Oh, don't be all *English*, Raff. How many times have you wanted to tell your parents to fu—'

'Sod off,' Freya cuts in. In all our years of friendship, she's never quite got used to me cussing like a trucker.

'Okay, fine – to *sod* off, then? How many times? Dozens, hundreds? They already pass judgement on you for working in marketing, despite your successes and all your promotions... What's the difference between that and them judging you for being a pastry chef? Oh, I know! You'll be living your dream!'

He looks away, his scowl intensifying.

Oops, I may have pushed too hard that time.

'Hey, I'm sor—'

'You are absolutely right,' he says, meeting my eyes.

'I am?'

'She is?' asks Freya.

He looks between us. 'For too long, I've sought approval that will never come. I could become the *prime minister* and my father would still find fault with my choices. And my mother's hardly any better. CiCi is more like a mum to me than my own mother ever has been, and she's giving me this incredible opportunity – *with* a massive safety net. Why have I taken so long to officially say yes? What's wrong with me?'

'There's nothing wrong with you,' I say.

'No, nothing,' Freya agrees.

'Other than your questionable taste in clothes,' I add.

Teasing him does the trick and he starts shaking with laughter. 'Oh, you're *hilarious*.'

'It made you laugh. Besides, none of your fans seem to care that you dress like a science teacher from the nineties.'

At that, Freya erupts into laughter.

'Hey, that's not nice,' says Raff through his laughter. Unable to keep a straight face, I join in.

'I know,' he says. 'Instead of telling my parents outright, how about I pop on some chef's whites, then take a photo of me out front of Baked to Perfection and send it to them?'

Freya grimaces.

'Too much?' he asks.

'Perhaps,' she replies right as I say, 'No way! Not extreme enough. CiCi should be in the photo, and you should both be flipping them the bird.'

'Ba-ha-ha-ha.' Freya's bellowing laughter echoes throughout the café and most of the other diners look our way.

We apologise, and everyone goes back to their brunch.

'I can imagine Aunt CiCi rather enjoying that,' Raff says to us quietly. Then he reaches across the table and steals a piece of sourdough toast from my plate.

'Hey, you know I was saving that!' I say, trying unsuccessfully to snatch it back. I always save one piece of toast that I like to eat cold – I know, don't judge me – with peanut butter – again, don't judge me.

Raff shrugs and takes a bite, then starts groaning with pleasure as if it's the most delicious thing he's ever eaten. It *is* good, but he's being an idiot.

'You keep that up, they'll kick us out.'

He shrugs again.

And even though I'm (mildly) pissed off he stole my toast, Raff is more relaxed than I've seen him in ages and I'd forego a thousand pieces of toast for that.

Twenty minutes later, after Raff insisted on paying, we're standing outside in the cold, Freya leaning against me and bouncing on her toes to keep warm. What began as a crisp, sunny fall day has turned wintry during brunch.

'Thank you so much,' says Raff, hugging us in turn. 'You've been amazing and if I ever feel myself waver, I'll just picture CiCi with her middle fingers in the air, telling my parents to sod off.' Freya giggles, but then her teeth start chattering. 'Go, go get to your train,' he says, waving us off.

'Say hi to CiCi and Devin for us,' I tell him.

'Will do!' He waves over his shoulder as he heads to the nearest street to meet his Uber.

'Now we're alone again, I want to ask you something,' says Freya, hooking her arm through mine.

'Sure – anything,' I say, not knowing I'll instantly regret giving her a blank cheque.

* * *

'No way, Frey, that's ridiculous,' I tell her adamantly. I didn't think it was possible for her ideas to get any more harebrained, but now she wants *me* to help choose Raff's perfect match.

'You said the same thing about matching Raff in the first place,' she retorts.

'Well, yeah, and part of me still stands by that.'

'But the interview... He was very clear about wanting to find love,' she insists.

'Okay, yes, but Raff has a lot on right now. I've told you – I'm not sure finding him "the one" should be our priority. He's going to need our support to transition to a fulltime pastry chef.'

'Oh, he'll be fine with all that,' she says dismissively. 'He's *Raff*, and besides, he's got CiCi and Devin. Ooh, can you imagine how incredible it would be if Raff had his dream job *and* met his dream woman in time for Christmas?'

'Christmas?! Now you're delusional. That's, like, five weeks away.'

'Thirty-three days to be exact.'

'Sure, okay, but why the rush? What's so special about Christmas?'

'You did *not* just say that.'

'Sorry – forgot who I was talking to.'

I love Christmas as much as the next person, but Freya makes Buddy from *Elf* look like the Grinch. She's a Christmas *freak*. And now she seems to have conflated matching Raff with her favourite time of the year. I need to step in here before she starts ordering poinsettias for the bridal bouquet.

'But, Frey, that timeline's way beyond wishful thinking.'

'Which is why we need to get cracking,' she retorts.

'Poppy has *already* got cracking. You said that she and Ursula are working on it.'

'They *are* and that's why I need you. I can't be part of the selection process, so I need you to step in as my proxy. *Someone's* got to ensure they choose the right potentials for my very best friend.'

'First, "very best friend"? Are you in the third grade?'

She shrugs, hitching my shoulder up along with hers.

'Second, what am *I*, chopped liver?'

She giggles.

'And third, how is Poppy going to feel about me interfering in her case?'

Mentally, I have my fingers crossed that Poppy will hate the idea and tell Freya no.

Freya stops, so I do too.

'I've already talked to Poppy and she's in agreement, I promise,' she says earnestly. 'Because you won't be interfering; you'll be helping. *Please*, Gaby. I'd feel *so* much better if you were part of the vetting process. Oh, *and* we'll need your help with the set-ups,' she adds casually as an afterthought.

'The set-ups? What do you mean, you'll need my help?'

Freya explains the agency's strategy for matching Raff while adhering to his sole caveat – that he doesn't have to go on dates. And without asking me first, Freya has volunteered me to help fabricate these 'happenstance' meetings.

Why did I ever agree to be part of this ridiculous caper in the first place?

'*Please*, Gaby. We can't do this without you,' she says, her pale-blue eyes boring into mine. They could melt even the hardest heart, so how can I, her second-best friend, say no? Simple – I can't.

'Fine,' I say with a resigned sigh.

Her expression transforms from pleading to elated in 2.1 seconds. 'Really?' she asks, bouncing on her toes.

'Really – but only if you don't second-guess me.'

'Of course not.'

'Come on,' I say, ushering her towards the train station. 'And don't say "of course not" as if it's a foregone conclusion. I won't be texting you a play-by-play or anything. And you'll have to accept whatever Poppy and I decide.'

'And Ursula.'

'And Ursula,' I reply. 'I'm serious, Frey.'

'I know. And thank you,' she says, squeezing my arm.

'Yeah, yeah. Maybe save your thanks for when Raff is loved up with his new girlfriend.'

We reach the train station and I send Freya off with a hug and her promising to text Poppy as soon as she gets on the train.

I don't live far from here, so I'll walk the rest of the way, wishing the entire time I'd Ubered straight home from Fortunella – it's *freezing*. I often get teased about how much I hate the cold. 'But you're from Seattle – doesn't it rain there nine months a year?' people ask.

No, actually, it doesn't. The skies are *grey* around nine months a year – with a respite over the ten or so weeks of summer – but even when it's raining, it doesn't get as cold as it does here.

Well, not usually. It *has* snowed in Seattle, which shuts down nearly everything. Seattle is *not* built for snow – there are hardly any snow ploughs and far too many steep hills. I've seen a bus filled with people spin all the way from the top of Queen Anne hill to the bottom. Terrifying. But other than a few freak snowstorms – 'Snowpocalypse' of 2019, as one 'clever' weather reporter dubbed it, comes to mind – the winters are reasonably mild compared with London.

All these thoughts of home make me miss Mom and Dad more acutely than usual. We often talk on Sundays – my evening and their morning. I'll give them a call later.

As I turn down my street, my phone alerts me to a text and I take it out of my coat pocket. Shocker, it's Freya:

> Poppy says to come to the agency tomorrow at 5 for a screening. xx

A screening? What the hell is she talking about? I send a reply to ask, but I don't hear back. What in god's name have I said yes to?

8

GABY

'Gaby, do you have a moment?' asks my colleague, Lorrie – fifty-something (but doesn't look it) and divorced (and deliriously happy about it). She and Quinn – twenty-four and semi-fresh out of college – who's also on my team, hover at the edge of my cubicle.

'Ahh, sure, what's up?'

They exchange a glance, then Quinn jerks his head in the direction of the nearest meeting room. 'I've booked Wordsworth,' he says. Some 'genius' named all the meeting and conference rooms after dead (entirely male) poets.

'Okaaay,' I drawl, intrigued. I get up from my desk and follow them into Wordsworth, then Lorrie closes the door behind us and rounds on me.

'Is Raff leaving?' she asks – point blank, no preamble.

'Oh, umm...'

'He's been in with Claire for an age,' Quinn informs me in a dramatic whisper. 'And it doesn't look like a very "market-y" discussion, if you know what I mean?'

'I really don't,' I reply.

'Gaby, please be straight with us,' says Lorrie.

'We love Raff,' adds Quinn.

'I know. I love him too.'

They stare at me. 'Well?' Lorrie urges.

I sigh. 'It's not my news to share.'

'Gaby!' they cry in unison.

'*Shh.*' I glance towards the glass wall but fortunately, no one on our floor seems to have heard their cries.

Just then, I see Raff leaving Claire's office and I swing open the meeting room door. 'Hey, Raff, can I steal you for a sec?' I ask casually. He changes direction and comes our way.

'Hello,' he says, looking between us. I signal for him to close the door behind him. He does, regarding us warily. 'What's going on?'

'You tell us, Rafferty,' says Lorrie, her eyes narrowing.

'Are you leaving us?' Quinn whines. I've suspected for some time that he has a huge crush on Raff – now I'm positive.

Raff's eyes flick to meet mine and I lift my hands in surrender. 'Don't look at me. I didn't say a word.'

He turns to Lorrie and Quinn. 'Well...'

Quinn sucks in a breath through his teeth and Lorrie appears distraught.

'Yes, I am. I've just given notice,' Raff adds.

'No!' they wail together.

'Seriously, did you two rehearse this routine?' I ask, but they both ignore me – they're too busy imploring Raff to stay.

He raises his hands to placate them, and they fall silent. 'It's done,' he tells them gently. 'I'm working up till the Christmas break, but I won't be returning in the New Year.'

'Where are you off to then? Those bastards at Zenith didn't poach you, did they?' Lorrie asks, switching seamlessly to interrogation mode.

'Lorrie, you know I'd never work for those bastards at Zenith.'

'Those bastards' include Cockwomble, the not-so-affectionate-but-apt nickname Lorrie's given her ex-husband. Cockwomble is a senior director at Zenith and Lorrie would consider working for him tantamount to betrayal.

She exhales a loud sigh while Quinn falls into a chair. This is hitting them harder than I expected.

This is hitting *me* harder than I expected.

In less than a month, Raff won't be occupying the cubicle next to mine. We've shared that fuzzy green wall for *years* – so long, I can't remember when we didn't share it. Even after Raff's promotion last spring – a role that came with an office as well as a raise – he asked to stay put. Claire couldn't understand why. *I* could – Raff is the epitome of a team player – he thrives on working with the 'little people'. He also *hates* it when I call us that – more evidence that he's a genuinely good guy.

'So where are you off to then?' Lorrie asks wearily.

'Why don't you sit down and I'll tell you everything,' he offers.

Lorrie and Quinn exchange another look, then Lorrie takes a seat next to Quinn.

'Um, are you guys cool if I sit this out? I'm already up to speed.'

Quinn shrugs, Lorrie waves me off, and when I catch Raff's eye, I mouth, 'Good luck.'

I leave Wordsworth and instead of going back to my desk, I take the elevator to the ground floor. I have about forty minutes before my next meeting and I need a breather. After exiting the Shard, I head towards the river.

I never get bored of walking along the Thames, especially watching the ever-changing river traffic. Sometimes, I'll stop and take in the dense and varied architecture across the river on the northern bank. London is steeped in history, for sure, but it also has this vibrant modern energy. And Tower Bridge is one of the most spectacular landmarks I've ever seen. It has been far easier for this city to feel like my second home than I'd originally anticipated.

Though I do get homesick for Seattle – and not only because I miss my family. Seattle is a truly beautiful place – the city itself *and* the natural beauty surrounding it.

There's a vantage point not far from my parents' place that has always been my go-to for when I need to catch my breath or to ponder some dilemma. I'll sit and stare at the view, taking in each incredible detail. The rough and rugged Orcas Islands nestled in Puget Sound. How the Olympic Mountains in the distance are silhouetted against the sky. The working port at West Seattle, with its enormous cranes and boat traffic. The ferries that cross the sound, miniscule from that high up. The converted buildings along the waterfront – once used for shipping but now restaurants, hotels, and events venues. And the city itself, including the iconic Space Needle, which is even more incredible at night. And on clear days, which are few and far between, you can see Mount Rainier in the distance – so tall and monolithic, it looks fake, like that logo at the start of a Paramount Pictures movie.

I stop at a spot along the granite wall next to the Thames and rest my forearms on top. It's another crisp fall day and the sun is doing an impressive job of shining, making the sky a milky blue.

Raff is leaving.

Not only will I see less of him, but he's taking this huge leap of faith. I haven't done anything that extreme in years – not since my move to London. And with Freya gone...

Maybe this is why Raff's departure from Global Reach is hitting me so hard. First Freya, now Raff... They're both pursuing their passions.

But what's mine? I enjoy my work, but if I'm honest with myself, I haven't been stretched professionally for some time. I wonder if I should throw my hat in the ring for Raff's role. Getting promoted would certainly help me shake off the doldrums.

Or what about moving back to Seattle? Gina would be thrilled –

so would Dad – but is that what I want? And would it be good for me?

I'm heading back in a few weeks for my cousin's wedding, then staying on to spend Christmas with my parents. I suppose I could check out the vibe while I'm there – jobwise, dating wise... Of course, I'd miss Freya and Raff if I moved back to Seattle – and CiCi and Devin, and Lorrie and Quinn – my London peeps. But I'd also be closer to my family.

Ahh, hell, there's so much to consider.

My bout of navel gazing is cut short when my text notification chimes – probably Raff telling me he's broken Lorrie and Quinn's hearts and needs me back at the office ASAP.

But when I check my phone, it's not Raff, it's Poppy. I read the text and break into a smile, chuckling to myself.

> Hi Gaby. This is Poppy. Looking forward to this arvo. And don't worry – will make it painless. Have a fully stocked bar! *LOL emoji*

The more interactions I have with Poppy, the more I like her. But I still don't know what the hell a screening has to do with matchmaking.

* * *

'Hey! Great to see you,' says Poppy. 'Come on through.'

She leads the way to the back of the office and – I'll be damned – there's an actual screening room. As far as I knew, only rich people and film directors have these. I half-expect someone to hand out popcorn.

'This is Ursula,' says Poppy, and the woman sitting in the front row turns around.

'Pleased to meet you,' she says with a taut smile. She's either not pleased to meet me or that's as much as her face can move. Her eyes seem warm and welcoming, so I guess it's the latter.

'Hi, Ursula.' I sit next to her and Poppy sits next to me.

'So, when you said "screening", you meant...?' I ask her.

'You'll see but, first, did you want a bevvie? I wasn't kidding about the bar.'

'You weren't?' I ask with a laugh. 'Matchmaking may be more fun than I thought.'

'Just a perk of working after hours.'

'Ahh, of course. For some reason, I had this image of bar carts and day drinking, like in *Mad Men*.'

Poppy, laughs. 'Yeah, no.'

'Oh, I adore that Jon Hamm,' says Ursula, and when I turn to her, she's wearing a dreamy expression. 'So dishy...' She says the last part to herself and I don't ask her to expound.

I turn back to Poppy. 'I'll have something if you are.'

'Cool.' She presses a button on a console between our seats.

'Hi, Poppy. What can I get you?'

'Hi, Anita. A G&T for me, please.' She leans past me. 'Ursula?'

'I'll have the same.'

Then she looks at me, her eyebrows raised. 'Umm, yeah, a G&T sounds good.' Until I moved here, I never drank gin, but when in Rome and all that.

We chit chat for a few minutes, then the agency's receptionist shows up with a tray bearing three highballs.

'Thank you, Anita,' says Poppy. 'Anita makes the *best* G&Ts,' she tells me as she hands out the drinks.

Anita chuckles. 'Only because I put myself through uni working behind the bar. Right, I'm heading off,' she says. 'I hope it goes well.'

So do I, even though I still haven't a clue what to expect.

'Mmm, that is good,' says Poppy, licking her lips. 'Okay, so how this works is: based on the client questionnaire Freya completed, the additions you provided, and the recording of the *Nouveau Life* interview, Ursula and I have assembled a longlist of potential matches. We'll take you through those now so you can help us create a shortlist.'

'Okay,' I say, still confused why we're doing this in here.

Poppy picks up a huge remote and presses a couple of buttons. Instantly, the room goes dark, and a photograph of a woman appears on the screen.

'This is Ritu,' says Poppy. As she progresses through a series of images of an attractive South-Asian woman with curly, shoulder-length hair, Poppy gives me an in-depth biography of Ritu. In broad strokes, she's a high school English teacher, the oldest of three sisters, and the only one who's not married. She's also an avid traveller and has three cats.

In my periphery, Poppy looks my way and I turn to her. 'Any preliminary thoughts on Ritu?' she asks.

'Umm, just that she's an avid traveller and Raff's about to be tied to London with his new role at Baked to Perfection – at least for the foreseeable future. That *could* lead to a clash in priorities and, eventually, resentment – on both their parts.'

Poppy's eyes meet mine in the semi-darkness. 'That's an astute observation. Though, Raff *has* travelled quite a bit in the past. Don't you think he'll come back to it once he's got the lay of the land at Baked to Perfection?'

'Hmm, maybe. But that could be months or even years from now.'

'She's only the first of eight,' says Ursula. 'I suggest we proceed.'

I turn back to the screen and at the press of a button, a blonde woman with striking green eyes appears. 'This is Eilidh,' says Poppy.

And just like that we've 'swiped left' on Ritu. I don't feel entirely comfortable being in this position, learning about these women and judging them on so little information. Maybe that's why I've never used dating apps for anything more than casual dates. What can you really tell about a person based on their most flattering photo and some BS they've written in their bio?

Eilidh seems nice enough, but she has celiac disease and how would that work? Sure, sometimes Raff bakes gluten-free recipes, but he's about to work in a bakery! What's he supposed to do? Wear a hazmat suit to work so he doesn't come home covered in flour and make his girlfriend sick?

What started out as a novel assignment becomes more laborious as we go on. By the time we finish, we only have two potential matches – Jane, who works for a not-for-profit, and Ava, who's a vet. We also have an alternate – Julia, an artist who I wanted to kibosh solely for her obsession with German rave music, something Raff can't stand. But Ursula insisted we make her the alternate in case the others don't pan out.

'And we're done,' says Poppy brightly.

She brings up the lights, and I blink until my eyes adjust.

'Thank you, Poppy,' says Ursula. 'Richard's taking me to dinner, so I'll be off. Nice to meet you, Gaby. No doubt we'll see you again soon.'

We say goodbye to Ursula and Poppy collects our glasses, then leads us out of the screening room. 'I'll pop these in the dishwasher and be right back.'

With the office to myself for a few moments, I feel a pang of... well, *something* – unease, maybe. Was I too harsh on those women? They all seemed nice enough – and interesting – and I know from Freya the agency prides itself on the calibre of its clientele, including potential matches. Maybe that's why it feels icky to dismiss them based on a single preference or trait.

'Ready?' Poppy asks, and I land back in the present.

'Yeah, sure,' I reply.

She stops by her desk to collect her handbag and we head towards the exit.

'Poppy?'

'Mmm?' she asks as she keys in a security code. A loud beeping sound blasts, and she ushers me quickly through the double glass doors, then takes a set of keys out of her handbag and locks up.

'Back there... was I too judge-y – about the women? It's just that I know Raff and—'

'No, no, not at all. It's important we get this right, and you're across details that may not seem to matter on the page but could be a dealbreaker in the real world.'

'Exactly. That's all I was trying to do.'

She presses the button to call the elevator and the doors open right away. As we step inside, something else occurs to me. 'Can I ask... if I hadn't come in today, how would you have... you know?'

'Narrowed down the shortlist?'

I nod.

'By further scrutinising every compatibility marker, then considering which of the potential matches to introduce to Raff first.'

'So, *matchmaking*?' I ask with a smile. 'It's much more complex than I originally thought.'

'It's not an exact science, but we have a high success rate and where we fail, we take those learnings and adjust. You've saved us several days' work.'

'Then I'm glad I could help. And do you always do it like that?'

'The screening?'

'Yeah.'

'Nah,' she says as the elevator doors open on the ground floor. 'But Freya said you'd get a kick out of it.'

'Frey—' I shake my head.

'She's cheekier than most people think,' says Poppy.

'That's one way of describing her,' I reply with a chuckle.

We head out into the already dark evening, then say our good-byes. But as I walk towards the bus stop, I can't help but wondering, *If I've been so helpful, why do I feel like shit?*

9

POPPY

'Good morning, everyone,' Freya chirrups as she arrives.

'Hey, can I talk to you when you have a sec?' I ask, keeping my tone light. I want to give Freya time to drop her stuff at her desk and make her morning coffee before I spring my suspicions on her.

'Ooh, yes, I can't wait to hear all about yesterday,' she replies. 'Five minutes?'

'Sure.'

I spend the time rehearsing what to say in my head. How do you tell your colleague, one you're close with and whose case you're handling, that you suspect her best friend has feelings for her other best friend?

I'm still undecided when Freya rolls her desk chair over, carrying her favourite mug with 'Sip, Love, Repeat' printed on it in scrawling letters. If the agency gave out an award for 'Biggest Romantic', Freya would win without question.

'I want to hear absolutely everything,' she says, visibly bursting with anticipation.

I launch into an account of the screening with Gaby, fielding every clarifying question Freya has.

'Wait – she rejected *Maria*? But she would have been *perfect* for Raff,' says Freya.

'I thought so too,' I reply, seeing the ideal opportunity to transition to the topic I really want to discuss. 'But apparently, she reminded Gaby too much of one of Raff's exes – Sheree.'

'Hmm, Sheree...' Freya stares into space as if she's trying to conjure a mental picture of this mystery ex. 'Oh right, yes, I remember her,' she says eventually. 'Irish girl Raff dated for a couple of months a few years back. I suppose she and Maria *look* similar – they're both tall, willowy brunettes – but...' She shakes her head in disbelief. 'Did Gaby *really* reject her because of that? It seems... I don't know...'

'Not pertinent?' I offer, wondering if Freya will connect the dots herself.

'Exactly.'

'She wasn't keen on Julia either.'

'But she and Raff share several compatibility markers – they're both highly creative, for one.'

'I know. Ursula pulled rank and made her our alternate.'

'Well at least there's that but, Poppy, I really thought Maria would be our frontrunner.'

'Me too. So, any thoughts?'

'About the shortlist? I mean, it's not exactly what I had in mind, but it's a solid list.'

She's not getting it. I'm going to have to be more explicit.

'Any thoughts on Gaby's reaction to the longlisted potentials, specifically the ones she rejected?'

She drops her gaze as she contemplates the question. 'I suppose it shows that Gaby and Raff are much closer than he and I are these days. She seems to have picked up on quite a few factors I hadn't considered.'

How is she not making the connection?

'Frey, I'm pretty sure there's something else going on here.'

'How do you mean?'

'Has it ever occurred to you that Gaby may have feelings for Raff?' I ask.

'Feelings?'

'Romantic feelings, yes.'

Her surprise is so extreme it's comical, and then she bursts out laughing – and not a snigger or a chuckle or even a giggle. We're talking full-on, throw-her-head-back-and-guffaw laughter. Soon, everyone in the office is looking our way.

'Oi, Freya. What's so funny?' Nasrin shouts over the laughter.

Freya waves her hand in front of her face as she tries to catch her breath. Nas and I exchange a glance and she rolls her eyes.

'Are you done yet?' I ask Freya, my patience wearing thin.

She inhales deeply and gets her laughter under control. 'Sorry,' she gasps, running her forefingers under her eyes and blinking back tears.

'What's all this about?' asks Ursula, suddenly appearing at our side.

'Poppy said the *funniest* thing just now,' Freya replies, still catching her breath.

Ursula's lips quiver disapprovingly. 'Do tell.'

'Just about Gaby being in love with Raff.'

Freya shakes her head at me, her mouth curling into an amused, almost patronising smile. I *really* don't enjoy seeing Freya behave this way – it's very unlike her and almost definitely a result of her being too close to this case.

'I didn't say she's in love with him,' I say coolly. 'I was positing that there may be some underlying feelings impacting Gaby's judgement.'

'Poppy, Gaby has never fancied Raff – and vice versa. They're like brother and sister.'

'Got it,' I reply.

She sighs noisily, then stands. 'But thank you for the update.'

As Freya rolls her chair back to her desk, Ursula leans down, overwhelming me with her signature scent, Chanel N°5.

'After the staff meeting, I suggest you and I meet with Saskia and Paloma,' she whispers.

I meet her eyes. 'So, you agree with me?'

'Oh, absolutely. If you hadn't raised it, I would have.'

After Ursula leaves, I lean back in my chair as I start sifting through Freya's OTT reaction. This is worse than I anticipated – she's completely blind to a major factor that could derail this entire case. Maybe agreeing to keep her in the loop was a mistake.

I take a sip of tea, discovering it's gone cold, so I leap up and head to the kitchen to boil the kettle. After that interaction, I need all the magical, soothing properties tea can bring.

* * *

'I can see why you brought this to us,' says Saskia, 'but perhaps it was merely Gaby's protective instincts kicking in. He *is* her closest friend. Maybe she's just concerned about him getting hurt.'

Paloma chimes in with, 'That sounds plausible.'

'Hmm...' I murmur, not really convinced.

'No,' says Ursula, rejecting this line of reasoning. 'What Poppy and I witnessed last night was more than protectiveness. And I'd say these feelings have only recently come on. For Gaby, the *concept* of matching Rafferty has now become *reality*, triggering this response.'

'Interesting,' says Paloma. 'So, now she's been confronted with the competition, it's made her realise there's more to the friendship than she thought.'

'Actually,' I say, 'I doubt she's even aware at this stage. And if she does become cognisant of her feelings for Raff, she may conclude on her own that they're misplaced. We also need Gaby to act as envoy between us and Raff – otherwise we won't be able to action our meet-by-happenstance plan.'

'In that case,' says Saskia, 'why don't you proceed as planned but keep an eye on Gaby. If she comes to realise her true feelings or the manifestation of her feelings escalates, then let's revisit this.'

'Sounds good, Sask,' Paloma agrees. 'And thank you for raising this issue,' she says to me and Ursula. And with that, we're dismissed.

Even though we have a way forward, I'm worried that achieving Raff's HEA may lead to Gaby and her feelings becoming collateral damage. And, based on our earlier conversation, I don't know that I can keep my promise to Freya about sharing updates on the case.

Both realisations make me feel sick.

* * *

When I arrive home, our flat is warm and well-lit (thanks to our automated system), making it the sanctuary I'm craving after the day I've had.

Tristan's keys aren't in the catch-all on the hallstand, so I've beat him home, something that's becoming less frequent as the year progresses. We're so busy at the agency, I'm hoping we'll take on another agent in the New Year.

I shrug out of my coat and hang it up, then call for Saffron.

Surprisingly – *not* – she doesn't come, so I go into our room and change into my well-loved trackies and a hoodie – about as daggy as my outfits get.

Back in the lounge, I tell Google to start playing my favourite playlist of upbeat pop songs, then go to the fridge and take out the fixings for an epic grazing board. I may be a rubbish cook, but I can assemble a killer array of nibblies.

I'm putting on the finishing touches when Tristan's key sounds in the lock.

As soon as he enters our flat, I fly into his arms, clasping my hands behind his back and burying my face in the collar of his wool coat. 'I'm so glad you're home,' I say, my voice muffled. Still holding his laptop bag, one of his arms wraps around my waist, holding me tightly.

'Did you have a bad day?' he asks.

'Not terrible, but definitely not great.'

'I'm sorry, my love.'

'But look,' I say, gently easing out of our embrace, 'I made dinner.'

He regards my triumph with obvious appreciation. 'Nice. I can't wait to dig in.' His eyes meet mine, his expression softening. 'Are you sure you don't want me to whip something up?' he offers.

I shake my head. 'I just want to veg out on the sofa and stuff my face with cheese and olives.'

'Sounds good,' he says, his eyes twinkling. 'Give me a moment to change out of this,' he says, glancing down, 'and I'll find us a nice bottle to go with your superb grazing board.' He kisses me on the nose. 'Be right back.'

While Tristan's getting changed, I take the board to the lounge and set out plates, napkins, and utensils. I sit on the sofa, tucking my feet underneath me right as Saffron comes out of her room, her mouth stretching into a wide yawn.

'Oh, hello, little minx,' I say. 'Did you wake up because Tristan's home?'

She ignores me, instead sniffing the air.

'You haven't been fed yet, but I'm sure your boyfriend will sort you out after he's changed.'

'Hello, Saffy,' Tristan coos as he enters wearing almost an identical outfit to mine. If it were possible, I'd love him even more for slumming it in tracky dacks with his dag of a wife.

Saffron runs to him and he scoops her up one-handed and holds her to his chest. Even when he takes her with him into the kitchen, I can hear her purring. I'm convinced she'd be happier if it was just the two of them. He quickly feeds her, then peruses the wine fridge, returning with a Pinot Noir and two glasses.

'How's this?' he asks, showing me the label.

'Great,' I reply. I barely know my Sauv Blanc from my Cab Sauv, but it's nice of him to ask.

He pours and hands me a glass, then lifts his. 'To tomorrow being better than today.'

'Hear, hear to that,' I say. I clink my glass against his and take a sip, savouring the tangy pepperiness.

A moment later, Tristan reaches over and runs his hand along my thigh. 'Now, tell me about your not-so-good day.'

'I don't really want to go into the details, but there's been a complication in my case – the one with Freya's friend.'

'I'm sorry to hear that, darling,' he says, peering at me intently. He doesn't say anything more – no solutionising or mansplaining, just unadulterated empathy – another reason I love him as much as I do.

'Thanks. I've got Ursula I can lean on and I'm sure we'll figure something out, but...' I shrug.

'You've had better days,' he says.

'Yep.'

Out of the corner of my eye, I spy Saffron sniffing about the grazing board.

'Saffron Dean Fellows! You get away from that cheese immediately, if not sooner!' I bellow.

Saffron freezes, her paw suspended in air above the brie, and to her credit, she slowly places it on the floor. Tristan's laughter fills the room, and I start laughing with him, the mental and emotional toll of my not-so-good day ebbing away.

10

GABY

'She promised she'd keep me updated,' says Freya, making another circuit of my apartment. When she gets like this, she can't keep still. 'I mean, ostensibly, *I'm* the client. I'm the one who asked Poppy to take the case. But then she and Ursula have a meeting with Saskia and Paloma, and does she tell me what it was about? No! I'm left completely in the dark.'

'Frey...' She doesn't seem to hear me. 'Freya, *please* come and sit.'

She finally loses steam and joins me on the sofa, grabbing my only throw pillow – a gift from her – and placing it on her lap. 'I feel so... *excluded*,' she says softly.

I should have seen this coming. Actually, I *did* see this coming. Freya was always going to feel territorial about this case. I'm surprised we got this far before she flipped out.

'Hey,' I say. She stares fixedly at the coffee table. 'You know how you told me to tell you when you're being a drama queen?'

I nudge her with my toe, and she finally lifts her gaze to meet mine.

'I rescind my previous request,' she says gruffly.

Okay, time for the big guns – tough love it is.

'Well, I'm reinstating your previous request and you're being a drama queen. You need to chill.'

She scowls at me.

'That's not you chilling. That's the opposite of chill. Seriously, Frey – you *know* this isn't your case. And it's unreasonable to expect Poppy to inform you of every little detail as they occur.'

'But she said she would!'

'I seriously doubt th—'

I'm cut off by someone buzzing my apartment.

'Oh, shit,' I mutter.

'Are you expecting someone?'

'It's Raff,' I say, getting up and crossing to the wall console.

'What? *Why?*'

'Because I invited him,' I tell her.

Her jaw and eyebrows shoot in opposite directions, but I ignore her – she really is being overly dramatic – and buzz him in. Turning back to Freya, I say, 'You texted to say it was an emergency, Frey. Of *course* I called in the cavalry.'

She's too stunned to respond, and thirty seconds later, there's a knock at the door. I swing it open.

'I didn't know which kind of emergency, so I brought wine, crisps, and Penguins,' he says, holding up a canvas shopping bag stamped with the logo of one of our clients. 'Hiya,' he says, stooping to kiss my cheek.

'Hi, Raff.' I close the door and look on as he greets Freya with a one-armed bear hug.

'Poor you. I'm sorry you had a rubbish day,' he says, his chin resting on her head. 'Now, before you tell me everything, sweet, salty, or boozy?'

Freya's agitated mood melts away before my eyes as she steps back and peers up at Raff. 'Boozy and salty,' she replies, completely disarmed.

'Coming right up.'

And that there is one of the many reasons Raff will make someone a terrific boyfriend someday – or even husband.

He drops the bag of chips – sorry, *crisps* – on the coffee table, then goes into the kitchen to pour the wine.

Freya beelines to me. 'We can't tell him the real reason I'm upset,' she whispers.

'Yeah, no shit.'

Her lips flatten into a taut line. 'Gaby!' she whispers harshly.

'Sorry. Just... come up with something.'

'Me?'

'Yeah, it's your crisis.'

'Here we are,' says Raff, holding three glasses easily in his huge hands.

Freya takes one and I take another. 'So, what are we drinking to?' he asks, looking at Freya. 'Oh, fuck, you and Freddie didn't break up, did you?'

'No!' she cries, indignant.

'It's not out of the realm of possibility, Frey. That's the first thing I thought when I got your message.'

She looks at me, horrified. 'Why would you say that? Freddie and I are doing fabulously.'

My eyes dart towards Raff and I can tell he's thinking the same thing I am. We like Freddie – he's super sweet to Freya, which is the most important thing – but he's not the most interesting guy, especially when he's being overly didactic and goes off on a tangent. There's only so much you can hear about exotic fish without wishing Freddie had a mute button.

'We're glad,' Raff says with a convincing smile.

'So glad,' I echo. 'Let's sit, shall we.'

Raff and Freya sit on the sofa, and I flop into my teal Lounge Pug. The others make fun of my beanbag armchair, but they're just jealous. It's like if a chair was a hug.

'Right, now, tell me what's going on,' Raff says to Freya.

She flicks a glance in my direction then launches into a heavily redacted version of what happened at work, telling Raff she was left out of a discussion she thought she should have been part of.

'Oh, poor you,' he says, leaning across to pat her on the knee.

'Raff, before you got here, I was working the tough-love angle. You know, Freya's overreacting, she needs to chill... So, yeah...'

'Oh, I've cocked things up then, haven't I?' He looks between us. 'Should I go out and come back in again?'

Freya giggles, then downs a glug of wine. And with that, he's 'done a Raff' and made everything okay simply by being here.

'So, Raff, how's the transition to full-time pastry chef going?' I ask, eager to steer the conversation away from Freya's (hyper-bolised) work issue.

'Good. I feel a bit manic trying to get my head around every-thing, though.'

'Anything we can help with?' Freya asks.

'Kind of you, but no. Gabs has been brilliant, helping with my handover at work – and thank you,' he says, tilting his wine glass towards me.

'Sure, it was either help make the transition as smooth as possible or throw myself on the floor, wrap my arms around your ankles, and beg you not to leave.'

Raff chuckles.

'Are you going to apply for Raff's role?' Freya asks, as if it's only just occurred to her.

'I've already recommended her,' he tells Freya.

'You've— Why'd you do that?' I ask him.

'Because you'd smash it. Wait... are you seriously not interested?' he asks, a deep crease between his brows.

'Of *course* I am,' I say, waving him off. Now is not the time to contemplate the trajectory of my career. Tonight is about supporting Freya.

'Well, you should be. And Claire plans to discuss it with you – *soon*, Gabs.'

'Great,' I say and, thankfully, he doesn't make anything more of it. I think I do want it – but that's what makes me nervous. What if I don't get it? Where will that leave me in the whole pursuing-my-passion endeavour?

'So!' I exclaim, signposting a drastic change of subject. 'What's up next for the famous pastry chef? Have you been asked to appear on *Ballroom Battle of the Stars* yet?'

'Hilarious,' he replies drily.

'That's for *proper* celebrities, Gaby,' says Freya, failing (as always) to filter her thoughts before they pop out of her mouth.

'I can see you're feeling more like yourself,' Raff teases her. 'And no to *Ballroom Battles*,' he tells me. 'But I *do* have an intensive Food Hygiene Certificate course – levels one to three – this Saturday.'

Freya and I exchange a look, and she scrunches her nose. 'Sounds, um... fascinating,' I say.

He raises his eyebrows. 'Doubtful, but hopefully it won't be too bad – and I do need to know this stuff.'

Suddenly, I have a brainwave. Jane, the potential match who works for a not-for-profit – it's an organisation that provides nutritious meals to elderly people who live independently. Maybe she needs to refresh her Food Safety Certification? And even if she doesn't...

'Hey, Frey, I need your help,' I say, leaping up and heading to the kitchen.

'With what?' she whines at my back.

'Freya Nilsen, stop your whining and get your ass in here,' I call out.

There's some insolent murmuring from the next room, then she appears in the kitchen doorway. I grab her wrist and pull her closer, then quickly whisper my idea.

'That's perfect,' she whispers back, and I grin at her.

'What are you two whispering about?' asks Raff from the doorway. How is he so stealthy for such a tall guy?

I surreptitiously poke Freya so she doesn't blurt out anything that will ruin this meet cute before it even happens. Instead, she peers up at Raff with those big blue eyes and says, 'Gaby wanted my thoughts on period pants.'

'Period pa— Oh.'

There's a moment of embarrassed silence, then Raff mutters something about more wine, reaching past me to get the bottle, and I crash into him while trying to get out of his way.

As Raff and I bumble around the kitchen, Freya leans against the countertop doing a shitty job of stifling a giggle, and when Raff turns his back, she gives me a thumbs up.

At least she successfully deflected his question, but I *will* kill her later.

* * *

'This is excellent work, Gaby,' says Poppy after I've explained my idea and given her the name and location of Raff's course. 'And I agree that Jane is the most suitable potential match to go with. Food safety is at least adjacent to her work. I'll connect with her and tee it up.'

'Great!' I reply, faking enthusiasm.

Ever since Freya and Raff went home, I've felt... I don't know... *flat*.

We're really doing this. We're *actually* matching Raff with real women and one of them could be his person. But what if she turns out to be like Winnie and doesn't fit into our friendship group?

This isn't like buying him a sweater that doesn't fit. You can't return a *person*. 'Hey, Poppy... Yeah, sorry but Jane isn't a good fit for us. She's too clingy and we're not seeing enough of Raff. Could you... you know, rehome her?' Yeah, I'm sure that would go over well.

'Have a good night, Gaby,' Poppy says.

'Thanks, you too.'

We end the call and I spin the phone in my hands, staring off into space. It's such a weird position to be in. I'm essentially girl-friend shopping for my best friend. Weirder yet is that he *knows* – well, he doesn't *know* know, but surely he didn't buy that crap about period underwear. He's got to realise that Freya and I are up to something. *Right?*

I check the time on my phone. It's around 2 p.m. back in Seattle, and my mom should be home from work by now as she's on night-shift this month. I call her, half expecting it to go to voicemail, but she answers on the second ring.

'Hi, hun. This is a nice surprise.'

'Hi, Mom,' I reply, breaking into a smile. Just the sound of her voice can lift my spirits. With a jolt, it hits me how much they need lifting right now. 'How was work?' I ask.

'Oh, you know, just saving babies,' she replies, and we share the in-joke with gentle laughter.

Mom is an OB-GYN, a term I've had to explain to British people enough times that now if anyone asks, I just say, 'She delivers babies.'

Our in-joke was born (pun intended) when my brother-in-law, Jon, who's a commercial realtor, shouted into his phone, 'We're not saving babies, here, Dan. That's my mother-in-law's job!' That was bad enough, but he did it at the dinner table during Thanksgiving, then *winked* at her. Mom's knuckles turned white, and I could tell she was seconds away from throwing the turkey at his head.

He's always been a douchebag. But Issy loves him, so Mom and I put up with his douche-baggy ways. And when it comes to Jon, Dad feigns ignorance and stays out of it.

'I can't wait for you to get here,' she adds.

'I know, Mom. Me too.'

'For starters, you can help me run interference between Monica and Chrissy.'

'Oh no. What's going on?'

Mom launches into a soap opera's worth of wedding drama. Poor Monica has been fighting with Aunt Christine, who has apparently become a total Momzilla. I mentally pop some popcorn and settle in, instantly absorbed by Gina's special brand of storytelling.

God, I love my mom. Even after a long shift at the hospital, she takes the time to make me laugh, enveloping me in a huge dose of motherly love across the Atlantic.

But even through the laughter, a quiet unease hums away.

Is it taking the next step in my career? This bizarro matchmaking BS? Homesickness?

Whatever it is, it seems to be taking root, which only makes me worry about it more.

* * *

'Ready?' I ask Raff.

The December issue of *Nouveau Life* goes live tomorrow and with it, the article about Raff. Tonight, he's telling his parents he's leaving Global Reach and partnering with CiCi, and I'm here to give moral support.

'Hardly. I'd rather have a root canal with a rusty spoon – without anaesthetic.'

'That's, um... *graphic*. You know, I'm still happy to join the call. They won't yell at you if I'm right there.'

'It's a generous offer, but no. And my parents don't yell. They simply scowl at me in disapproval.'

'Sounds fun,' I say, trying to lighten the mood. It doesn't work and Raff keeps staring at the wall across from us.

'They might also threaten to disinherit me,' he says, as if to himself.

'Seriously?'

'Mm-hmm.'

I can't imagine my parents threatening me. Even when I've made decisions they may not have agreed with, they've supported me, wanting me to be my own person – championing me.

His parents sound like total assholes. And I will gladly put myself in the firing line if it means they'll be less asshole-y about his exciting news.

'Maybe I *should* join the call.'

He breaks from his daze, his head snapping in my direction, then gives me a lipless smile. 'It's okay, Gabs. But thanks.' He takes in a deep breath. 'Right,' he says, collecting his phone and standing. He gives me another of those please-kill-me-now smiles and goes into his bedroom and closes the door.

I take out my phone and text Freya:

He's talking to them now. *cringe emoji*

fingers crossed emoji Keep me posted

I rest my phone in my lap and fall back against the sofa, closing my eyes. It's been *such* a hectic week – like last week was and next week will be – I could *so* easily fall asleep.

'Gabs.' I wake with a start, discovering Raff peering down at me and gently shaking me by the shoulder.

I scramble to sit up. 'Sorry. How long was I out?' I ask.

'Could only have been a few minutes.'

'Oh.' I glance at my phone. Seven to be exact. He was in his bedroom for seven minutes. 'Are you done? Talking to your parents.'

'Yes.' He flops onto the sofa next to me.

'But that was only— Never mind. What did they say?'

'That I'm wasting a perfectly good degree... That I'm throwing away a passable career for a pipe dream...'

'Wait, did they really call marketing "passable"?'

'My father did, yes.'

'And the inheritance?'

'Didn't come up. My mother made some excuse about them having to get back to their friends, then abruptly ended the call.'

What sort of mother does that to her only child?

'Oh Raff, I'm so sorry your parents are such assholes.'

He chuckles. 'Thank you. I think.'

'I'm serious. At least you have CiCi and Devin. And me and Freya. And you know my parents love you...'

My parents *do* love Raff. Mom calls him the son she never had. Issy overheard her saying that once and was pissed off when she realised she meant Raff and not (douchebag) Jon.

Raff doesn't respond; instead, he stares at the wall again. Is *anything* I say going to get through? I can commiserate but I can't relate – not even remotely.

I take his hand. 'At least it's done now,' I tell him. 'Don't you feel relieved?'

He looks at me and nods.

'I do, yes.'

I kneel on the sofa, then reach over and give him a hug. 'You're Britain's Best Baker, don't forget.'

When I release him and sit back on my heels, there's a hint of amusement in his eyes.

'So, screw your parents. And no cake for them!' I declare.

He chuckles – finally – and shakes his head at me. 'You're an odd bod, Gaby Rivera.'

I shrug. 'Whatever works, hey?'

His head tilts and he looks at me intently. 'Thank you, for being here.'

'Hey, I got you, boo. Now I have to stand up because—' Too late. As soon as I release my feet and they hit the floor, the pins and needles kick in. 'Ow, ow, ow!' I say, falling back onto the sofa and tapping on my feet to wake them up.

'Right, while you do *that*, I'm ordering in.'

'Pizza!' I shout through the pain.

'Pizza for the banshee, coming right up.'

11

GABY

'Hiya, sorry I'm late,' says Freya, climbing onto the stool next to mine. We're at Whiskey Ginger, which is close to work and one of my favourite haunts. They excel in a cool vibe, tasty cocktails, and burgers so good, they remind me of home.

'That's okay. Raff was held up in a meeting anyway. He just texted,' I say, holding up my phone. 'ETA: five minutes.'

'Brilliant – enough time to get a drink.'

She gets up to go to the bar, but I place a hand on her arm to stop her.

'*Or* enough time to talk strategy. This isn't a social gathering, Frey.'

She gives me a weird look.

'Well, okay, it is, but the primary objective is to see how it went at Raff's course – with Jane.'

'Primary object— You sound like we're executing a plot to overthrow a foreign power or something. Remember what Poppy said? This isn't *Mission Impossible*,' she says.

'Yeah, yeah, okay. But just think, we could be minutes away

from learning that Raff has met his match – so to speak,' I add, realising the unintentional pun.

'Oh, you're right,' she says, a grin splitting her face. 'Isn't it exciting? Ooh, I'll have enough time to order a Christmas stocking with her name embroidered on it.'

'Well, that may be getting ahead of oursel—'

'Hello, I'm late, I know – endless bloody meetings this time of year.'

Raff smacks a kiss on each of our cheeks, then unwraps the tartan scarf from his neck and slides onto the third stool.

'Though, worth it, of course, Gabs,' he tells me, still trying to sell me on a role I already want.

'Right, first things first,' says Freya – and for the life of me, I'm convinced she's going to dive straight into asking about Jane. I poke her under the table, and she frowns at me briefly before her gaze lands back on Raff. 'Congratulations, Baking Star on the Rise!'

Oh, right – the article about Raff. Phew.

A blush creeps up Raff's cheeks and he shakes his head as he breaks into a smile. 'Thanks.'

'None of that false modesty nonsense. It was a cracking article, and you looked so dashing in the photographs,' she says.

He accepts the compliment with *slightly* more grace than the congratulations, tipping his head and saying, 'Well, thank you – but that's just testament to what a good photographer can do.'

'And stylist,' Freya adds, likely not realising she's added a backhand to her compliment. 'Loved the outfit. Did you get to keep it?'

'Er, yes, actually.'

'I didn't know that,' I say, surprised. 'You didn't bring anything home with you.'

'Well, I mean sort of. The designer was so happy with the shots, they sent me two pairs of jeans and five dress shirts.'

'Nice perk, Delaney,' I quip, and he grins.

Maybe the next time Freya and I try to entice him to go clothes shopping – for clothes that actually fit – we'll be successful.

'Right, enough about me, what's that then?' he asks, nodding at my almost finished drink.

'Apple cinnamon spritz.'

'Ooh, yum,' he says. 'Another?' he asks.

'Sure.'

'Frey? What'll it be?'

'White wine, please.'

'This coming from Miss Christmas?' I ask, pretending to be aghast. 'Bah, humbug!' I declare. 'Try again.'

'Fine,' she says with a giggle. 'I'll have what Gaby's having.'

Raff disappears into the growing crowd, snaking his way to the bar.

'So, back to Jane...' she says, a glint of mischief in her eye. She takes out her phone and taps away, and ten seconds later, shows me a customisable Christmas stocking on an artisan website. 'What about this one?' she asks.

'Uh, no.'

'Why not?' She tilts her head as she regards her phone screen.

'Because you're putting the cart and all the hay it's carrying *way* before the horse.'

She blinks at me as if confused, then she leans in close. 'But Jane was the number-one potential,' she says loudly. We may be in a noisy bar but it's a good thing Raff's still getting our drinks, his reddish curls visible above the crowd.

'Yes, but you've told me a million times that matchmaking isn't an exact science,' I retort. 'Besides, Jane was only first because the perfect opportunity presented itself.'

Freya's mouth puckers and she slumps on her stool.

'Here we are: three apple cinnamon spritzes,' says Raff, setting them on the table.

He climbs back onto the third stool and takes a sip of his drink, then licks his lips. I shoot Freya a look. Stupidly, I forgot to tell her *I* would take the lead on bringing up the course – and Jane – so I do my best to convey this with my eyes.

My best isn't good enough.

'So, how was your course on the weekend, Raff? Meet anyone interesting?'

I exhale a frustrated sigh. Freya's about as subtle as a sledgehammer.

'What? Oh, er, it was fine, I suppose. Most of it was common sense. Just glad to be done with it.'

'And how many other people were there?' I ask, pretending to be enthralled.

'About twenty of us, I'd say.'

'Cool.'

We sip our drinks in silence.

'And what's the age range for that sort of course?' asks Freya, finally playing ball and asking a decent question.

'Quite broad, actually. I'd say between sixteen and sixty.'

'Fascinating,' I reply.

It's not, which makes it a stupid thing to say, and I'm not surprised when Raff squints at me curiously.

Then he starts laughing. 'There was this *one* woman...'

I exchange a quick glance with Freya, then look back at Raff. This might be it.

'She would *not stop talking*.'

'What do you mean?' asks Freya.

'I mean, we're all there for this intensive course and none of us *really* want to be there... It's just, you know... go, learn the content, do the test, get the certificate. But she wanted to chat the entire day – and so many questions. Where do I live? What do I like to do at the weekend? That sort of thing. I had to ask her several times to please be quiet, as I'd missed what the instructor was saying.'

'Sounds really annoying,' I say, mentally crossing my fingers that her name wasn't Jane. Although, this sounds exactly how I would behave if I was supposed to meet a guy 'by happenstance'. And it's not like Jane is a trained actor.

'Did you catch her name?' Freya asks.

'I didn't have a choice – she plopped down next to me right as we were about to start and introduced herself. Why do you ask?' His question comes with a confused expression, but Freya merely shrugs and takes a slug of her cocktail.

Think, Gaby.

'Sounds like this gal I used to sit next to in Chemistry my senior year. Total chatterbox. Would not shut up.' I pretend to try and recall her name, then snap my fingers. 'Calliope, that's right.'

'Well, at least she had an interesting name. This woman was called Jane. Nice enough but *really* not the time or the place for a chat.'

Shit.

Freya catches my eye, our two-second look conveying a myriad of thoughts, the primary one being: *Back to the drawing board.*

But the thing is, even though I'm disappointed that Jane was a swing and a miss, there's also a niggling feeling of relief. What the hell is that about?

* * *

Poppy

'Bugger,' I mutter to myself after I hang up from Gaby.

'What's happened?' asks George, his head popping up above his monitor three desks away.

'Seriously, how did you hear that?'

He comes over, even though I didn't ask him to, and props himself on the edge of my desk. 'I've told you before, I have outstanding hearing. So, what's up? Why "bugger"?'

'Potential number one didn't work out.'

'Oh, that *is* a bugger.'

While it's reasonably common to have to move down the list – only around a third of our clients are matched with the first potential – it's still disappointing, especially as the happenstance meeting with Jane seemed ideal – on paper anyway.

'So, who's number two?' George asks.

I regard him closely. He doesn't usually show this much interest in the minutiae of my cases, but this case is special – it's Freya's close friend and there's an unspoken added layer of pressure that Raff gets his HEA.

It won't hurt to get George's take on things – he's really good at brainstorming – so I tell him about Ava, who's a veterinarian.

'Hmm,' he says, 'too bad your client doesn't have a dog or a cat.'

I chuckle and prop my chin on my hand. *Typically*, he's good at brainstorming.

'And how would that help us, exactly? I mean, we're *good*...' I say, alluding to how often we successfully deploy our vast network of connections. 'But his pet would need to see a vet, his existing vet would have to be unavailable, *and* we'd have to somehow steer him towards Ava's practice.'

'Yes, yes, I see your point.'

We fall quiet – both of us noodling – and I lean back in my chair and stare at the peace lily on my desk. I've come up with some of my best ideas gazing into its waxy, deep-green leaves.

George leans closer and I look up at him. 'Why don't you ask Freya?' he suggests quietly. 'She might have something.'

I look over at Freya, who's seated at her desk with her back to me. She's been cool towards me since our conversation about Gaby and Raff, our exchanges limited to overly polite hellos and good-byes. I recognise there was a little tension between us when we spoke that day, but is she waiting for an *apology*? If so, I'm not sure what I have to apologise for.

Maybe she's just busy with her divorcée case. It sounds like a bit of a nightmare.

'I'll think about it,' I say noncommittally.

George straightens up and with a squeeze of my shoulder, goes back to his desk.

I'm about to check emails when my phone rings. It's Gaby again.

'Hey, Gaby,' I say, 'what's up?'

'I've been thinking about Jane.'

'Yeah, me too. Do you reckon Raff would buy bumping into her again at some random location?'

She chuckles. 'Yeah, I doubt that would fly. He's smart – he'd know something was up.'

'I figured.'

'*But*,' she continues, 'something occurred to me. Raff's always been terrible at recognising when someone's flirting with him – girls, guys, one of our non-binary colleagues – it doesn't matter. He's oblivious. Someone could strip naked in front of him and say, "Take me, Raff," and he'd reply, "Where do you want to go?"'

This makes me laugh out loud.

'So, you're saying that even if Jane had solid flirtation skills – which we don't know for sure – they would have been lost on Raff?'

'Exactly.'

I pause for a moment, considering the implications, then say, 'We need a new plan,' right as Gaby says the same thing.

We both laugh.

'I'm glad we're on the same page,' she says.

'Me too.' I glance over and catch Freya looking my way. She must have heard I'm on a call with Gaby. 'You available to meet after work?' I ask Gaby.

'Um, hang on...' There's a pause – presumably, she's checking her diary. 'No client events tonight, so free as a bird.'

'Great. I'll text you where and when.'

'Cool. See ya then.'

We end the call and I stare at the peace lily again. For someone who may have feelings for Raff, Gaby is certainly doing her part – and then some – to help him find his match. Maybe Ursula and I were wrong.

Or maybe Gaby *does* have feelings for him but still hasn't admitted them to herself. This isn't the first time I've encountered someone who's oblivious to their own feelings – especially romantic ones.

And there's another possibility, one I haven't considered before now. What if Raff is into Gaby – even if he doesn't recognise yet – which is why he didn't engage with Jane at the course?

The kernel of an idea flits into my mind, and I wait patiently for it to take shape. It only takes a few minutes before I know what our new plan is, and it should give me clarity about Gaby's feelings – possibly even Raff's.

Ursula's out of the office at the moment, but I'll fill her in when she returns. I'm positive she'll agree with my strategy.

I glance back at Freya, who's now typing on her laptop. I suppose now is as good a time as any to fall on my non-existent sword and make things right between us. Besides, even if she doesn't believe there might be something between Gaby and Raff, she'll be instrumental in executing stage one of my new plan, starting with meeting Gaby for drinks.

'Hey, Freya,' I call out as I stand and make my way to her desk.

When I get there, she looks up at me, her eyes filled with contrition.

'Hi, Poppy. I was about to come over.'

'Oh, yeah?'

She nods. 'I'm so sorry. I've been a nitwit...'

'Nah!' I say with a wave of my hand. She blinks at me slowly, as we both know this is a lie. 'Well, okay, maybe a little one,' I add gently.

* * *

Gaby

Poppy's chosen The Gin Palace for our meet-up, a hip cocktail bar in Covent Garden which she says is halfway between the agency and her apartment. Or close to. I'm the first to arrive but there aren't any seats available, even though it's only Tuesday, and I do my best to stake out a space big enough for me, Poppy, and Freya.

At first I was surprised that Freya's coming with her, but then it hit me – Poppy's good at people. Of course she got Freya to come. And Freya may be sweet as pie most of the time, but when she gets a bee in her bonnet... Well, kudos to Poppy for setting the bee free.

'We're here!' Freya declares, pushing between two burly banker types. They scowl in her direction, but she's oblivious. She gives me a cheek kiss as Poppy follows her into the three-square-feet of floor I've commandeered.

'Hey, Gaby.'

'Hey. Is it always like this?' I ask Poppy, scanning the room.

'To be honest, I wouldn't know – it's only my second time here and last time, Greta saved me a seat at the bar,' she replies. 'It's probably the lead up to the holidays.'

'Oh yeah.' Somehow, the Christmas decorations and a tinny

rendition of 'The Little Drummer Boy' blaring from the sound system escaped my notice till now.

'So, what are you having?' she asks us. 'My shout.'

'A Cosmo,' says Freya. I throw her a look. 'What?'

'Have we suddenly been transported back to 1999?' I quip.

'I'm finally watching *Sex and the City*,' she explains with a shrug. 'I've never had a Cosmo and I want to see what all the fuss is about.'

'Okay, sure,' I reply.

'I'm a Charlotte,' she adds thoughtfully, and I'd have to agree.

Which makes me what? Carrie's a romantic – not me at all. Samantha is a sex goddess – that's *definitely* not me. So, Miranda? She's way more career oriented than I am. Maybe I'm nobody.

'And for you, Gaby?' Poppy asks, her words cutting through my bizarre introspection.

'Whatever you're having is fine,' I say with a half-hearted smile.

Poppy disappears into the crowd, and I turn to Freya.

'So, you two are good?'

'We are. I was acting like a nitwit, and I apologised this morning. This is Poppy's case and it's not her fault I got my knickers in such a twist.'

I shake my head at her. I could have told her the same thing and it wouldn't have made a hill of beans difference. Come to think of it, I *did* tell her the same thing...

'What?' she asks.

'Never mind,' I say – it's not worth rehashing.

She tilts her head and regards me closely.

Now *I* say, 'What?'

Her lips disappear between her teeth as if she's trying to decide whether to tell me something.

She releases her lips. 'It's nothing,' she says.

'Wow, such sparkling conversation tonight. We should have a podcast,' I joke.

'Far too busy for that,' she replies seriously, and I let it go. 'Right, now, let's talk about Raff's case... Between the potentials you vetoed at the screening and Raff spending an entire day telling Jane to shush, we're much further down the longlist than I would have expected.'

'Wait, so you saw the longlist?'

'Of course.'

This is news to me, but it makes me curious.

'So, which one was your favourite?' I ask.

'I wouldn't say *favourite*, but I liked Maria.'

'Maria... Oh, no. She was *way* too much like Sheree – they look practically identical. And Raff was *heartbroken* after she moved back to Dublin.'

'Right,' Freya says slowly, her brow creasing into a frown. 'And what about Julia, the artist?'

'The one who likes German rave music. Raff can't stand that crap.'

'And apparently, neither can you,' she says.

'Excuse me,' calls out a familiar Australian accent. I look towards Poppy's voice and see that she's squeezing through the crowd carrying three cocktails aloft, the same way Raff does, but with much smaller hands. I relieve her of the Cosmo and hand it to Freya.

'Phoof,' sighs Poppy. 'Maybe we should have met at the agency. A triathlon would be easier than that.'

She hands me a highball garnished with a wedge of lime. I sniff it – it's gingery. 'Dark 'n' stormy?' I ask, and she grins.

'Cheers, big ears.' She clinks her glass against mine, then Freya's, and takes a sip of her drink.

I'm still stuck on her oddball toast, when Freya comes back with, 'To love, laughter, and happily ever after.'

'Cheers,' I say simply, raising my glass at them in turn. I take a drink and it's delicious.

'Right,' says Poppy, 'let's get to why we're here. I've been noodling on this since our call, Gaby, and if Raff really is as clueless about spotting signals as you say he is, then I reckon he needs a wing-woman for the next happenstance meeting.'

'Oh, yeah, that's a great idea,' I say, instantly imagining Freya and Freddie inviting Raff to something and (somehow) bumping into Ava. 'I wish I'd thought of it.'

'Stellar idea, Poppy,' says Freya, nodding at her earnestly.

'So, you're happy to be Raff's wing-woman?' Poppy asks, looking directly at me.

'Wait, *what*?'

12

GABY

'But why me? Freya would be a *way* better wing-woman than I would,' I say adamantly. 'She's a *matchmaker*.'

'Yes, but you're closer to Raff than I am, which makes *you* better suited,' Freya retorts.

She and I lock eyes for a beat, then I turn to Poppy. 'Seriously, why me?'

'Well, from what you've both told me, you *are* closer to Raff than Freya,' she replies. 'But you're forgetting that it can't be Freya – conflict of interest, remember?'

'But she'd be acting as his friend, not his matchmaker.'

Poppy makes a face that tells me I'm playing semantics, but I don't care. I'd make a shitty wing-woman – *period*.

'Help me out here, Frey,' I plead.

'I'm sorry, but I agree with Poppy. And with my trip to Sweden coming up and my divorcée case – she's *such* a handful – I don't have the capacity right now. *Please?* If we're going to find Raff a girlfriend before Christmas—'

'Wait,' says Poppy, interrupting. 'Is that your expected timeframe? Because that's pushing it, Frey.'

'See?' I say to Freya. 'And I've got stuff on too. I've got all my holiday campaigns, I'm going home in a couple of weeks, *and* I'm helping Raff tie things up at work... Maybe we need to wait till the New Year and pick this up again then.'

What I don't say is that by January, I might have talked Freya into playing wing-woman instead of me.

'Nooo,' she wails.

What is with her lately? All this whining and wailing. I frown at her, about to call it out, when Poppy addresses me.

'How about this,' she says. 'Is there anything coming up on your calendar that you could invite Raff along to?'

'You mean before Christmas?' She nods and when I turn towards Freya, she's nodding along, her eyes filled with hope.

'I've got a bunch of client events,' I say, taking out my phone and navigating to my calendar.

My personal stuff is in yellow, and my out-of-hours work stuff in red – and sadly, the coming weeks are drowning in red. With this many client holiday parties in the lead up to Christmas, my calendar looks like a crime scene. These events can be fun – some more than others – but they tend to follow the same format with the only distinguishing feature being the contents of the goodie bags.

'There's this,' I say, spying a client event Raff is also attending. 'Raff and I are both going to the LuxeLustre event next Tuesday.'

'LuxeLustre?' Poppy asks.

'Luxury jewellery designer.'

'Ahh,' she replies. 'I suppose that could work, but I was hoping for something a little less "corporate-y" and a little more personal. Is there anything else?'

My eyes land on this coming Saturday afternoon, which I've blocked out to go to a day spa. They're one of my newer clients – super upmarket and way out of my modest marketing manager budget. They've booked me in for 'the full treatment' – gratis for me and a guest. Only I'd forgotten about it till now and I haven't invited anyone yet.

Would Raff want to go with me? The thought of him wrapped in a white, fluffy robe with cucumbers on his eyes makes me chuckle.

'Care to share?' Poppy asks.

I hold up my phone. 'I've got this day spa thing on Saturday. A freebie from a client for me and a guest, but I doubt—'

'Perfect!' Freya chirps.

'A day spa? Raff?' I give her my you've-got-to-be-kidding look.

'He has been really stressed lately,' she replies earnestly.

When I glance at Poppy, it's clear she's amused. She gives a half-shrug. 'Couldn't hurt to ask. But could you get Ava in as well? The agency will cover the cost.'

'It's kinda last-minute but I've got a good relationship with them. I can ask.'

'It really is perfect, Gaby,' Freya reiterates.

I look between them. How have I gone from 'no frigging way' to 'I can ask' in a matter of minutes? Then it dawns on me.

'Oh, you guys are *good*,' I tell them.

Freya blinks at me innocently but Poppy owns it, quipping, 'Too bloody right we are,' before downing the last of her drink.

* * *

'Er, no thanks. I'll be very busy sorting my sock drawer on Saturday.'

As I predicted, Raff doesn't want to go to the day spa – shocker. And this is *after* my contact at Elysium Elite agreed to squeeze Ava into an already booked-out day – for *free*.

With one half of the plan now in place, I've got to get Raff to change his mind. As I'm in a time-crunch, I skip sweet talking, cajoling, bribery, and blackmail – though what I'd use against him is a mystery; he's too good a person to ever be blackmailed.

Instead, I go straight to begging.

'*Please*. Freya can't come and I *need* a day of pampering. I'm running around at work like a headless chicken...' This is a lie, as I'm organised as hell at work. 'And I haven't even packed for Seattle yet. I'm a huge ball of stress.'

'First off, you are smashing it at work.' I should have known he'd refute that. 'And second, your trip is more than a fortnight away and you *never* pack in advance, Miss "I'll pack the morning of and forget my knickers".'

'That was one time.' It was three times. 'Besides, you're leaving me at Global Reach all alone and you owe me.'

'Ah, so now we get to the crux of it.' His green eyes crease at the corners, betraying his stern expression. 'And I owe you because...?'

'You're my work husband and you're abandoning me.'

I do *not* like the way my voice hitches on 'abandoning'. What the hell is that about? I'm a big girl and Raff is one of my closest friends. Of *course* we'll still see each other.

And then it hits me – *hard*. When Freya left, our friendship transitioned to a new phase. We're still close but not *close* close.

I must be afraid that the same thing will happen with Raff. I suddenly feel queasy, which is unfair because Raff deserves this. He deserves to follow his passion.

He cocks his head, giving me a pitying look. I don't like that either, especially if it's a talisman of the inevitable change of our dynamic.

'You still have Lorrie and Quinn,' he says gently. 'Surely the two of them together add up to one work spouse.'

'It's not the same thing,' I say tersely. 'And we're getting off topic. Just come to the day spa. It'll be fun.'

He stares at me through narrowed eyes. 'I wouldn't have to walk about nude, would I?'

I cough out a laugh. 'What? No. It's not like that. It's "all genders" in the common areas, meaning everyone will be wearing robes. It's only in the treatment rooms that they make you strip naked.'

'Fuck. Really?'

'*No!* But you should see your face right now,' I say with a laugh, glad to be done with the heavy part of the conversation.

Raff's lips stretch into a mirthless smile. 'This is not the way to get me to agree, you know.'

'What is the way, then? Because I am not taking no for an answer.'

He throws his head back and heaves out a sigh of surrender. 'Fine!'

'Thank you!' I leap up to run around the conference table and wrap my arms around his shoulders in a hug. He pats my arm, his head shaking. I can tell he's still wary, but at least I've kept my promise to Poppy about getting him to the day spa.

There's a knock at the door and a colleague pokes her head in as three others huddle behind her.

'Sorry, but we've got Byron booked from one.'

'That's my fault,' I say, straightening.

Raff and I vacate the meeting room and go back to our respective desks. I text Poppy and Freya to tell them The Pamper Ploy is a go!

Poppy texts back almost immediately.

Cute name. Better trademark that. *winky face*

With Poppy briefing Ava, all I have to do before Saturday is mentally prepare for ultimate wing-womaning.

Whatever that is.

* * *

'I could get used to this,' says Raff, stretching out on a cushioned lounger.

We're only an hour in, but we've already been in the hot tub *and* the infrared sauna. Then we (stupidly and literally) took the plunge in the freezing-cold plunge pool. I lasted approximately 3.2 seconds before I shot up the ladder and stood on the platform shivering. Without waiting for Raff, who was laughing at my hasty retreat, I beelined for the hot tub and immersed myself in the steaming water up to my neck until I thawed out.

Plunge pools are hardcore, and I am anything but.

Now we have free time until our massages in thirty minutes. At first, the staff offered us a couples massage – hilarious! – but we set them straight and told them we're just friends.

An older woman enters the relaxation room wearing the spa's uniform. It looks like pyjamas and I'm a little envious she gets to dress so comfortably for work. She carries herself as if she does yoga three times a day, her movement graceful and fluid, and she sets down a tray on the table between us.

'Herbal tea,' she says. 'Lavender – good for relaxation,' she adds with a smile.

She leaves us to pour from a small glass tea pot into two teeny pottery cups. They remind me of the shot glasses I once brought back from Mexico.

'Shall I be mother?' asks Raff, reaching for the pot.

'Moth— Oh, right,' I say, remembering what that expression means. I've only heard it a few times and never once from anyone under the age of sixty.

Raff hands me one of the cups and I sniff. It smells incredible.

But when I take a sip, it requires all my willpower not to spit it out. Soap. It tastes exactly like soap. I swallow and glance over at Raff, who's making the same face as me.

'Tea shouldn't taste like potpourri,' he says, setting the cup down.

'I was going to say "soap",' I say, putting mine next to his.

'The thing is,' he tells me intently, 'floral notes can be wondrous in food – and in this case, tea. But you cannot overdo it.'

'I'm onto you. You're just quoting Vicky Harrington,' I say, referring to one of the judges on *Britain's Best Baker*.

'That's *Dame* Vicky to you,' he says with a smile.

'She flirted with you, you know.'

His eyes widen. 'She never did any such thing. She was only being friendly.'

My ass, she was, I think. She may be in her seventies but Dame Vicky always had a flirty smile for Raff. She also touched his forearm a lot and said 'Oh, Rafferty' so often, we should have turned it into a drinking game.

I snigger to myself. Unknowingly, he's just warranted me being his wing-woman.

I check the clock – a large disc of blond wood that blends in perfectly with the wall. We're only a few minutes off when Ava is supposed to arr—

'Excuse me, but you're not saving this for anyone, are you?'

Raff and I both look in the direction of the softly spoken voice. It's her. God, she is really pretty – *way* prettier than she seemed in the photos Poppy showed me. About five-six, with a chocolate-brown pixie cut, striking brows that frame almond-shaped brown eyes, and rosebud lips. Apt really, as she reminds me of a young Rose Byrne.

Raff looks between me and Ava – *twice* – then splutters, 'Oh no, all yours.'

Does that reaction mean Raff finds her attractive? I hope so.

Ava smiles at us sweetly, then lowers herself onto the lounger next to Raff's and reclines, sighing serenely as her chin tips towards the ceiling. We could take a photo of her exactly like that and use it in one of Elysium Elite's ad campaigns – without having to edit it.

'Isn't this place divine?' she asks, looking over with a smile.

'Is this your first time at Elysium?' I ask, leaning past Raff.

'First, but definitely not the last. You?'

'First time for us both.' I lean in closer and whisper, 'It's a perk. I'm their marketing manager.'

'Ooh, nice perk.' We exchange smiles. 'And what do you do?' she asks Raff.

For a pseudo-celebrity who hates being recognised, Ava pretending *not* to recognise Raff is a slam dunk. No wonder he grins. 'I work in marketing as well,' he replies.

Trust him to downplay his big win *and* omit his career change. He really is hopeless.

'But not for much longer,' I tell her.

Raff's cheeks turn pink. 'Er, yes. That's right. I'm becoming a baker.'

If I could, I'd backhand him. There's modesty and there's ultimate understatement.

'Raff recently won *Britain's Best Bakers*,' I say. 'The Christmas edition.'

'Oh,' she says with a laugh. 'I should have recognised you. My nan loves that show.'

There's a beat of silence, then we all snigger, and a middle-aged woman on a lounger across the way shoots us a filthy look.

'Eek,' Ava whispers. 'I'm Ava, by the way.'

'Rafferty – well, Raff,' he says, pointing to himself.

'And I'm Gaby, Raff's friend.'

Raff's head snaps in my direction, a scowl passing over his face.

I can almost *hear* him wondering why I clarified that we're not a couple.

'So, what treatments are you having?' she asks.

Raff turns back to Ava, his eyes staying locked on mine until the last second. 'Er, massages, then a facial.'

'And pedicures,' I chime in.

'But I'm only doing the bits without nail polish,' he's quick to add.

'Sounds fab,' she says, and we all fall silent.

Say something, Raff, I think, willing him to engage. Maybe me being here is the issue. I should excuse myself.

'I'm going to the bathroom,' I state, climbing off my lounger.

Without looking back, I leave the relaxation room and head out into the corridor. I don't need the bathroom, but I may as well scope it out. If it's anything like the rest of this joint, including the locker room, it will be something to behold.

It is. It has the same aesthetic as the rest of the day spa right down to the soft, warm lighting. I glance at myself in the mirror and I look incredible in this light – my skin especially. Note to self: buy new bulbs for the bathroom in my apartment. No matter how rested I am, or how good I'm feeling about myself, one glance in my bathroom mirror and I feel like Gollum after a big night out.

I take my time, trying out some of the free toiletries on offer.

Stupidly, I spray two different perfumes onto my wrists and now I smell like a beach birthed a bouquet. I run my wrists under water and rub them together but that only makes it worse.

I check the time. There are clocks everywhere here, so clients arrive at their treatments on time, and it's been fifteen minutes since I left Raff and Ava. Surely that's long enough for her to have done whatever it is that Poppy coached her to do?

I head back to the relaxation room and Raff's there on his own, sitting on the side of his lounger.

'Where's Ava?' I ask.

'She had her massage. Speaking of, we'd better get going. I was worried you'd fallen in.'

'Uh, no... I was, uh...'

He sniffs the air. 'Is that you?' he asks. 'A bit strong, Gabs.'

But before I can refute his mild insult, Raff stands, then tightens the sash of his robe. 'This way,' he says, leading the way to the massage wing.

I jog to catch up to him. 'She seemed nice,' I say.

'Who? Oh, yes, I suppose. Can I ask... Is that really the done thing?'

'What?'

'Chatting up strangers in the relaxation room at a day spa? Hardly very relaxing if you're having to make small talk, is it? *And* you left me alone with her.'

'I went to the *bathroom*, Raff. It's not like I left you for dead.'

He stops suddenly and regards me. 'I know. Sorry. It's just... Now that we're here, I'm quite enjoying myself and...' His eyes flick to the wall behind me. 'Oh bollocks. Come on, we'll be late.'

He strides off again and I rush to catch up.

Needless to say, it is *not* a relaxing massage. How can it be when I spend the entire hour bombarding myself with questions? One prevails, my mind landing on it at least a dozen times.

How can Raff be so clueless?

Especially when he gave us a green light to match him. How can he not have cottoned on that Jane and Ava were *plants*? Maybe I need to make a poster – with glitter – and hold it up in front of him:

Potential girlfriend alert!

But he's so clueless, he probably wouldn't even get *that*.

13

GABY

'Wow, that's a bit forward, following me like that,' Raff mumbles to himself.

I glance over and he's on his Instagram account – his personal one, not the one set up by *Britain's Best Bakers'* social media team.

'Who's following you?' I ask, knowing it's got to be Ava.

'The woman from the spa – Ava.' He holds up his phone to show me her profile. *Well, at least he's shown enough interest to check it out*, I think, but he immediately goes back to his main feed and starts scrolling with his thumb.

I swallow my frustration. 'Why is it forward of her to follow you? You had a conversation – she's not some rando, Raff.'

'I suppose,' he says thoughtfully, then he barks out a laugh. 'You do realise that's twice in as many weeks that a perfect stranger has accosted me with questions.'

Seriously? How is he not getting this?

'So?' I say, my patience stretched thin. 'She seemed nice.'

'Why are you so stroppy all of a sudden?' he asks.

I regard him closely, going back and forth on what I should – and shouldn't – say to him. I *could* come clean and shout, 'You were supposed to ask her out, you idiot!' but instead I reply, 'Because I was all relaxed and Zen and now we're packed into public transit, and I already feel like I need another massage.' It's the truth – just not the whole truth.

Raff puts his phone in his jeans pocket.

'No doubt their usual clients make their way home lolling about on the backseat of town cars.'

He's smirking at me, and I nudge him gently in the ribs with my elbow. 'You're teasing me.'

'A little bit.'

I lean against him, and he switches to holding on with his other hand, then wraps a reassuring arm around my shoulder. He knows how I feel about crowded trains and buses *and* the Tube (which also goes underground – the horror). I can never fully relax until I'm above ground, on terra firma, and free and clear of the crowds.

A crowded bar? Fine – I can take myself outside if I need to. But crowded PT? I'd rather stick a fork in my eye. And in the lead up to the holidays, it's worse than ever.

Only three more stops until Kingston, I tell myself.

'So, what did you two talk about while I was in the bathroom?' I ask.

'This and that. She's a veterinarian.'

That's all he found out in fifteen minutes? Raff doesn't need a wing-woman; he needs a wing-*squadron*.

It looked so easy on the show – how well he got along with the other contestants. And he's great with clients – super charming. So why is it that when it's one on one and he just needs to be himself, his communication skills fly out the window? He was a pink-faced, spluttering mess when Ava first joined us at the spa.

God, is that how he is on first dates? If it is, then it's a wonder he's dated as much as he has. Although, it's likely that many women find him charming simply because he's not a cocky asshole who's only out for sex.

If it weren't thwarting our efforts, I'd find it endearing how royally he's botched these meetings – first Jane and now Ava.

'Much on for the rest of the day?' he asks. 'Hot date?' he adds.

I shake my head. Who has time for dating this time of year? The last date I went on was in October, and it was over nearly before it started. He was one of those guys who only dates so he can flex. And I mean that figuratively – he couldn't stop talking about himself – *and* literally. I lost count of the number of times he adopted some sort of pose and tensed his biceps.

I got out of there after one drink. Even if I could have put up with his annoying personality for a hookup, there's no way a guy like that is anything but selfish in bed.

'Hardly,' I reply, steering clear of the gory details. 'I feel like I haven't dated since the Nixon administration.'

'Huh?'

I glance up at him. 'Stupid joke. Never mind.'

'You know, you really should put yourself out there more, Gabs. You're an attractive woman, clever, accomplished, *kind*... Any bloke would be lucky to have you.'

Oh, the fucking irony, I want to shout across the train carriage. Instead, I blink at him, wondering for the umpteenth time how he can be so clueless. He's got Alicia Silverstone beat a thousand times over.

* * *

Poppy

I'm waiting at Ursula's desk when she comes in.

'Good morning, Poppy.'

'Good morning. Have you much on today?'

She pauses a moment, her lips tensing, highlighting my 'fatal' error. I'm so keen to discuss Raff's case, I've jumped on her the second she's arrived.

'I'll give you a minute.'

'Mm-hmm,' she murmurs.

I scamper back to my desk and plop into my chair, reaching for my phone. Gaby's message is still on the screen.

> Well, he did it again. Raff the Oblivious reigns supreme. Ava is a no-go even though I left them alone to talk. Nice gal and very pretty but no date. *shrug emoji* We did have a nice day at the spa. *smiley face emoji* So what's plan C? *thinking face emoji*

Plan C is I take Raff by the shoulders and give him a shake.

No, that's not fair. As far as clients go, I have had far bigger challenges. My own husband comes to mind. Pre-me and a clause in his grandfather's will requiring that he marry before his thirty-fifth birthday or lose his inheritance, he was anti-relationships, anti-marriage, and vehemently anti-love.

Of course, matching *myself* with a client is a one-time-only thing.

Maybe our whole approach is off. Maybe Gaby's right and we should wait until the New Year then regroup. Or we're upfront with Raff about what we're doing and ask him (nicely) to fall into line. I certainly don't want to keep frittering away solid potential matches because he's so oblivious to what's going on.

I look over at Freya, who's at her desk chatting animatedly on the phone. How likely is it that I can convince her to put this case on hiatus for now?

I re-read Gaby's message a third time – not even the slightest hint of hesitation on her part. She *seems* 100 per cent all-in on matching Raff, but...

It's rare that I am completely off-base when intuiting someone's true feelings – the same for Ursula, who's far more experienced at matchmaking than I am. So, I'm not abandoning my suspicions just yet.

'I'm free now, Poppy,' says Ursula.

'Great,' I say. 'I've booked us a meeting room.'

Once we're in the meeting room – my favourite one that looks out over the Thames – I quickly take her through our two failed matches. Even though her expression remains mostly static, tension in her jaw belies her calm exterior.

While we match around a third of our clients the first time, most of the others match with the second potential. It's rare that we need to move further down the list – in this case, to our alternate, Julia.

'It sounds to me like it's the set-ups that are the issue,' she says. I refrain from mentioning that happenstance set-ups were her idea. I need her onside. 'Perhaps he's one of those people who does better in a group,' she adds.

'Could be,' I say hesitantly. 'But Gaby says he hates being the centre of attention.'

'That's it exactly. In a group, he doesn't have to be the centre of attention. He's simply one of many. You know, when I saw him on *Britain's Best Bakers*—'

'Oh, I didn't know you were into that. Tris and I love it.'

She gives me the Ursula equivalent of a smile. 'It's one of Richard's favourites, but I quite like it too. Anyway, if you'll remember, when Rafferty was amongst his fellow bakers, he was friendly, charming, *so* chatty – a total natural.'

'You're right.'

'Perhaps that's where he thrives.'

'On a TV show? I don't follow.'

'No, I mean when he's amongst others, when the spotlight isn't entirely on him – it's shared with other people.'

'Ahh, interesting.' As I consider her hypothesis, I walk over to the window and glance out at the Thames. It's a grey day with light drizzle and the river is a dull greyish-brown and flowing sluggishly. I turn and face Ursula, then lean against the windowsill. 'So, when he's been approached by these two potentials – first at the food safety course and then at the day spa – it was a one-on-one engagement...'

'Putting Rafferty in the spotlight of sorts,' she says, building on my point.

'So, he's in the spotlight, it makes him uncomfortable, which means he misses all the signals that these women might be interested in dating him.'

'That would certainly explain how he can be a serial dater *and* a deer in headlights when he's approached out of the blue,' she says.

'Because when he's dating, he's in control. He may not feel completely comfortable – at least not right away – but he's there by choice.'

'Exactly.'

'So how do we bottle *that* Raff? How do we get the affable, chatty Raff to meet potential number three?'

'This is Julia, right? The artist?' she asks.

'Yes.'

'Can you bring up her profile?'

I go back to the table and pick up my tablet, then navigate to Julia's profile. 'What am I looking for?'

Ursula holds out her hand and I give her the tablet, then go to the other side of the table so I can read over her shoulder.

She scrolls the screen, stopping intermittently to read, then taps the screen three times with a scarlet fingernail. 'There. Look.'

'She's on London's "Forty Under Forty to Watch" list,' I say.

'One of my clients was on the list in 2018. They always have a meet and greet – a cocktail party – the first week of December. It's late notice, but if we could snaggle Rafferty an invite...'

'Ursula! That's brilliant. I could kiss you!'

'Well, let's not get ahead of ourselves. That invitation might be hard to come by.'

'But we must know *someone* at Forty Under Forty, surely? Let's raise it at the staff meeting and see.'

'Good idea. Paloma's bound to know someone.'

* * *

'Good news,' I tell Gaby when I call her after work. 'You and Raff are going to the "Forty Under Forty to Watch" cocktail party on Wednesday night.'

It took a dozen phone calls and most of the day, but we did it. We brought Ursula's inspired idea to fruition.

'Wait, what? But I've got drinks with the people at MouMou that night.' MouMou is an established luxury handbag label – they must be one of her clients.

'Can you make an appearance and duck out early? Or send someone in your place?'

She's quiet for a moment, then sighs. 'Obviously, this is about Raff – matching him, I mean – but...' Her words trail off, reminding me of Freya. 'Poppy, you do this for a living, but I'm *really* not cut out for this kind of thing – especially after the spa day. Can't Freya go with him?'

Her hesitation is warranted, I'll admit – this case has put a lot of pressure on her – but is it also evidence of Gaby wanting Raff for herself?

'I'll ask Freya,' I reply.

'Thanks,' she says, her relief obvious. 'And how are you planning to get Raff to show up?'

'He's going to receive a personal invitation from the director herself. She's an old school friend of Paloma's – you know, our head of client relations.'

Gaby chuckles. 'We really are in entirely different spheres, aren't we?'

'Says the woman who hobnobs with designers,' I quip.

'That's *work*.'

'So is this.'

'And it's not *hobnobbing*,' she continues, ignoring what I've said. 'It's putting on my one designer cocktail dress and making small talk all night – and at a MouMou party, that will be with wannabee influencers and C-list celebrities. The only benefit is that the booze will be top shelf – oh, and their goodie bags are the apex predator of goodie bags.'

'Yeah, doesn't really sound like my scene,' I say. 'Even with the goodie bags. But do you know what *does* sound fun? A fancy cocktail party for London's forty most fabulous people under forty!'

'Nice try, Poppy. Ask Freya – she can go with him. That's if Raff agrees to go.'

'Okay,' I say, letting her off the hook – for now. 'I'll let you know how it goes.'

'Thanks.'

We end the call and I tap my phone against my chin.

Freya's onboard with my wing-woman strategy, even if she doesn't know its additional aim is to unearth how Gaby really sees Raff, so I'll elicit her help.

I want both Raff *and* Gaby at that event.

Not only did Paloma have to call in a slew of favours to secure the invitation, but it's *exactly* the type of occasion that could lift the veil from Gaby's eyes. They'll both be dressed to the nines, it will be festive as well as fancy, and Julia is a very attractive and charming woman. If Gaby can witness Julia's charm offensive and *not* want Raff for herself, then her feelings for him are most likely platonic and nothing more.

Before packing up for the day, I send a quick message to Freya, explaining what I need from her to ensure Raff and Gaby go to the Forty Under Forty event.

As I gather my belongings and put on my coat and scarf, I look around the office. Only George is still at his desk – everyone else has gone home, as it's now past six – so he'll lock up when he's done.

'Bye, George, see you tomorrow.'

'Bye, Poppy.'

'And don't stay too long.'

He chuckles at that. Like me, he often disregards the agency's culture of clocking off at five. But it's not always possible – especially not when you have a high-stakes case like this one *and* you're prepping three cases for the New Year.

That means long days, as well as being on-call evenings and weekends.

I really do hope we employ another agent soon, ease some of the burden on the five of us. But it's not the sort of role that gets advertised on job sites.

As I step out into the darkness and head towards the Tube station, I can't help but wonder how compatible a baby would be with the life of a matchmaker.

Not very, is my guess.

14

GABY

'Thanks for coming with me, Gabs,' says Raff, tugging at the collar of his shirt.

'No problem,' I reply.

If he truly understood the extent of this favour, he'd offer me his first-born child in payment. Or an Aston Martin. I'd prefer the latter.

But I should have learnt by now that Poppy Dean can work wonders. Not only did she get Raff to accept the invitation to this little shindig, but after Freya gave a resounding no, she got *me* here as Raff's plus one. She didn't even have to resort to begging. She went with bribery, dangling a carrot so enticing, I couldn't resist – professional hair and makeup, and a stylist. Apparently, Greta hooked her up. Well, hooked *me* up.

And once I said yes, I had to bribe Quinn to take my place at the MouMou event. Somehow, I'll need to convince Elysium to comp me another spa day for Quinn and a friend.

All these backroom deals were signed, sealed, and delivered within twenty-four hours of Poppy's call to tell me the 'good news'.

Now here we are – me and Raff – in the back of another town car, looking better than either of us has looked before, or likely will again. Tonight is like prom on steroids.

'You look lovely, by the way,' he says, regarding me intently across the backseat.

'Thanks,' I say, suddenly self-conscious. It shouldn't feel weird that Raff's complimenting me, considering how well we know each other, but it does.

He *is* right, though (if I do say so myself) – the hair and makeup team, *and* the stylist, did a stellar job. I feel... well, maybe not beautiful but at the very least, pretty.

My shoulder-length hair has been dried pin-straight (which necessitated a quick trim to even out the ends), and the hair stylist parted it on the left, pinning the right side behind my ear with a diamante-encrusted hairpin. The style is reminiscent of 1930s movie stars and my hair is so glossy, Raff can probably see his reflection in it.

The makeup artist gave me a smoky eye in dark green, a hint of peach-coloured blush, and a glossy nude lip. They even gifted me the tube for touch-ups.

But the dress!

It's *so* pretty – a sleeveless sheath in slinky, forest-green silk that skims my body, its hem landing mid-thigh. As I have a boyish, athletic figure – no cleavage and not even a *hint* of a butt, so very un-J.Lo – I've gotta love a dress that makes the most of what I *do* have, namely shapely arms and well-defined legs from working out three times a week.

Rounding out the look are forest-green heels and a matching clutch, both from the Lorenzo/Elle Bliss Mile High Club collection. Global Reach pitched to them last year, but we didn't land the account. A pity – I'd *love* to work with them.

Raff looks great too. His hair is in a similar style to the one he had for the *Nouveau Life* photoshoot, and he's wearing a modern-cut, dark-grey suit, crisp, white dress shirt, and a patterned tie that has the same hue of green as my dress.

We're dressed like a couple, I suddenly realise. Ha-ha! Hilarious.

'If it's too cold when we arrive, you can borrow my suit jacket until we get inside,' he offers.

'Nah, that's okay. We'll only be in the cold for a few seconds. The price you pay for beauty, huh?'

He smiles at me. 'Indeed.'

The car pulls up outside The Leadenhall Building (AKA the Cheesegrater). It's not the most inspired-looking building. It has some incredible views, though, especially from the forty-second floor where the event is being held. We take the elevator with several couples, excited whispers filling the air.

The last time I was here was for the launch of (yet another) sparkling mineral water brand – not my campaign but a colleague's and a fairly run-of-the-mill event.

But as we step out of the elevator, I'm left breathless.

The space has been transformed into a winter wonderland. Thousands of fairy lights twinkle and dozens of strategically positioned candelabras make the large room feel warm and cosy. White and silver garlands adorn the walls, and each table has a huge vase filled with silver glass baubles as its centrepiece. There's a string quartet playing 'It's Beginning to Look a Lot Like Christmas', and I'd have to agree.

Wait! Is that *snow*? I reach out and several tiny flakes land on my hand, melting away in an instant.

'Wowser,' says Raff, stooping to talk in my ear. 'This is way beyond anything we've ever done – and we've organised some cracking events.'

I don't have time to agree, as we're instantly greeted by a

perfectly coiffed woman, who appears to be in her mid-twenties. 'Mr Delaney, Ms Rivera, welcome,' she says with a warm smile. 'These are for you.'

She hands us nametags embossed on stiff card. Raff's says: *Rafferty Delaney, Winner of Britain's Best Bakers*. Mine says: *Gabriela Rivera, Guest of Rafferty Delaney*. I affix mine to the neckline of my dress and help Raff clip his onto his breast pocket.

'That's quite the party trick,' I say to him quietly.

'I know – she must have had to study our photographs or something,' he mutters back.

I straighten his nametag then step back.

'This way, please,' says the woman.

She leads us to the end of a short cue where people are waiting to be photographed against a large backdrop, a landscape that is either Lapland or a Lapland wannabe. Gentle, glistening, snow-covered slopes, stands of conifers, their branches so thick with snow it looks like they've been frosted in fondant, and a deep-purple-hued sky with traces of the Aurora Borealis. It could be right before sunrise or right after sunset.

The photographer is a pro and efficiently directs the pairs and trios into elegant poses, prompting smiles where none were only moments before. Now it's our turn.

'Madam, sir...' he says, indicating where we should stand. 'Sir, if you could place your hand on madam's waist, and madam, turn slightly towards sir.'

'Oh, we're not—' I say, about to correct him.

But he steps forward and moves Raff's hand to rest on my hip, then positions me. 'Perfect.' He steps back and regards us. 'Madam, chin lifted, please.' I lift my chin. 'And soft smiles as if something is mildly amusing.'

Actually, that *is* mildly amusing – and possibly the cleverest tactic for eliciting an enigmatic smile I've ever encountered.

He takes several shots and after each one, I feel Raff's grip getting stronger. He *really* doesn't like having his photo taken. 'Are we done yet?' he mutters wryly, and I snigger.

'Perfect,' says the photographer, snapping a final shot, one in which I was laughing.

He gently waves his hand for us to clear the landscape and our hostess is waiting for us on the other side. 'This way, please.'

She leads us towards a small group of people who are standing around bar tables, drinking and talking. As we approach, she turns to us.

'Grace is making the rounds,' she says, referring to Grace Wong, the founder of Forty Under Forty, 'so you'll meet her shortly. In the meantime, we've grouped our guests into specialty areas as an ice breaker. You're with the creatives, Mr Delaney. And of course, please feel free to mingle with other specialty areas at your leisure. Have a lovely evening.'

She smiles politely, then dips her chin in a half-nod and strides off.

'Gabs,' says Raff, leaning in, 'this is already one of the best parties I've ever been to.'

'One of? I'm going with *the* best, and we've only been here five minutes.'

'Ten,' he says, and when I look up at him, he smiles.

'Madam, sir?' We're interrupted by a waiter bearing a tray of brimming Champagne flutes.

'Oh, yes please,' says Raff, relieving him of two glasses. He hands one to me, then holds his up in a toast. 'To my best friend, thank you *so* much for being my plus one. I would never have said yes to this if you hadn't agreed to come with me.'

I clink my glass against his.

'My pleasure. *Literally.*'

He downs a generous glug and I take a sip. This is the real deal

– *actual* Champagne and it's so delicious, I could cry. That is, if I hadn't been made up by a thousand-pounds-an-hour makeup artist.

'Ready?' he asks, licking his lower lip.

He means am I ready to mingle, and as someone who grew up with a large extended family – on both sides – I'm prepared to do the heavy lifting here.

I take his hand to reassure him, and he smiles down at me.

'Hello,' I say, approaching a trio at the precise moment their collective laughter dies down. They turn to us, smiling, and I introduce us. Then I ask, 'So, what brings you here tonight?' – a question that's designed to spark conversation with strangers and my go-to at this type of event.

Mere minutes in, it's like a switch has flipped and Raff is engaging with the others, charming and confident, and holding up his end of the conversation with ease. We've never really discussed it, his social anxiety or how he overcomes it to be this version of himself. But I know from experience he'll be comfortable with these people for the rest of the night.

I nod and smile and contribute when it's appropriate, but mostly I'm looking out for Julia, the artist. She hasn't arrived yet as far as I can tell.

I think back on what I learnt about her at the screening. Overall, I thought she was a decent match for Raff – it was her obsession with German EDM that put me off. If he likes her, I suppose he can decide if it's a deal breaker or not.

If he likes her...

The surrealness of where I am and what I'm doing suddenly smacks me in the face.

I'm at the party of the season, looking like I belong here (thanks to an incredible style team), wing-womaning my best friend in hopes of matching him with one of London's Forty Under Forty to Watch.

My life is weird sometimes.

I cast my eyes towards the Lapland landscape to scope out who's recently arrived and there she is! Oh, she's with a guy – a very handsome guy. He looks remarkably like Jude Law did in *The Holiday*.

I glance at Raff, trying to see him through fresh eyes – *Julia's* eyes. He really does look good – his hair suits him like that. As if on cue, he laughs, his head tipping back, and he looks so handsome, my heart could burst.

If he and Julia hit it off tonight *and* they're a match, she had better be good to him or I'll...

'Hello, everyone. I hear this is where the fun people are.'

Talk about making an entrance.

She's even more gorgeous up close. Tall, curvy (she's down the J.Lo end of the spectrum), with long blonde hair worn in a deliberately messy up-do, and a very pretty face, right down to her large hazel eyes and pouty pink lips.

Essentially, the opposite of me.

Julia introduces herself to our little group, then says, 'And this is my brother, Peter.'

Oh! Her *brother*! Well, hello, Peter! Added bonus of playing wing-woman for your bestie? The hot brother.

After introductions are made, Julia starts chatting to Raff. I sip my Champagne and look around, doing my best to hide that I'm watching them out of the corner of my eye as well as eavesdropping.

'Full confession,' she says, 'I'm a die-hard *Britain's Best Bakers* fan – *and* I read the article in *Nouveau Life* – so I know who you are.'

Raff chuckles at that – a far cry from the pink-faced stammer he typically trots out when confronted with being recognised.

'Well, you have the advantage,' he replies, 'as I'm afraid I'm not familiar with your artwork. Sorry.'

She waves her hand modestly. 'Plenty of time to talk about that. I want *gossip*.'

'Gossip?' he replies, his mouth curling into a curious smile.

'Yes. Tell me, is Dame Vicky really that fun in real life or is that only for the cameras?'

'Oh, I see.' I can tell from his tone that he's amused.

'It's just... I adore her, you see, and I need to know it's not an act – that she's not a total cow off camera.'

Raff laughs, then spills the tea on Dame Vicky – that she *is* as lovely offscreen as she is onscreen, and just like that, it's finally happening! Raff has met his match.

Well, hopefully, but this is looking way more promising than our previous attempts.

With no further wing-womaning required in the foreseeable future, I sidle up to Peter, who's been left on his own. 'So, how did you get roped into this?' I ask.

He laughs and it may be the sexiest sound to ever grace my ears.

'My sister and I drag each other along to all sorts of things this time of year. This is me returning a favour.'

'Really? For what?'

'My work Christmas party. I'm a project planner for the City of London in the most boring division ever – traffic management – so it's always dull as dishwater. Catering by Tesco – including the plonk – soundtrack by Radio 1, excruciating party games, and a visit from our boss dressed as Father Christmas, handing out gifts from Poundland.'

'Sounds like torture,' I commiserate – even though it sounds like his boss is doing their best to spread Christmas cheer on a budget.

'It is. The sort of do you only take a date to if the relationship is in its final days and you're looking for an exit strategy.'

'Right, so cause of death: work Christmas party.'

'Exactly.'

Peter sounds like he might be a bit of a player.

'So,' he says, leaning closer, 'is he your boyfriend?' He jerks his head in Raff's direction.

'Best friend. I'm also here as a favour,' I add, even though he didn't ask. He's hot but he's not the best conversationalist.

'And what do *you* do, Gabriela, guest of Rafferty?'

'I'm a marketing manager.'

'Sounds interesting.'

How can it when I've only given him a job title? It's a sloppy line but he's so gorgeous, I play along.

'Far more interesting than traffic management, that's for sure,' I say. I take a deliberately timed sip of my Champagne and look around the room, feigning disinterest.

He moves even closer, taking the bait, and I get a whiff of his cologne. He's wearing Aventus by Creed – an expensive cologne for a public servant. But then, I know from his sister's profile that their family has money – *serious* money.

'You're rather sexy,' he says, low in my ear.

I meet his eyes, then smile serenely, as if I hear that all the time. I don't.

Peter may be a player, but he is hot as hell and I haven't had a hot-as-hell guy in my bed for so long, I've forgotten the last time.

'Gabs?'

Crappy timing, Raff. Can't you see I'm being seduced by the hot guy? Or am I doing the seducing? Either way...

'Yes?' I say, stepping back from Peter, who emits an audible groan of disappointment.

'Julia here has been to Seattle.' He waves me over.

I can predict how this conversation will go: we'll compare favourite haunts, saying, 'Oh, yeah, that place is great,' then we'll run out of places we have in common and that will be that.

But the real issue is that Raff is supposed to be flying solo now.

And, yeah, having done my duty, I was about to cut out early with the Jude Law lookalike.

I plaster a smile on my face and join them. 'You don't say?'

15

GABY

'What a brilliant night,' Raff says. If we were in a room, not a town car, he'd be bouncing off the walls. 'I mean, the event itself was wonderful, of course, but I never in a million years thought I'd meet someone out of the blue like that!'

Out of the blue! Hah! If you only knew.

And given that he recently gave Freya carte blanche to find him a girlfriend, he *should* know.

'So, you liked Julia I take it?' I ask, sending a forced smile across the backseat.

'Yeah, she's great,' he replies, beaming back at me. 'I'm hoping to see her at the weekend.'

'But this weekend is CiCi and Devin's Christmas party.' Oh shit, is he considering bringing *Julia*?

'I meant Sunday. A bit early for "meet the family", don't you think? Even for me,' he quips.

I smile again, then turn and look out the window. I should be happy for him. He met Julia and they hit it off – exactly as Poppy and I planned. But I'm not happy for him. I couldn't be further from happy for him.

Which makes me a shitty friend. A shitty friend who's had a shocking realisation.

As we ride in silence through the mostly deserted streets of London, scenes from the night pop into my head like jump scares in a horror movie.

Raff and Julia laughing, sharing a joke. Julia touching Raff's forearm and Raff briefly covering her hand with his. Julia asking Raff to help when a tendril of hair caught in the clasp of her neck-lace. Raff watching her walk across the room when she went to the bathroom, then sighing. Them exchanging phone numbers at the end of the night. Him texting her while we waited for the car.

I witnessed all this firsthand because the second I was called away from Peter the Player to talk about the hotspots of Seattle, he disappeared into the crowd to find a surer thing. I saw him leave twenty minutes later with a petite, dark-haired woman who had balloon lips and eyelashes so long she could sweep chimneys with them.

I tried to leave soon after, but Raff insisted I stay and 'have a good time' because I 'deserved it'. What I *deserve* is a swift kick up the butt for not realising sooner how I feel. Because I know the signs of Raff falling for someone – I've seen them before, dozens of times.

But I've never been jealous before.

A sudden wave of nausea crashes through me, and I stab at the button to lower the window, but the switch must be locked.

'Excuse me,' I say to the driver, tapping him on the shoulder, 'could I please have the window down?'

'Of course, madam.'

The window lowers and I suck in great gulps of the cold night air.

'Are you all right, Gabs?' I feel Raff's hand on my back, patting gently, and I want to flick it away. But it's not his fault I feel sick. 'Too much champers, do you think?'

His back patting ramps up and I raise a hand to make him stop – it's not helping. I focus on steadying my breathing – in through my nose, out through my mouth – and soon enough my stomach settles – well, mostly – and I swallow the build-up of saliva in my mouth, then sit heavily against the seat.

'I'm okay now,' I tell the driver. 'Thanks.' The window slides up silently.

'Are you all right?'

I exhale slowly, then shoot Raff a weak smile. 'Yeah, I'm okay. You're probably right – too much to drink and not enough to eat.'

This is an outright lie. I only had a glass and a half of Champagne all night. Once Peter disappeared and I became hyper aware of Raff and Julia hitting it off, I switched to soda water and downed so many canapés, the waiters started giving me a wide berth. Raff obviously didn't notice any of this.

He pats my leg – my bare leg – then rests his hand on my thigh right above my knee. As he stares out the side window, wearing a dreamy smile, I drop my gaze to his hand, mesmerised by his thumb moving gently back and forth.

Raff and I have been close for years and there must have been hundreds of times when he's hugged me, or grabbed my hand to cross a busy street, or patted my back, or rested his hand on my leg reassuringly.

But this is the first time that I've wished it meant more.

And that's why I nearly vomited out the window.

I have feelings for my best friend – *romantic* feelings. And like a frigging idiot, I may have realised too late.

* * *

When I wake up to my alarm and peer into the pre-dawn darkness, there's a moment of ignorant bliss before I recall last night's realisation. Then it all comes screaming back and I roll over and groan into my pillow.

I wish it were Saturday and I could stay in bed all day and wallow. But I've got a meeting with the analytics team first thing to review stats on my clients' holiday campaigns.

The not-so-glamorous side of marketing.

I'm also meeting with Claire this afternoon about the director role. And of course, Raff will be in the office, as he doesn't finish up until the end of next week.

But at least I don't have a client event tonight.

I roll onto my back and stare at the ceiling. Why don't I have a cat? If I had a cat, I could curl up with it and tell it all my problems.

Well, *one* problem.

One big, fat, stinking, stupid problem.

How the hell didn't I see it sooner? And who the hell am I supposed to talk to about it when one of my best friends is laser-focused on finding Raff a new girlfriend and my other best friend is the problem itself on legs?! I can't even talk to Lorrie about it, because as close as we are as colleagues, we're not really friends outside of work.

Poppy. She's the only person who comes to mind.

I heave out an ugly, ragged sigh, then throw the covers back and get out of bed.

Today is going to suck no matter what; there's no point in stalling any longer and making it worse by being late.

* * *

Even anticipating how much today would suck, it feels like the suckiest day to ever have sucked. And it's only 11 a.m.

My 9 a.m. meeting ran long and, despite three out of four of my holiday campaigns killing it and the fourth hitting its targets, I found it difficult to care. My mind kept wandering to last night, and my colleagues had to repeat themselves – *repeatedly*. I looked like an idiot.

Then after the meeting, I remembered that I left the dress I wore last night at home. A courier was supposed to collect it from the office today and take it back to the designer. Now I'm going to have to cover the cost of the courier myself, which I discovered during a tense call with the designer's assistant is £120. I could have bought my *own* designer dress at TK Maxx for that.

And in my rush to leave the apartment this morning, I also forgot my gym bag, meaning I can't work out at lunchtime – and with how busy I am, that makes three workouts in a row I've missed. I *need* my workouts – just as much for my mental health as my physical health. They're my meditation, when I can switch off my over-active mind and just *be*.

Also, Claire just stopped by my desk to tell me she needs to bump our meeting up to one, meaning the preparation I'd planned to do between one and three needs to be done now.

Oh, and Freya texted:

> Heard from Raff – he liked Julia! And Poppy said it's mutual! So excited. Thanks again for going with him. *kissing face emoji*

No wonder I'm still feeling queasy.

Is an emotional hangover a thing? Is this how I felt after Eric announced he was in love with Donna and they were getting married?

Maybe. I can't remember, it was so long ago. I was also a different Gaby back then, full of hopes for the future and imagining a life with Eric. A house in the suburbs, 2.4 kids, a dog, and an SUV – the American dream.

Hah! If we'd got married, we'd be divorced by now. We had *zero* in common other than we both loved the Mariners. Baseball became the only thing we ever talked about.

'Gaby!'

I've been so lost in thought, I've missed that Lorrie is trying to get my attention.

'Sorry.' I smile up at her wanly and she frowns back at me.

'Are you ill? If you are, you should probably go home.' She eyes me warily, keeping her distance.

'That's sweet, but—'

'You don't want to be the person who brought a lurgy to the office and made everyone else sick right before the holidays,' she adds, talking over me.

'I'm not sick,' I reply tartly.

'Oh, a fun night then,' she concludes, her demeanour changing in an instant. She perches on the edge of my desk and wags her eyebrows. 'So? How was it?'

I *could* tell her the truth, but that would only make this shitshow worse.

'It was great,' I say, busting out the biggest fake smile in my arsenal.

Quinn comes over. 'Gaby, have you seen this? You and Raff on the "Forty Under Forty" website? They've posted the photos from last night's event.' He holds up his phone and there we are, me and Raff, looking very much like a couple on a date – right down to the matching dress and tie.

Well, fuck.

'Gaby, are you all right? You look like you've seen a ghost,' says Quinn.

Lorrie steps forward and places a hand on my forehead. 'You've gone pale.' This is saying a lot because I may have inherited my mom's boyish figure, but I got my complexion from my dad, who's Hispanic.

'I'm fine. I just—'

'Did I miss an invite to a team meeting?'

Wonderful, now Raff's here. He joins the others and all three of them stare at me, Lorrie with her arms crossed.

'Gabs? Are you ill?' Raff asks, a concerned frown on his face.

But I don't want his concern. I want him to go away because – *damn him* – he looks great. Last's night's hairstyle is still going strong, his shirt actually fits him – it must be one of the shirts the designer sent over – and he's wearing an air of confidence that is *incredibly* attractive.

He's hot.

Raff – longtime best friend, who's been like a brother to me for years – is hot. *Fuckety, fuck, fuck, fuck.*

I inhale deeply, then smile as serenely as possible. 'I'm fine,' I reply. 'Only I didn't sleep well last night and I've got a packed schedule today. So, yeah...' I make the can-you-please-go-away-and-leave-me-alone? face.

'Oh!' Raff is the first to understand. 'Sorry, of course, we'll let you get back to it then.'

He shepherds the others away, but Lorrie stares at me over her shoulder, her eyes narrowed. She knows something's up, but I don't have time – or the mental space – to worry about Lorrie right now.

It's hard enough trying to wrap my brain around how 'Just Raff' transformed into 'Hot Raff' overnight.

I need to focus, and *not* on him.

If my discussion with Claire goes well, I may be offered the role without having to formally apply for it. I slide my laptop closer, navigating to the shared drive and pulling up the data on my holiday campaigns. As I read through the figures again, 'work mode' kicks in and the queasiness and all the errant thoughts of Raff start to subside.

This. *This* is what I need to get through the day – focusing on work. Focusing on work while trying to ignore the little voice in my head that's wondering what Poppy will say when I give her my news.

I'm guessing she won't be pleased.

* * *

I guessed right. I've dropped my bombshell and Poppy's gone quiet on the other end of the call. Never a good sign when someone is completely silent after you tell them something important. I start pacing the small meeting room.

'Poppy?'

'Sorry – I was processing what you said. Does Raff know?'

'How I feel? Ah, no. No, I barely worked up the courage to tell you, let alone bare my soul to Raff the day after he meets his dream girl.'

'Okay. So, when do you plan on telling Freya?'

Argh! I was hoping *she'd* break it to Freya.

'I don't... I don't know how,' I reply.

'Gaby, she's your bestie. You have to tell her – and as soon you can. She'll understand.'

'That's just it. I don't know that she will. What if she's pissed at me? It's shitty timing.'

'The timing's... yeah, it's not great.'

Understatement of the year.

'But consider this...' she continues. 'If last night hadn't

happened, maybe you never would've realised how you feel about Raff.'

'Are you saying some things happen for a reason?'

'Something like that.'

'Because I don't really believe in fate or that *que sera sera* crap. My dad does – he's a total romantic – but I didn't get that gene.'

'Gaby, you're waffling,' she says, calling me out.

'Yeah, I know. What if *you* told her?'

'I already tried, but she didn't believe me. Bugger. Sorry, I shouldn't have said that.'

'What do you mean you already tried?' I ask.

She sighs heavily. 'You remember the screening?'

'Yeah, of course.'

'Well, I suspected something back then – Ursula did too.'

'Wait,' I say with a wry laugh. 'You're saying you knew before I did? But how? Am I that readable? Oh shit – do you think *Raff* knows?' I screech.

'I said we *suspected*. Based on how oblivious Raff can be about this sort of thing, I doubt he knows. And Freya discounted the possibility entirely.'

This is all too much. The screening was weeks ago. That means people have been talking about me and how I feel about Raff for *weeks* now. Well, my *suspected* feelings.

'Ugh,' I groan.

'Gaby, I need you to take a breath.'

'Easy for you to say. This is *humiliating*.'

'I can understand how it must feel that way. Look, I'm going to have to discuss this with my colleagues and determine what happens next. Actually, it might be best if you hold off on telling Freya for now.'

'I wasn't going to tell Fr— Never mind.'

'Just wait until you hear from me, okay?'

'Okay. Poppy, I really am sorry.'

'You have nothing to apologise for,' she reassures me, but I don't agree. I should have seen it sooner. How did I not see it sooner?

'Hang in there and I'll be in touch,' she says.

'Thanks,' I say glumly, and we end the call.

Hang in there. But *how*?

16

POPPY

I end the call and set my phone on my desk, then rock back in my chair. 'Bugger, bugger, bugger,' I mutter to myself.

I should know better than to say anything out loud that I don't want George to hear, and he's at my desk in an instant.

'Dish.'

'You're such a gossip,' I say, shaking my head at him.

'*Or* I'm simply a concerned colleague and am offering my services.' He bows dramatically as if he's in a Regency romance.

I cast a glance at Freya. She seems immersed in a potential's profile, but even so, this isn't something I can discuss within cooee of her.

'Come for a walk?' I ask George as I stand and put on my coat. 'I need a coffee,' I say a little louder, establishing a cover story for our sudden departure from the office – even though I rarely have coffee this late in the day.

'If you're buying, always,' George replies.

A few minutes later, we enter the café on the ground floor of our building. It's busier than usual, like most places in the lead up to Christmas. Mariah is singing her ubiquitous song and there is tinsel wrapped around everything. Above the counter, there's a well-loved sign that's missing one of the Rs and reads, 'MER Y CHRISTMAS!'

We queue up, George chatting about a Christmas party he's going to on the weekend with a guy he's seeing, which reminds me that Tristan and I have his mother's party this weekend, something I'm dreading. It will be Tris and me drowning in a sea of Helen's posh friends, making polite conversation until it's a suitable time to leave.

At least if Helen asks us about grandchildren again, we might have a different answer for her. That is, if I ever broach the topic with my husband. But there are too many other things on my mind right now.

Coffees in hand – a cappuccino for George and a flat white for me – we head to the back of the café and squeeze around a tiny table, perching on even tinier stools.

'*Now* dish,' says George.

I recount my earlier conversation with Julia, in which she told me it went well and that she really likes Raff, then Freya's update that Raff feels the same way about Julia.

'Wait, I'm confused. The match is made, so what's the problem?'

'The problem is what Gaby told me on the phone just now.'

As I explain Gaby's realisation – and my part in it – George's eyes get larger, and his jaw drops dramatically. He looks absurd and I'd laugh if this weren't so serious.

'So, yeah...' I say, finally taking a sip of my flat white. Only with how unsettled I am, it curdles the second it hits my stomach and I push it aside.

'Blimey, that *is* a sticky situation,' George concludes.

'Yeah.'

'And on top of all that, you don't know how to break it to Freya because she didn't believe you the first time – about Gaby, I mean.'

'Exactly. Wait, I never told you that.'

He tugs on his left earlobe. 'I was in the office that morning, Poppy. I heard the entire conversation.'

'Of course you did.'

I look down at the tabletop. 'George, I feel sick,' I admit. 'Either I did my best with the information I had, or I screwed up. And I'm worried it's the latter.'

We say matchmaking isn't an exact science and as we're working with people and heightened emotions and high-stakes situations, there are a multitude of factors that can go wrong in a case. *And* we're human and just as fallible as everyone else.

But all that said, we're experienced and professional, and we're expected to stay on top of the ins and outs of our cases. Like nimbly handling the romantic feelings of someone who is heavily involved.

'You couldn't have known for sure how this would pan out,' he says reassuringly. 'Or that the timing would be so... *ironic.*'

I meet his eye. 'I spent a decade as a psychologist, George. A decade of analysing the inner machinations of people's minds and helping them acknowledge their truths. I *should* have known better. I'm slipping.'

'You're not slip— Poppy, you're not a psychologist any more. You haven't been for years, and yes, those skills come in handy sometimes, but they're not the only thing that make you a good matchmaker. If they were, then what does that make me? I'm not a former psychologist – I'm an art school dropout – but I like to think I'm damned good at my job.'

This may be the first time George has spoken so frankly to me and I couldn't appreciate it – or him – more.

'Thank you,' I say, reaching the short distance between us to give his hand a squeeze. 'Normally it's Nas who doles out the truth bombs, but you're right. I can't be expected to know everything that's going on inside everyone's head at any given moment. That's too much pressure for anyone to bear.'

'Precisely.'

'And you *are* damned good at your job.'

'I know.'

We share a smile.

'But I still feel like I've made a misstep here, even if it's forgivable,' I say, my smile falling away. 'And now I have a woman who might be in love with her best friend and there's every chance he's been successfully matched with someone else. Oh, and my colleague – the one who got me into this mess in the first place – is going to be *so* upset when I tell her.'

'Freya will understand.'

There's silence for a second, then we start chuckling at the same time.

'Well, she *might*,' he says.

'Hmm.'

'But if she doesn't, she needs to consider that she's culpable too. She should have trusted your judgement when you first brought it up.'

'I know. Ugh. Tell me why I agreed to take this case in the first place.'

'Because you're a good egg, Poppy.'

'A good egg bearing bad news.'

'Was that you trying to be funny?' he asks.

'Trying and not succeeding, apparently. Come on, we should get back.'

* * *

'In here, darling,' Tristan calls out from the bedroom as I close the front door.

'Be right there,' I call back. I'm not sure I'm up for a sexy interlude right now, but maybe he's in there waiting to administer a huge hug.

I drop my handbag on the hallstand, then shrug out of my coat and hang it up and toe off my shoes. The flat smells delicious – Tristan's famous pasta sauce is simmering on the stove – and on the stereo, Michael Bublé is enticing it to snow.

God, is Christmas really only a couple of weeks away? This time last year, Tristan and I were packing for a quick trip to Tassie so he could meet Mum and Dad and have his first hot Christmas.

This reminds me that I won't get to see Mum and Dad till Easter when they're coming here for a holiday. Tris and I haven't told Saffron that they'll be taking her room and she'll have to slum it in ours – a distracting thought that makes me smile before I get too melancholic about missing my parents.

I wander into the bedroom, but Tristan's not here. I gently push open the door to the en suite and my darling, gorgeous husband is in the tub, surrounded by candles and chin-deep in bubbles. Next to the tub, a bottle of Champagne is chilling in an ice bucket.

'It's a Bublé bubbly bubble bath,' he declares, grinning proudly.

I burst out laughing. 'You dag, I love you so much right now!'

He reaches over and retrieves the bottle, then pours me a glass of bubbly. 'Well, come on! The water's starting to cool down.'

I head back to the bedroom to quickly undress, then return and slip into the hot water. '*Oh, that feels divine.*'

Tristan hands me a Champagne flute and holds up his. 'I'm sorry you've had another not-so-good day. To a better evening.'

I take a sip, then set my glass on the table beside me. I lean my head back against the rim of the tub and close my eyes, right as Tristan captures one of my feet in his hands and starts rubbing it.

'Ahh,' I sigh. 'Truly, you may just be the perfect man. What did I do to deserve you?'

'You saved me from being a miserable, lonely bachelor for the rest of my life. I'm positive I've come out on top in this arrangement.'

I crack open one eye and he's regarding me lovingly. 'Want to talk about it?' he asks. All he knows is what I messaged him earlier – that my case has gone sideways, and Saskia and Paloma have scheduled an all-hands-on-deck meeting for tomorrow morning to figure it out.

'Not really,' I reply. 'I'll know more after tomorrow's meeting. How was *your* day?'

'Not great. Patrick lost twenty million pounds today.'

I sit up suddenly and water sloshes over the side of the tub. 'What? That's... Why didn't you tell me?'

He chuckles. 'I am telling you.'

'I mean before, when I messaged that I'd had a shit day, you could have replied, "Me too".'

'I didn't want to worry you, not when you have so much on your plate.'

'Tristan, *you* are my plate.'

He gives me a funny look.

'Well, you know what I mean. No one – and no case – is more important to me than you are. So, when you have a shit day, you tell me, okay?'

'Consider me suitably reprimanded,' he replies with a smirk.

I slide back into the water and run my foot along his arm. 'Sorry for telling you off.'

'Forgiven.' He winks.

'Do you want to talk about it? Patrick's fuck up?'

'Definitely not.'

'Okay,' I say, reaching for my bubbly and taking another sip. 'So, what should we get to welcome Baby Sharma?' I ask, changing the subject to something a lot more fun.

He laughs. 'Darling, that's months away.'

'Yes, but Jacinda has three older brothers – all married – and I want us to be the baby's favourite aunt and uncle.'

'Ahh, yes, the winning-the-child's-love-by-buying-them-extravagant-gifts strategy. That's bound to work. I know *I* loved that as a child.'

Tristan's childhood was vastly different to mine. He had a distant father and a cold and critical mother. No wonder he and Ravi gravitated towards each other at boarding school, becoming lifelong friends at the age of seven.

'Hmm, good point. I mean, you did turn out *okay* but—'

'*Okay?* Such ringing endorsement.' His narrowed eyes are betrayed by his twitching mouth.

'You turned out to be the best husband I could ever have hoped for – if I'd ever hoped for a husband before I met you,' I say, mostly serious.

'There might be a compliment in there.'

'Believe me, babe, there is.'

* * *

All-hands-on-deck meetings aren't unheard of at Ever After, but they're rare enough that I didn't sleep last night. Well, Saffron doing zoomies at 3 a.m. didn't help, but the main culprit was worrying about how to get this case back on track.

If that's even possible.

We're in Saskia's office – me, Ursula, Paloma, and Saskia. It was decided (not by me) that we wouldn't bring in Freya until I'd briefed the others.

It's probably the best approach considering Freya was gushing to me this morning about how much Raff was gushing to *her* about meeting Julia 'out of the blue'.

I've just finished explaining where we're at, including how I 'interfered' to tease out Gaby's true feelings. Fortunately, Ursula backs me on that unreservedly, and there are no admonishments for my chosen strategy. Well, none from my bosses, that is. I've been admonishing myself plenty since yesterday.

'Poppy, has there been *any* indication that Rafferty might return Gaby's feelings?' Saskia asks.

I sigh. 'As far as I know, none. But I can only go by what Gaby's told me. I haven't seen them together, not recently. The last time was months ago at a dinner party at Freya's – and I didn't notice anything unusual. They behaved like best friends.'

'Sask,' says Paloma, 'are you thinking what I'm thinking?'

They exchange one of their Saskia-Paloma-mind-meld looks.

'You're right – it's time. Poppy, can you ask Freya to come in, please?'

A couple minutes later, I'm back in Saskia's office with a confused-looking Freya. She sits on the sofa next to me, then looks between the rest of us, her large eyes even wider than usual.

All I told her was that we needed her in a meeting about Raff's case.

'Freya, there's been a development in Poppy's case,' says Saskia.

Freya visibly relaxes. 'I know! Isn't it brilliant?' she asks rhetorically. 'Third try lucky, right Poppy?'

'Uh...'

'Actually, that's not the development we meant,' says Paloma. 'There's something else, something we need to discuss with you.'

Freya frowns in obvious confusion. 'Sorry, so you didn't want to talk about Raff being matched? But I thought...'

I catch Ursula's eye behind Freya's back, hoping *she'll* explain what's going on. I feel like I'm too entangled in this case to talk about it sensibly.

I also fear that I've let Freya down. If I'd been more insistent when I first suspected Gaby had feelings for Raff, maybe we wouldn't be in this mess.

Thankfully, Ursula understands that I'm handing over to her, giving me a slight nod, then placing her hand on Freya's forearm.

She gently explains the situation to Freya, making it clear that Gaby's feelings for Raff have come to the fore and are undeniable. As she talks, Freya's face displays a gamut of emotions from incredulity to amusement to befuddlement.

Finally, there's acceptance.

She shakes her head at herself. 'You should have heard Raff on the phone this morning,' she tells us. 'He's so excited about Julia. Apparently, they messaged each other through the night, and they already have plans to see each other on Sunday. And Raff moves *fast* when he connects with someone. He's already invested – I can tell.' Freya slumps further into the sofa. She's even more upset about this than I expected.

'So, what do we do about Gaby?' I ask the group, hoping *someone* will have a magic-bullet solution.

I've always liked Gaby, but over these past few weeks, I've got to know her quite well and it pains me to think of her heartbroken because she discovered too late how she feels about Raff.

'Considering what Julia has told Poppy – and what you've just relayed to us, Freya – I suggest we see how this pans out,' says Saskia.

'Pans out?' asks Freya, lifting her head. 'You mean with Julia?'

'Yes,' says Saskia, softening her tone to couch the blow.

'I agree,' Paloma chimes in. 'Julia could be his match, or it might burn brightly for a short while then peter out. It's a waiting game now.'

'But what about Gaby?' Freya asks them, clearly fraught, and I'm with her.

'We're not trying to be callous,' says Paloma, 'but our primary duty is to our client – Rafferty. If we interfere at this point, we might destroy a match in the making. A reminder that we're match*makers*.'

If she was trying not to be callous, she didn't succeed. Ursula shoots her a pointed look, then turns to Freya, her eyes softening.

'Freya, consider how Rafferty would feel if he found out you'd interfered, and he and Julia were over before they even started. It really is for the best to see how their match plays out.'

'I suppose,' Freya says glumly. She drops her head into her hands. 'How did I fuck this up so badly? I only wanted to help Raff find love... And now Gaby's going to be heartbroken. Why did I meddle in the first place?'

I rest my hand on her shoulder to comfort her, a feeble gesture considering how much she's beating herself up. Ursula and I exchange glances and it's clear we're on the same page. The situation is grim.

Eventually, Freya lifts her head and looks at the others. 'I should probably call Gaby...' Without another word, she leaves.

'Well, this is one for the books,' says Paloma.

'Ugh,' I reply.

'It will all work out as is intended,' says Ursula confidently. She is decidedly in camp *que sera sera*.

I have no idea what camp I'm in right now, but I *am* certain that a Bublé bubbly bubble bath is not going to fix this.

17

GABY

Freya's on her way over to my apartment. Part of me feels relieved that she knows how I feel about Raff. And the other part is nervous. There's every chance I'm about to get reamed by my bestie.

I also got a text from Poppy earlier and I open my phone to read it again:

> Let me know if you want to talk after you see Freya.

No reassurance. No 'everything's going to be fine'. No 'London's best matchmaking agency has saved the day and you and Raff are going to be together'.

As if.

At least I got through today without my mind wandering *too* much. I simply kept my head down and focused on work. Since meeting with Claire yesterday, I now have a clearer picture of what it might be like to take over Raff's role in the New Year. It's exciting and terrifying, with a little 'don't count your chickens before they hatch' thrown in.

It's better not to let yourself want something in case you don't get it, right?

Like wanting your best friend to fall in love with you.

'Argh!'

I check the time. Freya should be here by now. I turn on the TV, but I can't concentrate and I end up flicking through everything on my Netflix queue. Nope. Nope. Nope. It's like being on a dating app, only without the eye candy.

I give up and turn off the TV right as Freya buzzes my apartment. I let her into the building, then wait out the thirty seconds it will take her to get to my front door. It takes a thousand years, then there's finally a soft knock.

I bust out a huge smile – fake it till you make it, right? – and open the door. 'Hi!' I exclaim, as if it's been months and not days since I last saw her.

Head tilt. Sad eyes. Pouty bottom lip. *Weird*. She steps inside and without a word, wraps her spindly arms around my neck, enveloping me in a hug.

What is happening right now?

'Poor you,' she says, her voice muffled by my hair.

She steps back and regards me thoughtfully, then takes my hand and leads me over to the sofa. She sits, tugging on my hand, and I plonk down beside her wordlessly, as this feels very much like an out-of-body experience.

Seriously, what is happening right now?

'Tell me everything.'

'Tell you— Wait, I'm confused. Aren't you pissed at me?'

'No,' she replies, clearly puzzled. 'Why would I be?'

'Oh, I don't know,' I say, getting up and pacing because I'm so antsy, I can't sit still. 'Maybe because you've had me running all over frigging London playing wing-woman for Raff and now he's met Julia and is already swept up in that whole thing, which is exactly what you wanted, but then I have this sudden realisation that hey, Raff might be the guy for me, and the timing couldn't possibly be worse and... and...'

Drained, I fall into my Lounge Pug.

'But why would I be angry at you for how you *feel*?' she asks.

'Because you had this elaborate plan and now I've gone and fucked it up.'

'You haven't... *messed* it up,' she says, sidestepping the profanity.

'Really? Because if you'll recall, I've had a front-row seat to this shitshow. I know how much work has gone into matching Raff and—'

'Gaby...' She lifts her hand, palm towards me, and I stop talking.

Probably a good thing because I've worked myself into such a lather, I've buried myself in the Lounge Pug. I may have to spend the rest of my life here.

I climb out awkwardly and return to the sofa. 'Sorry.' I point to myself. 'Drama queen.'

'Well, at least it's you this time – it gets exhausting carrying the mantel all by myself,' she says, teasing me with a gentle smile.

'Frey, seriously though, now what?'

Freya takes a deep breath, which doesn't set me at ease at all. In fact, it does the opposite. 'Just tell me,' I say.

'Oh, Gaby, I wish I could just wave a magic wand and get you your happily ever after.'

I laugh – it's a dry, raspy sound. 'But life doesn't work that way.'

'No.'

'So, what's going to happen with Raff – with Raff and Julia, I mean?' I ask, hating the sound of her name now she's essentially my rival.

'We need to see where things go,' she says softly.

I don't know what I expected. But it wasn't this and the words land with full force, despite Freya's gentle tone.

'I'm so sorry,' she says, grasping my hand and sliding closer. 'I shouldn't have disregarded Poppy's suspicions. But you and Raff – I thought it was laughable and...' Her voices fades away.

Laughable.

But isn't it? And not only the concept of me falling for Raff, but the timing. If Alanis Morissette got wind of this shitshow, she could add a whole verse to that irony song of hers.

But none of this is Freya's fault. 'This isn't on you,' I tell her.

'I do this for a living, Gaby. How could I miss the signs?'

'What signs? Until two days ago, I thought of Raff like my dorky younger brother. I've never thought of him *romantically*. If you *had* believed Poppy and confronted me, I would have laughed it off.'

'But Poppy and Ursula...' she says, confused.

'They must be soothsayers, because whatever they saw, I didn't have even the *slightest* clue.'

'I suppose.'

It strikes me as funny that Freya came here to comfort me, and now I'm comforting her.

'And you're forgetting something,' I add. 'You're way too close to this – that's why you weren't allowed to match Raff yourself. You *couldn't* see it – you're too emotionally involved.'

'Only because he's—'

'Your first best friend – I *know*,' I say, calling back to our dumb conversation from last week.

She gives me a weak smile.

'Can I ask...?' She hesitates. 'Are you in love with Raff?'

I inhale deeply and drop my gaze to the floor.

Am I in love with Raff? Great question.

'I love him, of course I do – the same way I love you.' I look up and she's peering at me intently. 'And I feel safe with him – like I can be myself – or at least I did until Wednesday night,' I add with a dry chuckle. It falls away and I'm serious again, as I delve deeper into my feelings for Raff.

'I always look forward to seeing him and when we spend time together... it's like it fills me up inside. But, again, that's how I feel about you too. Hell, I don't know. What's "being in love" anyway? I've never experienced anything close to it.'

'Not even with your ex?' she asks.

'In retrospect, no, definitely not. Any time I look back on my relationship with Eric, I can't believe I stayed with him as long as I did. We never really *talked*, you know. And if I needed solace, if something terrible happened, like when my grandma on my mom's side passed away, Eric was *not* the person to go to. Not even for something as simple as having a crappy day. He'd tear his eyes away from the TV, say something trite or condescending like, 'It'll be okay,' or, 'You're worrying about nothing,' then crack a beer and go back to watching ESPN.'

Freya squeezes my hand. 'That sounds awful – and *lonely*.'

'Yeah.' I'm quiet for a moment – seriously, why did I put up with Eric for as long as I did? *Six years!*

'Frey,' I say, meeting her eye. 'You're the professional. What do you think turns friendship into love?'

She's thoughtful for a moment, then she smiles and says, 'You realise that you fancy them.'

'Really? That's it?' I ask with a snort. 'Geez, I can see why they pay you the big bucks.'

She purses her lips at me, trying not to laugh. 'It's more than that, of course,' she says, 'but it's also very difficult to identify. Everything you described about your friendship, that's all foundational to a good relationship. Then there's the added layer of attraction. But in between is something... *indefinable* – a spark of sorts.'

'Chemistry?' I ask.

'Some people call it that, yes. Believe me, even at the agency, we wish we could pinpoint precisely what it is and bottle it. But it's either there or it isn't. And "it" is different for every person.'

'It's there between Raff and Julia,' I say quietly. A lump lodges in my throat and I stare at the floor again.

'You don't know that – only *they* know that. And it's still very early days. They haven't even been on a date yet.'

'I know what I saw.'

'And I'm telling you that you don't,' she says with unwavering assuredness.

It's not often that Freya takes a stand like this, and even though I'm not convinced she's right, I don't press her.

'So, that brings us back to "now what?",' I say instead.

'Now, we wait and see.'

'Wonderful. God, with how fast Raff moves, they could be engaged by the spring.'

'*Or* it fizzles out before it even begins,' she says reassuringly. 'But until we know for sure, *please* protect your heart, Gaby.'

'Protect my— How the hell do I do that?'

'Just... try not to dwell on things, and if Raff starts talking to you about Julia, maybe change the subject.'

'So, essentially, take a knife to a gunfight.'

She looks confused. 'I don't know that one – is that something Americans say?'

'It means there's no way this isn't gonna suck.'

She gives me a pitying smile. 'Probably not.'

'Ugh,' I groan. 'I *really* don't want to go to CiCi and Devin's tomorrow.'

This additional realisation lands with so much force, I feel like I've been hit by a bus. This might be how it is from now on – me avoiding Raff. Well, at least until I get over him.

'But you *have* to,' Freya replies vehemently. 'It's *Christmas*. And you know CiCi will have been baking for weeks.'

'That's BS,' I say with a laugh. 'CiCi always hires a caterer.'

'Well, there's her famous Christmas cake – you don't want to miss that. *Please* come. It'll be fun – their parties are always fun. And if Raff corners you to talk about Julia, you can signal me, and I'll come rescue you.' She jostles my shoulder. 'Please, Gaby, please come.'

'Okay, geez!' I say, more to shut her up than anything. 'You're like Mrs Claus over there with all your Christmas spirit.'

She grins at me and I roll my eyes. I'll make an appearance, then get the hell out of there.

* * *

What is it they say about best-laid plans? I should have known there was no way I could show up to CiCi and Devin's, then make an exit thirty minutes later.

For one thing, despite the team of caterers who are buzzing around the kitchen, CiCi's put me to work replenishing a tray of hors d'oeuvres.

Like they do every year, she and Devin have gone all-out – and not only with the generous spread of food and drinks. Their spacious home is decked out in garlands made from real fir-tree branches, each decorated in gold trim, tall pillar candles cover every flat surface, emitting a warm glow, the scent of L'Occitane's Noël permeates the air, and a roaring fire is crackling in the living room fireplace – above which are hung uniform Christmas stockings (for decorative purposes only). And their next-door neighbours, who perform on the West End, are at the piano in the library, playing and singing Christmas carols.

The *pièce de résistance* is the fourteen-foot Christmas tree dominating the foyer, teeming with every gold decoration in existence.

'Make sure each blini gets a sprig of dill,' says CiCi, looking over my shoulder.

'Yep, no problem,' I say, expertly placing a delicate frond of dill.

Why am I here again? And not only in the kitchen, but at this party? So far, I've steered clear of Raff, but how long can that last?

'Something's off with you today,' says CiCi, leaning against the counter to face me. 'Are you all right?'

I look up and she's got the concerned-look-head-tilt combo going on. Ah, so that's why she's got me in here – she wants me to spill the tea. Only, I am so not spilling so much as a drop of tea about her nephew. Just, no.

'Oh... you know,' I say breezily, 'winding up at work with end-of-year stuff, planning my trip home... It's been intense these past few weeks.'

She nods, but I can tell she's not buying it – a reminder why CiCi is my 'mom away from my mom'.

'And is everything all right between you and Raff?'

Good thing I don't have a mouthful of anything, or I would have spat it out all over these blinis.

'Yeah, totally. Why are you asking?'

She shrugs with a half-smile. 'Well, you're typically joined at the hip at these things, but not today. You also arrived separately, so I wondered...'

Wow, she's good. But I can't have CiCi worrying about me – or more to the point, me and Raff.

'Oh,' I say with a laugh. 'I had something on this morning, so it made sense to make my own way here.' I leave it at that, deliberately omitting an explanation for why I've avoided Raff since I arrived.

'Glad to hear it.'

But I can tell she doesn't buy my feeble excuse – or my evasion tactics – as there's a knowing glint in her eye that reminds me of Gina. Mom calls it her 'bullshit detection radar'.

'Would you mind taking those out to the buffet?' she asks.

Glad to be out of the hotseat, I flash her a bright smile and say, 'Happy to.'

I'm making room on the buffet table for the blinis when the distinctive chink-chick-chink of someone striking a glass with something metal rings out across the living room.

'Hello, everyone,' says Devin, who's standing on a small wooden stool near the fireplace. 'If I could have your attention, please. And could everyone come in from the other rooms?'

Pairs and trios of people come in from the other parts of the house, swarming into the living room.

Once everyone's crammed in, Devin says, 'I just wanted to say on behalf of CiCi and myself that we're so happy you could all be here today. This is one of our favourite events of the year and what makes it so special is being with the people we love.'

He made a similar speech last year – and the year before – but it always comes from the heart. I scan the room for Raff and when I find him, he's looking at me, smiling. I smile back, then look away.

He's wearing that Christmas sweater – the one he wore to the photoshoot – only this time, he doesn't look like a dork. He looks cute. That may also have something to do with his hair, which he's now wearing off his face – the hair stylist at *Nouveau* probably taught him how to do that. Regardless, with his hair worn like that, he's more handsome than ever.

Even in that stupid sweater, he looks good.

I steer my attention back to Devin and he's making a toast. I chorus, 'To absent family and friends,' along with the other guests, my mind going straight to Mom and Dad and Issy – and (poor) Monica, who must be freaking out with her wedding only a week and a half away and my aunt being a total nightmare from hell.

'Now, this part is a surprise,' says Devin. 'CiCi, my love, where are you?'

'Here, darling.'

He holds his hand out to her, and guests step aside as she makes her way to Devin, eyeing him curiously.

She mouths something to him, but I can't make it out. Devin laughs and says, 'You'll see.'

'Now,' he says, addressing the rest of us. 'All of you know that my darling CiCi here is one of the hardest working people in England.'

The guests murmur in agreement.

'And on top of running a business at one of the busiest times of the year, she's organised this lovely party. So, in appreciation of all you are and all you do, my love, I have a surprise.'

CiCi looks up at him, her smile asking, 'What are you up to?'

'After saying we would for years but never getting around to it, we are *finally* spending Christmas in Lapland. I've booked us a romantic holiday, just the two of us, and you won't need to lift a finger.'

'Devin!' She claps a hand to her chest and for a second, it's hard to tell if it's a good surprise or not. Then she bursts into tears, and he steps off the stool and envelops her in a hug. There's a moment of total silence, then the room erupts into applause.

Witnessing how happy CiCi is, and how in love she and Devin are, brings tears to my eyes.

I want that.

And I want it with Raff, says the little voice in my head.

18

GABY

I look towards where Raff was standing earlier to share the moment, but he's not there and I start scanning the room. Where did he go?

'Isn't that the most romantic thing ever?' asks Freya, who is unexpectedly at my side. 'I adore Freddie, really I do, but I'd die of shock if he ever made such a grand romantic gesture.'

This is the first time Freya has disparaged Freddie in this way, instantly making me want to defend him. I must like him more than I realised – probably because he's so sweet to her.

'Have you told him that you'd like him to be more romantic?' I ask. 'You're, like, the biggest romantic I know – surely you've at least hinted?'

She shrugs, which is Freya for 'no'.

'You know Freddie would do anything for you. Why don't you just tell him what you want?'

'Because I shouldn't have to. We've been together over a year – doesn't he know me well enough to figure it out on his own?'

So, she's expecting Freddie to guess what's in her head, which is unfair and could eventually undermine their relationship. I suppose even a matchmaker doesn't always get it right.

'Frey, *tell* him. You'd be honest with him if there was something more he could be doing in bed, right? How is this any different?'

Freya's eyes widen in horror. Oops, I've crossed a line. In many ways, we're as close as sisters, but we've never been the type of girl-friends who discuss our sex lives. If I need to talk about sex, I do that with Issy or my mom.

'Sorry,' I say, and she shakes her head as if she's trying to dislodge something.

'Have you seen Raff?' she asks, abruptly changing the subject.

'Not since Devin's speech.' I scan the room again and festivities have resumed, but no Raff. Something feels off.

'Come on,' I say. 'Let's go find him.'

Freya and I do a whole circuit of the ground floor before we find Raff and CiCi in the conservatory, one of the few places in CiCi and Devin's home that doesn't scream 'tasteful opulence'. It looks like it was furnished with cast-offs from the set of *The Golden Girls*: a wicker two-seater and matching cane chairs, the cushions covered in a palm-leaf motif, a circular rattan rug on the floor, and more plants in terracotta pots than in most greenhouses.

I'm about to knock on the open door when Raff says, 'It's fine, Aunt CiCi, I *promise*.'

Only it doesn't seem fine – whatever 'it' is. Despite the brave face, Raff is obviously distraught. And it's rare to see him like this – shy, embarrassed at being the centre of attention, sure, but not riled up. He's usually unflappable.

That's why he's the rock of our trio.

'Hey,' I say, stepping into the room, Freya close behind me. 'What's going on?'

'Ah, love,' CiCi says to me. 'I had no idea Devin had gone and booked that trip. And *he* had no idea that you two were going abroad. He thought Raff would be sorted – have a friends' Christmas.'

'Oh no, Raff!' exclaims Freya. 'You'll be all alone.'

'It appears so, yes,' he replies tautly.

'I'd invite you to come to Sweden with me,' says Freya, 'but we're staying with my dad's cousin and I'll be sleeping in a tiny bedroom in a child's bed. I wasn't even able to ask Freddie.'

'No, no, I wouldn't want to intrude anyway.'

'How about you come with us?' CiCi offers. 'We can see if there's another room available in the lodge.'

I can tell that Raff considers it, but only for a second. As upset as he is, there's no way he'd gatecrash his aunt and uncle's romantic getaway.

He fakes a smile. 'I'm sure Uncle Devin would have something to say about that, don't you?'

Speaking of...

'Here you all are,' says Devin.

'We're hardly hiding, darling,' says CiCi, still frowning.

'Sorry, lad,' he says to Raff with a pained expression. 'I suppose I can see about changing the trip to the New Year...'

CiCi's head swivels in his direction. I doubt she was expecting that, and she doesn't seem too pleased about it.

'Why don't you come home with me for Christmas?' I blurt, only realising the second the words are out of my mouth what I've done.

'What? Really?' In an instant, Raff's countenance changes from distraught to hopeful. 'Are you sure that wouldn't be an imposition?'

An imposition? No. Stupid on my part? Abso-fucking-lutely.

'Hardly,' I say with a forced laugh. 'You know Gina adores you. So does Dad. And you can sleep in Issy's old room. You'd have to be my plus-one to my cousin's wedding on Christmas Eve but other than that, Christmases at my parents' place are pretty chill.'

Good god! Has Gaby-the-best-friend had a brain fart, forgetting there's a new Gaby in town, one that's fallen for Raff? Why, yes. Yes, she has!

Raff breaks into a wide grin. 'If you're sure?' he asks hopefully, melting my heart. There's no way I can rescind the offer now.

'I'm sure. It'll be great – *better* than great. It'll be a blast. *And* if I bring you as my date to the wedding, I won't have to fend off sleazy groomsmen or field questions about why I'm still single. Nothing worse than relatives asking me when I'm going to find myself a decent man, especially my Aunt Christine. She *never* lets up.'

Now I'm rabbiting on like a moron. Because I *am* a moron. I've not only invited Raff home for the holidays, I've also volunteered him to be my fake wedding date! And I've had *one* mug of spiced rum since I arrived, so I can't blame alcohol for my stupidity.

Fortunately, the only person who appears to have noticed my SNAFU is Freya, who stares at me, gobsmacked. The others, including Raff, are talking over each other excitedly.

'Thank you, love,' says CiCi, giving me a quick hug. 'It means the world to us to know that Raff will be with family over Christmas.'

'Sure thing. All good. Totally fine.' My mind adds, *Nothing to see here – just a total trainwreck waiting to happen.*

'Right, now that's sorted, if you wouldn't mind re-joining the party...' says Devin, his eyebrows raised.

'That's Devin's polite way of saying "Everybody out",' says CiCi with a laugh. She shoos us through the conservatory door and closes it behind her, and she and Devin stride off to the main part of the house to return to their party.

'Seriously, Gabs, you're a total lifesaver,' says Raff, stopping me with a hand on my arm. 'I know it's silly, my reaction...' He gives me a lipless smile.

'Not at all. I'd be pissed if my parents pulled something like that. But don't thank me yet. Apparently, my aunt is being a total Momzilla. You may have to help me run interference.'

He laughs. 'Sounds almost fun.'

'It won't be, I promise, but the rest should be.'

I'm doing my best to avoid looking at Freya, who's standing close by wearing her I-need-to-talk-to-you-urgently expression.

'Well, this is cause for a celebration,' says Raff. 'I'll grab us some champers.'

Raff leaves to get us drinks and now there's no avoiding Freya.

'Is this really a good idea?' she asks.

I heave out a sigh. 'Honestly? Probably not, but by the time I realised what I'd said, it was too late. You saw his face, Frey. He was crushed. I haven't seen him like that since Winnie broke up with him. And what was I supposed to do? Leave him here to have Christmas by himself?'

'He could have gone to Lorrie's.'

'Well, no, because Lorrie and her kids are off to Majorca for Christmas.'

'Oh.'

'It'll be fine, don't worry,' I say, but who am I trying to convince – her or me? Because there is every chance it will be weird and uncomfortable and, quite possibly, heartbreaking.

'It's going to be a busy week anyway,' I continue, affecting a casual lack of concern. 'Lots of family around in the lead up to the wedding, and the wedding itself will eat up a day. Then Christmas with Mom and Dad, and home on the twenty-seventh. It'll go like that,' I add, snapping my fingers.

'But your *feelings*, Gaby,' she says, her eyes teeming with worry.

'My feelings will have to wait. I mean, they have to anyway,

right? Until there's some clarity around Julia? And if Raff chooses
her, they'll have to wait indefinitely, so I may as well get used to it.'

I've gotta be honest – not loving how cynical I sound right now.

Freya mustn't either and her shoulders slump, her expression
becoming even more distressed.

'I'm not convincing you, am I?'

'No.'

'That's okay. I'm not convincing me either. Fuck, Frey, what have
I done?'

She rubs my arm soothingly, which is about as effective trying
to snuff out a raging house fire by spitting on it.

* * *

'Hey, Mom, I have some news.' I'm ensconced in my Lounge Pug,
needing every ounce of its comforting properties now that I've
committed to spending twenty-four-seven with Raff over the holidays.

'Good or bad?' she asks. 'I can't tell from your tone.'

'Uh, good news. At least I hope it is. I *may* have invited Raff to
come home with me for Christmas.'

She chuckles. '*May* have? Or *have*?'

'Have.' I am 99 per cent sure it will be fine, but in the time it
takes for Mom to respond, my stomach clenches with doubt.

'Oh, hun, what a treat for us! I'll start thinking about something
to put under the tree for him. Oh, and I can have Rosemary make
him a stocking.' Rosemary is one of the night nurses on the ward
who does crafts at the nurses' station when it's quiet.

I chuckle – trust my mom to start planning Christmas presents
for Raff the second I give her the news.

'Are you sure, Mom? It's not too much of an imposition?'

'Hardly! We love Raff. He's welcome any time.'

'I know I should have checked with you first but Devin surprised CiCi with a trip to Lapland, meaning Raff would be on his own, and you should have seen him, Mom – like a lost little boy. I couldn't bear the thought of him all alone on Christmas.'

'You did the right thing, Gaby. You always do.'

If I did the right thing then why am I seriously questioning my choices? I think.

What I *say* is, 'Thanks, Mom.'

'Will he be on the same flight as you?'

'Unsure. He's looking at flights tonight, but I'll let you know.'

'Okay, hun. And don't worry, I'll smooth things over with Chrissy – about the seating arrangements for the wedding.'

'Oh, right. Yeah, she's not going to like me very much.'

'Chrissy doesn't like anyone right now – you're in good company.'

I laugh.

'Listen, I've gotta go but talk soon, huh?'

'Bye, Mom. Love you.'

She says she loves me too, and we end the call.

'It's only a week, Gaby. You're entirely capable of spending seven days under the same roof with Raff, without doing or saying anything to let on how you feel.'

Somehow, saying this out loud is not convincing – shocker. No wonder Freya was compelled to talk me out of it. She even sent a text after the party:

> Have asked my parents if we can take Raff to Sweden with us. They said yes, but he'll need to stay in a hotel. Better than nothing though, right? *shrug emoji* Should I ask him?

I replied:

Let me talk to Gina first.

She replied back with an 'okay' emoji, but I read between the lines (so to speak). She's worried – about me, about Raff, about this whole thing blowing up in our faces.

And she's gone to a lot of trouble. Her family are nice people, but inviting a last-minute guest to a Nilsen family Christmas would have been a big ask – even bigger than bringing Raff to my cousin's wedding. Freya's doing her best to help me out of this mess.

'Argh, what are you *doing*, Gaby?' I ask myself. 'Besides now talking to yourself, you dork.'

Wait, am I looking at this the wrong way?

Maybe there's a silver lining here. With Raff out of London so soon after meeting Julia, there's less time for their budding relationship to develop into something, right?

And by spending time together – out of work, away from Freya and CiCi and Devin – maybe Raff will see *me* in a new light, like I've recently seen him.

Maybe Raff coming to Seattle is the best thing that can happen under the circumstances.

'Hmm, maybe...' I mutter.

There's only one person I can ask. Freya's too close to it, and CiCi may suspect something's up but she's not the right person to discuss this with.

It's a risk, because she won't just tell me what I want to hear – she'll give it to me straight – but if there's any hope at all...

I navigate to Poppy's contact details in my phone and hit the call button.

19

POPPY

'Thank you *so* much for having us over,' I say as Shaz lets us into their flat. She captures me in a hug and I whisper, 'I need to de-Helen after that.'

She laughs, understanding immediately. Lauren welcomes us in, taking our coats and offering us a glass of wine from the open bottle on the coffee table.

'Yes, please,' says Tristan.

Relieved of his coat and suit jacket, he loosens his tie while I toe off my shoes and wriggle out of my pantyhose, doing my best not to show my undies – though, it is just Tris and my closest friends.

'Make yourself at home,' says Shaz with a laugh.

'Sorry, don't mind me.' I ball up the pantyhose and shove them in my handbag.

Tristan and I have spent the afternoon at his mum's, dressed to impress, sipping Champagne, hobnobbing with crusty old men and their pinched-face wives, and eating canapés right out of a seventies cookbook: vol-au-vents, pigs in blankets, devilled eggs, and cheese-and-gherkin skewers.

Helen may have money, but it's old money, which may be why her party planning hasn't evolved since before Tristan was born.

The one saving grace was that she only serves *extremely* expensive Champagne – her way of flaunting the fortune she inherited from Tristan's late father – and it is dee-lish! I've arrived at Shaz and Lauren's slightly tipsy and ravenous. There are only so many chunks of gherkin a person can eat.

I eye the generous platter of nibblies on the coffee table – olives, oozing camembert, crumbly cheddar, hummus, fancy seeded crackers, and prosciutto *and* salami – and fall in love with our friends even more.

I dash over to the platter and shove a stuffed green olive in my mouth, then get comfy on the sofa next to Tristan.

'So, how was it?' Lauren asks, handing us glasses of a Bordeaux-style blend from Washington.

Tris and I exchange an amused look.

'*Over*,' he answers drily, his eyebrows raised sardonically. 'At least for another year.'

'That good, huh?' asks Shaz with a grin.

'How would *you* describe it, darling?' he asks.

'It was about as festive as a trip to the gynaecologist.'

Shaz coughs out a laugh and Tristan sniggers.

'Wow,' says Lauren, 'sounds painful. Well, you're here now.'

'On that...' I say. I wriggle, trying to get comfortable, but no luck. 'This dress is strangling me.' I throw a pleading look towards Shaz.

'Help yourself,' she says, waving her arm in the direction of their bedroom.

I leap up and return to the lounge room a couple of minutes later, wearing a pair of Shaz's trackies and a T-shirt.

'Much better,' I say, plopping down next to Tristan.

He's regaling Shaz and Lauren with the sole amusing anecdote from the party: his father's former business partner and recent widower cornered Helen under the mistletoe and kissed her on the mouth.

'Oh my god! Helen would have *died*,' exclaims Shaz, one of the few people Helen has ever warmed to, having succumbed to Shaz's charms at our wedding.

'I had to remind myself where the smelling salts are kept,' he quips.

'She *did* look like she was about to faint,' I say through a mouthful of cheese and crackers.

Lauren, who has never met Helen – lucky thing – chuckles. I'm pretty sure she's convinced we're exaggerating. If she ever does meet Helen, it won't take her long to discover that we're not.

'Oh, I totally forgot,' says Shaz, 'Jass and Ravi told us their news. How exciting, eh? A little bubba on the scene.'

'I know. I can't *wait*,' I reply. 'And confession time: I've been trawling baby websites for presents. Everything's so little and cute,' I coo.

Tristan laughs. 'If you buy every item you've shown me in the past couple of weeks, Ravi and Jacinda will have to move into a larger home.'

'But I want Baby Sharma to have everything their little heart desires,' I say.

'Yeah, that's what aunties are for, Tris,' Shaz agrees, 'spoiling their nieces and nephews.'

'Sooo...' says Lauren, who's sitting on the rug cross-legged. She looks up at Shaz, who nods at her, smiling, then turns back to us. '*We're* actually talking about it.' She takes a sip of wine, eyeing me over the rim of her glass.

'Having a baby?'

'Yep!' She breaks into a wide grin.

'Really?' I ask excitedly. 'So, which one of you...?' I look between them.

'Hah – not me,' says Shaz. 'Can you imagine *me pregnant*?' She takes a swig of wine to punctuate her point.

'So, *you'll* carry the baby then, Lauren?' asks Tristan, ignoring Shaz's crass outburst.

'That's what we're thinking.'

'When?' I ask.

'Oh, we haven't even found a fertility clinic yet. We're going to do that in January.'

'New year, new beginnings...' says Shaz wistfully. She'll make a great mum – they both will – and I am *so* happy for them.

We're all quiet for a long moment and in the silence, that question pops into my mind again, about *us* having a child. I look over at Tristan and he appears contemplative. I wonder if his thoughts have gone to the same place mine have.

It would be amazing to raise a child alongside our closest friends' children. We'd be one big extended family and the kids would grow up like cousins.

But there are so many other considerations, including the one Tristan just raised about having room for a baby. We'd probably have to move – and would that be closer to or further away from our friends?

And what about my parents? It would be hard on them having their only grandchild living across the world. Could I do that to them? But what's the alternative? I don't want to move back to Tassie. And even as a thought experiment, it's unimaginable to see city-dweller Tristan making a life in rural Tasmania. *Or* me. I'm a proud and happy Londoner now.

'*Poppy.*'

I snap out of my trance to find the three of them staring at me.

'Sorry – off with the fairies,' I say lightly, not wanting to explain what I was thinking about.

'Your phone, darling,' says Tristan. 'It's ringing.'

'Oh! Shit.' I leap up from the sofa and rush to my handbag. I take out my phone, seeing Gaby's name on the screen, and answer right away.

'Hi, Gaby, what's up?'

'Sorry to disturb you – I know it's Saturday evening,' she says.

'No worries, but can you hold on a sec?' I turn to the others and signal that I'll take the call in the bedroom. They know the latest – about Gaby falling for Raff – but I don't want to disrupt their evening with a work call. I close the door behind me and sit on the edge of the bed. 'So, how are you doing?' I ask.

'Um... okay.'

After Freya messaged last night to say that she'd been to Gaby's, I sent Gaby a supportive text, but this is the first time we've spoken since she told me about her feelings for Raff.

'I imagine it's been hard, especially as we're seeing how things go with Raff and Julia.'

'Well, yeah,' she says, 'but that's not why I'm calling. I've done something...'

'Okay.'

I have no idea what's coming, but Gaby sounds almost cheerful.

'And before I tell you what it is, you should know that it's done now, and I can't take it back. But I do need your take on it if you're okay with that?'

Oh bugger. She hasn't confessed her feelings to Raff, has she? I mean, she has every right to but...

'What is it, Gaby?' I ask, masking my unease.

'Raff's coming to Seattle with me for Christmas. And to my cousin's wedding on the twenty-fourth.'

'Oh.' At face value, that isn't necessarily a bad thing, but I'd wager there's more to it than a simple trip. 'Does Freya know?'

'Yeah, she knows. She was there when I made the offer.'

Gaby goes on to explain how it came about and I have to say, I would have done the same thing. No one should be alone on Christmas – especially someone who loves Christmas as much as Raff seems to.

'And I know I'm supposed to let the whole Raff-and-Julia thing unfold without interfering, and that includes not telling him how I feel, but…'

I catch the shift in her tone when she says 'Raff and Julia' and I sympathise with her all over again. This is just shitty luck and even shittier timing – and neither of those things are her fault. You can't schedule falling in love like you do a dental appointment.

She's gone silent. 'But?' I ask, prompting her to finish her thought.

'But…' She sighs. 'What if something happens between me and Raff while we're there? You know, *organically*?'

The way she says 'organically' is loaded with justifications, rationalisations, and a generous serving of hope.

'In a roundabout way, are you asking for my permission to act on your feelings?'

'Maybe. That's wrong, though, isn't it?'

'Gaby, I can't tell you what to do – and neither can the agency. Our decision was based on what *we* would do – or in this case, wouldn't do. We've decided to see how the match with Julia pans out, but you aren't bound by that decision. You're not beholden to us.'

'But is it the right thing to do? Let something happen with Raff – if it comes to that, I mean.'

'Only you can know that.'

'Okay,' she says, her tone betraying her disappointment in my response.

I'm very familiar with this specific brand of hope, having had many patients over the years who sought my 'permission' to do one thing or another. Only I am not here to dole out permission. Gaby isn't my client. She's only informally connected to this case, and if she wants to make a play for Raff, then I can't stop her. Actually, I wouldn't *try* to stop her, but I'm also not going to tell her to go for it outright. That would be overstepping.

'What did Freya say?' I ask instead.

'She's freaking out. She even asked her parents if Raff could go to Sweden with them.'

Yikes – that's a big ask for Freya. From what she's told me, her family prefer to keep to themselves. She *must* be freaking out, and I sympathise with her. She only wanted to do something nice for Raff and now her two closest friends are embroiled in a love triangle. There's no way she would have seen that coming.

'But he's not going to Sweden?' I ask to be sure.

'No. He's definitely coming home with me. But, Poppy, he's seeing Julia tomorrow. They've got a date. And we're not leaving for Seattle until the end of next week. What if he sees her every day between now and then?'

'He might, and you need to be prepared for that. You and Freya have both mentioned how fast he moves once he's interested in someone.'

'Yeah.' She's quiet for a moment. 'I feel sick when I think of them together,' she says, her voice strangled.

'That's understandable. Look, I can't tell you what to do, but I will say this: you love Raff – as a friend, I mean – and you want him to be happy, right?'

'Of course.'

'So, if you see that he's happy with Julia, then—'

'Then I should leave well enough alone,' she says, talking over me, her voice steeped in sadness.

'Something like that – though much harder to do when you're staying under the same roof.'

'Yeah... Oh god, this is a huge mistake, isn't it?'

'It's not an ideal situation, no, but you're being a good friend ensuring that Raff's not alone for Christmas. You've put him and his feelings before yours. But your feelings matter too, so do what you can to safeguard your heart.'

She makes a sound, but I can't tell if it's a cough or a laugh or a little of both. 'Freya basically said the same thing,' she says.

'Well, Freya's smart – like I am,' I say, making her chuckle. '*And* she cares about you. *Both* of you.'

'Yeah.' She's quiet for a second. 'Hey, Poppy, if I need any advice or just to talk...'

'You mean while you're in America?' I ask.

'Yeah.'

'You can message me – or call. I can't promise advice – especially if it goes against the agency's stance – but I can be a friendly ear if you're not comfortable talking to Freya.'

She exhales noisily. 'Thanks. I can't ask for any more than that.'

'You're welcome. Hey, I should chuff off – I'm at my friends' place.'

'Sorry again about intruding on your evening.'

'It's completely fine. Look, whatever happens in Seattle, do your best to keep Raff's happiness in mind, but also be true to yourself. If those are mutually exclusive, do what you think is right in the moment.'

She laughs freely at that, which is fair. It may be the most vague non-advice advice I've ever given. 'Thanks, Poppy. I'll do my best.'

We say our goodbyes and I return to the lounge.

'Everything all right?' asks Tristan.

'Yeah, how's Gaby?' Shaz adds.

'Oh, no biggie – she's only gone and invited Raff to go to Seattle with her over Christmas – *and* to be her date at her cousin's wedding.'

'Oh, that's...' says Lauren with a grimace.

'That's a *move*,' adds Shaz. 'What could possibly go wrong there?'

'I know. Argh, this case!' I drop onto the sofa next to Tristan and lean my head on his shoulder. He lifts his hand to cup my cheek, patting it gently. 'I've also agreed to play agony aunt for the duration.'

'Shouldn't Freya be on the hook for that?' asks Shaz. 'They're her friends.'

'Oh,' I say sitting up. 'You've reminded me – I should message her.'

'About?' Shaz asks as I start typing.

'Hang on...' I hit send, then answer Shaz. 'Freya's feeling it too. She's really upset.'

'Because she thought she was doing a good thing?' Lauren asks, getting it instantly.

'Yep,' I reply.

'What is it they say about the road to hell being paved with good intentions?' asks Shaz.

'*That*,' I tell her. 'That's the whole saying.'

Tristan sniggers, then draws me gently towards him and I nestle in the crook of his arm.

'Meanwhile,' I say, 'Raff's living in ignorant bliss and about to go on his first date with Julia Mendelssohn.'

'Wait – *that's* who he matched with?' asks Lauren.

'You know who she is?' I ask.

'Doesn't everyone?' she asks with a laugh. Lauren loves

celebrity gossip and reads all the society pages, poring over who went where with whom. She's a walking *Who's Who?* guide.

'Well, *I* do, of course. I vetted her as a potential but—'

'I have no idea who she is, babe,' says Shaz.

'Well, she's an artist and she's *gorgeous* – total bombshell.'

'Don't you love how my girlfriend is always talking about how gorgeous other women are?' Shaz asks me and Tristan.

'But I chose *you*. It's only to establish how high my standards are, so you know how gorgeous *you* are in comparison.'

'Nice save, babe,' says Shaz.

Their banter does the trick and I'm able to set Gaby and Raff and the whole messy palaver aside – at least for tonight, or until the next disastrous turn in this case.

Whichever comes first.

20

GABY

It's amazing how fast a week can go by.

The days – and nights – between CiCi and Devin's party and the flight to Seattle are jam-packed with end-of-year meetings, client parties, last-minute Christmas shopping, packing, and trying to ignore the mounting panic about taking Raff home with me for the holidays.

I've also done my best to be a supportive friend every time Raff has gushed to me about Julia, nodding and smiling and saying things like, 'You don't say.' What's been going on inside my head is a whole other story.

'Julia said the funniest thing at dinner the other night.'

Move over, Taylor Tomlinson. Julia should take that act on the road.

'Did you know that Julia has a painting hanging in the Tate Modern?'

I did know that because my new favourite hobby is googling your new girlfriend, then stress eating a packet of cookies.

'Julia and her family are off to St Moritz for Christmas. Can you *imagine*? Maybe next Christmas, I'll be joining them.'

Please, kill me now.

I feel like I've perfected the that's-amazing-and-this-isn't-making-me-die-inside-at-all smile. I can't even *bear* the idea of them sleeping together. Which means it's torture that I've been thinking about it non-stop, right down to the nausea-inducing details. The only saving grace is reminding myself that Raff may dive headfirst into relationships, but he typically holds off on sleeping with someone until he's been dating them for at least a few weeks.

Although Raff is *also* capable of packing a month's worth of dates into just one week.

And now we're an hour into our flight to Seattle and he's already mentioned her three times. Only nine hours to go!

'Hey,' I say, when there's a brief pause after his description of Julia's next collection – something about shades of blue. 'How about I brief you on the family? So you're extra prepared.'

'Oh, er… sure.'

He probably wasn't finished telling me how incredibly talented Julia is, but I've heard about as much as I can tolerate for today. And I've never really had low self-esteem – I was raised with a healthy ego, a balance of valuing myself and being thankful for good fortune and the opportunities that have come my way. But a week of 'Julia this' and 'Julia that' has started to make a dent. Even Zendaya would be having doubts about how she measured up against the gorgeous, talented, hilarious Julia if she were in my shoes.

I also spent *way* too much time imagining what their couple name would be. I went through Rulia, Jaffia, and Rajul before landing on Raffia, which made me laugh out loud at my desk like an idiot. When Lorrie peeked around the wall of her cubical with a quizzical look, I tried (and failed) to pass it off as a cough. She gave me a you're-being-weird frown, then went back to work.

'Okay,' I say, angling my body towards him, 'all my dad's family are in Texas, so you'll only be meeting Mom's side – the Johnsons.'

'Well, your mother is an absolute darling, so if they're anything like her...'

'Umm...' I give him a cheesy, apologetic smile. 'Some of them are. Others, not so much.'

'And is there a reason you waited until we were in the air to tell me this?'

'Absolutely – I'm not stupid. If I'd revealed some of what I'm about to say ahead of time, you'd be in Sweden right now, sleeping head-to-toe with Freya in a doll's bed.'

This makes him laugh again, and we're instantly back to being Gabs and Raff, cracking each other up like this is any other day and not the end of 'Raffia's Intense Week of Dating'.

'You know those families where everyone talks at once and no one's really listening and it's constant mayhem, but you can also feel the love in the air?'

He narrows his eyes. 'I'm not sure.'

'You know. It's sounds like everyone's fighting but, really, they love each other?' I ask.

'Not firsthand. I grew up in England, remember. As rowdy as it ever got at CiCi and Devin's was a heated discussion about which to put on a scone first – jam or cream.'

'Wow, sounds *heavy*,' I say with a smirk.

'Actually, *clotted*.'

'Sorry?'

'The cream – it's clotted cream, not heavy cream.'

'Now you're being obtuse on purpose,' I retort.

He grins at me, then tips an imaginary hat.

'So, who won the great scone showdown?'

'Who do you think? Aunt CiCi, of course. She always wins –

and when it comes to scones, which she is famous for, she's a Devon girl all the way.'

'Which is?'

'Cream first.'

'Ahh, fascinating.'

He grins. 'No, it isn't but I'm surprised you've known her all these years and it's never come up.'

'Now that you mention it,' I say, recalling the many times I've had scones at CiCi's, 'I just follow what she does – and yeah, she's a cream-then-jam woman all the way.'

'Is this the sort of sparkling conversation I can expect from your family?' he teases.

'Hey – *you* brought up scones.'

'Fair. So, what topics should I brush up on then?'

'Probably easier if I list the topics to avoid,' I reply.

'All right.'

'Politics,' I say, counting off on my fingers.

'Well, obvs. Wait, just in case, which way do they lean?'

'Left. Only... Aunt Christine *still* hasn't come to terms with Washington legalising marijuana, which was in 2012. She calls it a "gateway" drug. Do *not* let her get started on that.'

'Noted. Anything else?'

'We are a Mariner's family – that's Seattle's baseball team. My cousin's fiancé is from Kansas, but he follows the Oakland As – that's a Californian team – and it's a *huge* deal to my Uncle Marvin.'

'*Marvin?*'

'Yeah, like Marvin the Martian,' I reply. It may be an unusual name to some, but I've had an Uncle Marvin my whole life, so it's not weird to me. 'Anyway, if either Uncle Marv or Brian even *mention* baseball, get out of there immediately. I mean it. Clear. The. Room.'

'But you said the bickering was all in good fun.'

'Baseball talk isn't bickering. It's war.'

'I feel like I should be writing this down,' he says with a pretend frown.

'Nah,' I reply. 'Now Monica, the bride, is a total sweetheart. She's like a little sister to me and Issy – she's eight years younger than me – and Issy and I babysat her all the time. Super cute kid, always singing and dancing. Issy and I would play our favourite songs, like "Hips Don't Lie" and "Crazy in Love", and the three of us would make up these little dance routines.'

'What does Monica do now?' he asks.

'She teaches dance.'

'Wow. Look at you, helping mould young minds.'

'I take zero credit. That was all Monica. Even at a young age, she was a good dancer – way better than me or Issy.'

'You're not really selling yourself as a wedding date,' he teases.

The reminder cuts through the fun of our banter.

Not only are we going to yet another formal event together – and I still don't know if it's a good idea or just plain stupid – but my aunt freaked out *way* more than anticipated when Mom told her I was bringing a plus one after RSVPing that I was attending alone. She had to add a *tenth* place setting to *one* table – the horror! Mom says I'm firmly in the bad books and that some next-level grovelling will be in order when I see Aunt Christine.

I laugh off Raff's comment, ignoring the turmoil it has stirred up. 'I can do the basics. I'm also half Rivera, don't forget. I'm a pretty decent line dancer *and* my dad taught me to salsa when I was little.'

'Maybe *I'll* be the rubbish date then.'

'You'll be...' I can't say the one thing I want to say, which is 'perfect'. I settle on, '...fine.'

He laughs. 'High praise indeed.'

Just then the drinks cart rolls by, followed by the food cart, and suddenly I'm ravenous – for *airplane food*.

'It's the best part, isn't it?' Raff asks.

'What is?'

I glance over and we lock eyes. He's smiling and his eyes seem greener than usual – it's probably his teal long-sleeved T-shirt doing that. I've always liked him in teal.

'Mealtimes,' he answers, and I have to remind myself what we were talking about.

'Oh right – well, they help pass the time.'

'This might sound strange, but I actually *like* airplane food.'

I scrunch my face at him. 'That is strange.'

'I don't know what it is – possibly all the little compartments. Like a bento box in the sky.'

'Spoken like a marketing whizz,' I quip. 'You should call BA when we land and sell them that. Or maybe ask the flight attendant to pass it along.'

He sniggers. 'So, are you expecting to hear from Claire before Christmas?' The change of subject to Global Reach catches me off-guard.

'I'm not sure,' I reply. 'I'm trying to put it out of my mind. You know – just in case.'

'Good tactic, focusing on other things until you hear from her.'

Yes, 'other things', such as all-consuming thoughts of you and Julia.

'That's prudent of you,' he continues. 'It's easy to become obsessed when you're waiting on news.'

News like whether you and Julia will 'stick' or if I'll get actually get a look-in?

I glance at him and he's looking at me reassuringly, so oblivious to the irony of what he's just said, it's laughable. Only I don't laugh, because if I start it will be impossible to stop, and I'd rather not be that bizarre woman on the flight who laughed hysterically for the entire Atlantic crossing.

'Mm-hmm,' I say instead.

One thing is clear: I can't keep obsessing about Raff and Julia – rather, *Raffia*. I'll go nuts.

'Can I tell you something?' I ask.

'Anything.'

Hah! If you only knew how untrue that is.

'I want it, the role – I *really* want it,' I say.

This is the first time I've expressed it to another person in such certain terms, and it feels fucking great.

Raff's face splits into a grin. 'I *thought* as much,' he says, nudging me softly with his elbow. 'You've played things very close to your chest, you have.'

I have but not for the reasons he thinks. And now I've told him how much the role means to me, the floodgates open.

'It's been a combo of you leaving and helping with your handover and picturing myself in the role that's helped me realise how much I want it. *And* that I've been coasting for far too long.'

'You haven't been coasting,' he insists.

'That's generous, but I don't mean I've slacked off or anything – just that it's been way too long since I stretched my abilities. Everything for the past year or so has felt *safe*. Now I'm craving excitement. You know, those projects that make you wonder if you can pull it off – you get the brief, and it comes with a side of adrenalin.'

'Well,' he says with a laugh, 'you'll certainly get that. I can't tell you how many times I've been bricking it.'

I regard him with renewed curiosity. 'I would never have guessed that.'

'I suppose we don't know *everything* about each other,' he says, and I give him a lipless smile.

He's right though. Even best friends keep secrets from each other. Like the one I'm keeping from him.

'Anyway, it sounds like you're ready for the challenge,' he says.

'Yeah, it'll be good to switch things up.'

That's true of my personal life too but a relationship with Raff is unlikely. At least being offered the role at Global Reach is within the realm of possibility.

'Mmm,' he mutters thoughtfully. 'That's certainly what *I'll* be doing.'

'You have no idea how much I admire you, Raff. Here you are, having had this meteoric rise in marketing and now—'

He scoffs, interrupting me. 'I'd hardly call it meteoric, Gabs.'

'Because you're you. And that's how it's always been for you. Whether you know it or not, you're the golden child. You've always excelled at whatever you've put your mind to.'

'So have you.'

I shake my head. 'No. I got good grades – in high school and in college – and I've had a solid career, but none of this comes naturally to me. I have to work twice as hard to achieve half as much.'

'Wait, is this a gender equity thi—'

'*No*. This is a Gaby equity thing. I'm not naturally brilliant like you are. I'm not saying you don't work hard – of course you do – but when you apply yourself, you get further along than I do when I apply myself.'

He frowns at me. 'I don't follow.'

'You're smarter than I am, Raff.'

'I am not!' he insists, as if it's an empirical truth.

'But—'

'You're *wrong*.'

I sit back against my seat. I don't want us to fight, especially not mid-air, and it seems there's no convincing him. The food cart is only three rows ahead of us now. Good timing – we can eat our bento boxes in the sky and cool down.

'Gabs,' he says, leaning close. 'I only meant that there are different ways a person can be clever. There are so many things that you're better at than I am.'

'Like what?' I ask, tossing out the challenge.

'Handling social situations, for one. You always know how to set people at ease – you can talk to practically *anyone*.'

'So can you.'

'Ah... no. I *pretend* to be articulate and charming, when inside I'm scouting for the nearest exit. And that's just one of the many, *many* ways you're cleverer than me.'

'Nice backpedalling,' I say.

'It's not back— I'm serious, Gabs. You're so brave. You moved across the world all by yourself and made a life in London. I could never have done that, especially in my twenties. And you're lovely and kind and the *best* friend. I can't think of anyone who would do a better job taking over my role. Claire will be lucky to have you. Global Reach is lucky to have you.'

Tears unexpectedly prick my eyes and I'm momentarily left speechless.

'Thanks,' I whisper, not trusting my voice.

He grasps my knee and squeezes, and our eyes meet for a long moment. I can't help but wish he already knew how I felt and that he felt the same. Because moments like this, where the lines of friendship blur, are going to become more difficult to endure. Especially with the week coming up.

Raff breaks eye contact, looking past me excitedly. 'Ooh, the pasta looks good, doesn't it?' he asks, craning his neck.

The flight attendants show up with their carts, doling out food and drinks, and our moment vanishes.

'Would you like to watch a film after we eat?' Raff asks. He points to the screen on the seat back in front of him. 'Look. They've got *When Harry Met Sally* – your favourite.'

It's not my favourite but it's up there. I saw it with Gina for the first time when I was about fifteen because it's *her* favourite movie. Other than the mortifying experience of sitting next to my mom while Meg Ryan faked an orgasm, I liked it. And since then, I've seen it at least ten more times.

Only watching it with Raff? The film about two people who've been friends for years, then fall in love? Uh, no.

'If you wanna watch something we've already seen, how about *Antman*? We both liked that one.'

'Yeah, all right,' he replies, giving me a funny look.

21

GABY

'Gaby!' I can hear my dad's voice, but it takes a moment to find him in the crowd of people, all of whom are on tiptoes scouring the emerging passengers for their loved ones.

I finally see him and when our eyes meet, we break into matching grins.

I glance over my shoulder at Raff. 'This way,' I call out, and he nods. The poor guy looks exhausted. We landed over an hour ago and I was straight through immigration, but the non-US-citizen line took a lot longer. I was waiting for him in baggage claim with both our bags by the time he cleared immigration.

'Hi, Dad!' I say, throwing my arms around his neck. I'm super close to my mom, but I've also been a 'daddy's girl' since forever.

'Hey, sweetheart.' He squeezes me tightly.

We step back and regard each other, him with a mock-appraising eye. 'Your mom is going to tell you you're too thin,' he says, a longstanding joke between us.

He means *he* thinks I'm too thin – though compared to his mom, my *abuela*, his sisters, my female cousins on the Rivera side, and even Issy, I am. Abuela calls me 'her little stick girl', something my older cousins used to echo mockingly.

Dad looks past me and grins at Raff, his hand outstretched. 'Rafferty,' he says.

'Roland,' Raff replies. They shake hands and do the manly back-slap hug.

'Okay, let's get out of this chaos,' says Dad, taking the handle of my suitcase. 'Come on, I got a great spot next to the elevator.' This means he drove around for at least twenty minutes until a spot near the elevator opened up.

We follow Dad through the crowded arrivals hall, then outside towards the parking garage. The air seems colder and crisper than I expected – none of Seattle's trademark 'mizzle' – but it's not likely to stay this way.

We pack our luggage into the back of Dad's SUV, then Raff and I fight over who gets the front seat. He insists I take it, and I lob back with, 'You're a foot taller than me and need more leg room. Besides, it'll give you the best view of the city.' He relents and gets in next to Dad.

As we drive onto the freeway, Dad runs us (well, me) through the latest news from the Rivera family – mostly good, although Abuela is being stubborn about taking her medication because it makes her head fuzzy. As she's typically a quick-witted, super-sharp octogenarian, I can understand why that would frustrate her.

Dad also wants to know all about his baby girl's new role. It doesn't matter to him that I haven't landed it yet.

'Just a technicality, right Raff?' he asks.

'Absolutely,' replies a transparently jetlagged Raff, stifling a yawn.

'You'll get it, sweetheart,' says Dad, doubling down on his fatherly reassurance.

I hope so.

Raff has done a stellar job as marketing director, creating a team culture of thinking outside the box, but there's a lot more we could be doing with emerging tech. It will take some convincing to get established luxury brands to agree, but I want to try. I raised it with Claire in our meeting and from what I could tell, she's also keen. I took that as a good sign, mentally crossing my fingers that my suggestion would be the decider and she'll appoint me to the role.

Dad asks Raff about working with CiCi and despite being exhausted, Raff perks up and talks animatedly about the plans he has for launching a new division of Baked to Perfection, creating a range of high-end specialty cakes.

There's a particular swooping curve of the 509 I'm waiting for, and when we get there, I reach forward to tap Raff's shoulder, interrupting him.

'Look.'

Seattle comes into view, lit up in the distance like one of those Christmas villages people have in their living rooms over the holidays.

'Oh, wow,' he says, and Dad and I exchange satisfied smiles in the rearview mirror. 'I had no idea it would be so… *pretty*.'

'Yeah, it's a tech hub, the birthplace of Grunge, and has the worst weather in the world—'

'Hey now,' says Dad, stepping in to defend my hometown.

'But Seattle sure is *purdy*,' I finish with a southern twang.

Conversation stalls while Raff gawps out the window and I see Seattle through fresh eyes – *his* eyes. It is a beautiful city and it's good to be back but, oddly, this doesn't feel like a homecoming. More like a visit.

'Here we are,' Dad says as we pull into the driveway of their two-storey Queen Anne home twenty minutes later. 'Welcome to the madhouse,' he adds.

'Dad!'

He chuckles, the deep timbre of his voice resonating through the car.

He helps get the bags out of the trunk, and soon the three of us, plus two suitcases and two carry-ons, are standing in the entry.

'Gina! They're here!'

'You're here!' says Mom, bursting through the door from the kitchen. She heads straight for me, grabbing both my hands and holding out my arms so she can get a look at me. 'Even more beautiful than the last time,' she says, tears in her eyes.

'Mo-om,' I drawl as she envelops me in a hug. Every time I visit, and the few times she's been to London, she greets me the same way. But with Raff standing right behind me, it's the first time I've been embarrassed.

She releases me, then reaches up to hug Raff. 'And even more handsome than the last time.'

'Hi, Gina,' he replies. His cheeks flush, so at least I'm not alone. 'And thank you so much for having me.'

'Oh, it's no trouble at all,' she says with a flap of her hand.

'Raff, want to help me get these upstairs?' Dad asks, indicating our suitcases.

'Happy to.'

Just then, my cousin, Monica, appears at the top of the stairs. 'Gaby!' she exclaims.

'Hey!' I reply, brightly. I hadn't expected Monica to be here. I glance at Mom, trying to catch her eye, but she and Dad are exchanging an unreadable look.

Monica flies downstairs and flings herself into my arms. 'I am *so* glad you're here,' she says in my ear.

I give her a squeeze, then let her go and introduce her to Raff, only now noticing that she's in her pyjamas. My mind leaps to the obvious conclusion.

'Are you staying here?' I ask, tempering my tone to sound ultra-happy about it.

'Just till the wedding. Mom is being impossible and I swear if I had to spend another night under that roof...' She looks lovingly at Mom. 'That's why I asked Aunt Gina if I could crash in Issy's old room.'

'Oh, cool! That's awesome,' I say, faking a smile. I finally catch Mom's eye and she grimaces at me guiltily.

'Plenty of time to catch up on that over dinner,' says Mom. 'Raff, Roland, how about you take the bags upstairs to Gaby's room and, Gaby, you can help me in the kitchen.'

'I'll bring these,' says Monica, grabbing a carry-on with each hand and jogging up the stairs.

I turn to Mom, my eyes narrowed. 'Sooo... I just flew long-haul. Do you mind if I freshen up first?' I ask, jerking a thumb towards upstairs.

'Plenty of time for that too,' she says *way* too cheerily. She beckons me with her hand and heads back to the kitchen. I follow, catching a waft of the aroma from the stove as I enter the kitchen. She's making creamy salmon and dill linguine – my favourite.

'So, busting out the big guns, I see.'

'What's that?' she asks, playing dumb.

'You're buttering me up with my favourite dish.'

She shrugs as if it hadn't occurred to her.

'Anything you want to tell me?' I ask.

'Monica is staying in Issy's old room,' she tells me in a stage whisper.

'Yeah, I got that part,' I retort drily. 'But *why*?'

'You heard her. Chrissy's being impossible and it's getting worse every day. Yesterday, the embossed paper napkins arrived. Now, keep in mind these are only for cocktail hour, which is immediately after the ceremony, so Monica and Brian have time to get their photos taken…'

'*And?*'

'Oh.' She shakes her head at herself. 'The napkins. They were – get this,' she says pausing for effect, '*ecru* and not *eggshell*.'

'Are those colours?'

'Yep.' She widens her eyes and nods as if this one anecdote says everything about my aunt's behaviour. And it does.

'Monica didn't care – they're basically the same colour – but Chrissy went through the roof! I offered Monica sanctuary to avoid World War Three.'

Mom and Uncle Marv are the only people who still call my aunt 'Chrissy', a name she abandoned when I was around five. I have a vivid memory of her shouting at me when I forgot to call her 'Aunt Christine'. You would have thought I'd called her a bitch. It was a lot for a five-year-old – I avoided her for nearly a year after that.

'That's very *nice* of you, Mom, and Aunt Christine clearly needs to chill. But where's Raff supposed to sleep?'

'Your dad's put an air mattress on your bedroom floor.'

'An air mat— But I get headaches if I sleep on an air mattress.'

I had to be collected early from 7th Grade camp because my head was pounding well into the next day. I missed out on ziplining, which for a 7th-grader was devastating.

'I remember. It's for Raff.'

'Raff is six-four, Mom. He's not going to fit on an air mattress.'

'What do you want me to do, Gabriela?' she asks, chopping the dill with far more ferocity than required.

Uh-oh, I've been here ten minutes and Mom's already using my full name. If I'm not careful, she'll ground me and I'll miss the wedding – or worse, *Christmas*.

'Sorry. It's fine. You're a good aunt.'

Her expression softens and she sets the knife down. 'I just figured... well, you two are best friends and I know you've shared rooms in the past.'

She's referring to the *one time* Freya, Freddie, Raff, and I went to Spain for a long weekend and they'd overbooked the hotel, so Raff and I had to share a room. But we each had our own bed. And it was nearly a year ago – as in *way* before Raff was anything more to me than a friend.

But there's no point in splitting hairs. This is a big house, but my dad's study is off-limits because he takes calls at all hours of the day and night. And since I moved out to go to college, my parents have slowly let the guest room deteriorate into a catch-all junk room. You can barely *move* in there, let alone lay down an air mattress.

This means Raff and I are either sharing a room, or I need to find decent-but-not-too-expensive accommodation in Seattle – a week before Christmas. Hah – unlikely!

'It'll be okay. Now do you really need my help with dinner, or can I go shower now?'

'I don't need help, but it's nearly ready so if you're showering, be quick.'

'You know you could have eaten earlier, Mom.' My parents usually eat around seven. 'Raff and I could have fended for ourselves.'

'No way! You're only here for seven nights. I'm making the most every second before you leave.'

'We literally just got here and you're already talking about us leaving?'

She ignores me, instead grabbing me by the shoulders. 'Shower.' She spins me towards the door, then pats my butt like she used to do when I was a kid.

'Is this your way of telling me I stink?' I call out over my shoulder.

Her high-pitched laugh follows me upstairs where I find Dad giving Raff the nickel tour.

'This is the door to the bathroom,' he says. 'It's a Jack-n-Jill you're sharing with Monica, so take it from a man who has lived with women for the past thirty-eight years, it's always a good idea to knock.'

'Noted,' says Raff with an amused smile.

'So, that's about it – and help yourself to whatever you want in the kitchen. *Mi casa es su casa.*'

'Thanks, Roland.'

'Oh,' he says, pausing next to me. 'And don't let me catch you trying anything with my daughter.'

'Dad!' I exclaim, horrified.

He laughs and Raff joins in, so I do as well – even though inside I just died a little.

* * *

Dinner is delicious but by nine, which is 5 a.m. London time, I'm totally wiped and so is Raff. There's staying awake to acclimate to a new time zone and there's the torture of (essentially) staying up all night in your thirties.

Monica gets up to clear the table, and Mom fends off our feeble offer to help with the dishes.

'No need,' she says. 'You two get some rest and we'll see you in the morning.'

I send Raff up first to shower and get ready for bed.

'Do we have anything planned for tomorrow?' I ask.

'We're decorating for Christmas,' Dad declares excitedly, and it suddenly dawns on me that there's not a single Christmas decoration in or on the entire house. This is very strange – my parents usually start decorating the day after Thanksgiving.

'Wait, you guys didn't hold off because we were coming, did you? Because that's sweet but you didn't need to do that.'

They exchange one of their married-forty-years-and-we-can-communicate-telepathically looks.

'Only partly,' says Mom. I narrow my eyes at her, and she turns to my dad. 'You take this one.'

'We've just had a lot going on, sweetheart. Franchising has taken on a life of its own – we're launching *eight* stores down the west coast next year, instead of five...' My dad owns World Emporium, a gorgeous store in downtown Seattle that imports fairtrade goods, mostly from Central America.

'And your mom's busier than ever at the hospital...'

'The pandemic caused a baby boom,' she says with a smile. 'And of course, there's the wedding,' she adds, lowering her voice. It's doubtful Monica can hear us – she's in the kitchen and it sounds like she's washing pots and pans.

'Do us a favour,' says Mom. 'If you ever get married, *don't* have a wedding during the holidays. Everything's twice as expensive and even more difficult to source.'

'Well, no wonder Aunt Christine is being such a Momzilla.'

Mom makes a face that it says, 'That's not the only reason,' and we exchange knowing smirks.

'Anyway, we've set aside the whole day tomorrow,' says Dad.

'Meaning?' I ask.

'Meaning,' he says, leaning closer, 'we're having a Christine-free day.'

I look at Mom, confused.

'I asked her to let us have some family time,' she explains. 'Just for tomorrow, then she can go back to catastrophising and bossing us around.'

I laugh. 'There's no way you said *that* to her.'

'Well, no. I'm not a novice at handling my sister,' she replies with a sly smile.

'Anyway,' says Dad, 'I'll take Raff down to the tree lot first thing.'

'Will they still have decent trees this close to Christmas?' I ask.

Dad shrugs. 'Doesn't matter. If we have to, we'll save a scraggly tree from the woodchopper – give it a good home.'

'That's so cheesy, Dad.'

He chuckles to himself.

'You and I will be on decorations – *inside* ones,' says Mom. 'No Christmas lights outside after last year.' She throws Dad a pointed look.

'Why, what happened last year?' I ask.

'Your father nearly fell off the roof.'

'What?' I ask, my mouth wide with horror.

'It was... I caught myself. It was fine. I was fine.' He rolls his eyes, but Mom's mouth flattens into an unimpressed line.

'Anyway,' she says to me, 'you and I will get started on decorating. And...' she says, as if she's prefacing something controversial. I brace myself – I have no idea what it could be. 'It might be a good time to go through all your old ornaments.'

'My old... Wait, are you talking about the ones I made in elementary school?'

She maintains eye contact, nodding slowly while her mouth twitches.

'So, you're telling me you no longer want my macaroni masterpieces on the tree? Because isn't that part of the parent–child contract? I bring home pasta that's been spray-painted gold, and you give it pride of place on the tree for perpetuity.'

'I don't recall signing anything. How 'bout you, Roland?' she asks Dad.

Dad looks off with a squint, pretending to scour his memory.

'Yeah, you two are hilarious,' I say. 'But if my painstakingly made ornaments are being relegated to the junk pile, I get something in return.'

'Like what, sweetheart?' asks Dad.

'It's time for a moratorium on the "Gaby wet her pants on the gondola at Whistler" story. You're never allowed to tell it again.'

'Ha-ha-ha!' laughs Mom, her head thrown back. Dad laughs along and so do I, even though I'm ostensibly laughing at my six-year-old self.

Or maybe it's simply the hysterical laughter of a jetlagged woman who has fallen for her best friend.

'Sorry to interrupt.' Raff's standing in the doorway, a wistful smile on his face. He holds up his phone charger. 'I've stupidly arrived without an adaptor.'

'I've got one.' Dad leaps up to retrieve one from his stockpile – can't have daughter number two unable to plug in *all the things* when she comes home to visit.

'Raff, while I've got you, I was going to ask... If it's not too much trouble, I mean...'

I suspect I know where she's going with this. 'Mom, just ask him.'

'Does it have anything to do with baking, by chance?' he asks, his eyes creased at the corners in amusement.

Mom grins at him. 'Only if it's not too much trouble,' she adds quickly. 'I've been so busy, I haven't had a chance to do my Christmas baking.'

'Which is not such a bad thing,' I say under my breath.

'Gabriela – that's not nice.'

'But true,' I add, also under my breath.

She tuts at me.

'I will happily bake some Christmas goodies while I'm here,' Raff offers magnanimously.

'Oh, excellent!' Mom's acting like there was a chance he'd say no. 'And I can run to the store and get everything you need – or Gaby can,' she adds, volunteering me.

Raff starts naming recipes and with each suggestion, her eyes widen even more. I haven't seen Mom this excited since Dad gave her a vacation to Mexico for Christmas five years ago.

Then again, Raff *is* Britain's Best Baker!

* * *

We're both in bed – me in the double canopy bed my parents bought me for my sweet sixteen and Raff on the shitty air mattress they've had since the nineties – and I'm staring up at the ceiling, exhausted but wired and annoyingly wide awake.

'Gabs?' whispers Raff.

'Yeah?'

There's a plasticky fart-like sound as he rolls over, and I scooch closer to the edge of the bed and look down. In the dim light, I can see that he's on his side, his head propped up with his hand.

'What's up?'

'I adore your family.'

I smile. 'They adore you too.'

He's quiet for a beat, then says, 'I hope you don't mind, but when I came down for the adaptor, I... I saw how you are with your mum and dad – teasing each other, making jokes...'

I hadn't known Raff had witnessed all that, but it explains the wistful expression when he interrupted us.

'I wish I had that sort of relationship with my parents,' he says, an undercurrent of sadness in his voice.

'Raff, your parents are—' I cut myself off. He knows his parents are assholes. He doesn't need me reminding him. 'Look, my parents love you and you love them, so my parents are your parents, okay?'

He chuckles softly. 'Is that the family equivalent of *mi casa es su casa*?' he asks.

'Something like that. Just know that this is a place where you're loved, so it's your home too, okay?'

He blinks a few times and I wonder if he's holding back tears.

'Thanks, Gabs,' he says, his voice choked with emotion. Now I'm blinking back tears of my own.

'Sure,' I say lightly. 'Now go to sleep. Big day tomorrow.'

He rolls over again, the noise of the air mattress making us both laugh.

'Dork,' I say to the darkness, and Raff chuckles softly.

22

GABY

When I wake, I'm so groggy, it takes me a moment to remember where I am. As it starts to crystalise – I'm in Seattle in my old bedroom – there's a jolt of panic as I sense someone else in my bed.

I crack my eyelids and Raff's lying on his side facing me, fast asleep, his lips parted.

Oh, yeah, we're sleeping together now.

Well, not *sleeping together* sleeping together but after twenty minutes listening to Raff's restless – and valiant – attempt to fall asleep on that shitty, farty air mattress, I sat up and said, 'Just sleep up here with me.'

He objected, like he did when I offered him the front seat of Dad's SUV, but I insisted harder than him. Eventually, exhaustion won the fight and he climbed into my bed. He was asleep in seconds.

I, however, lay awake for another half-hour, listening to him breathing and wondering how the hell I'm supposed to get through the next week. The man is now in my bed. All I want to do is snuggle up close to him and nestle into the crook of his arm.

It also hit me in the middle of the night as I tossed and turned for the umpteenth time that the last man who slept in this bed with me was Eric.

Raff inhales deeply and scrubs a hand over his face. Slowly opening his eyes, he says, 'Morning, Gabs.' Then he frowns at me. 'Wait, is it morning? I feel like I've slept for two days.'

I reach for my phone, which is charging on the bedside table. 'It's a little after seven, so yeah, it's morning. And fair warning, Gina and Roland will already be up, showered, dressed, and raring to go.'

He protests the arrival of the new day with a dramatic moan and I giggle. 'Aren't you supposed to be a morning person?' I tease.

'After flying long haul, it turns out I am a nothing person. I feel like I've been hit by a steam train.'

'How very nineteenth century of you. Come on,' I say, jostling him. 'Don't forget, there's an action-packed itinerary today – Christmas tree shopping, decorating the tree – *and* the house.'

'Right. How much of that can be done from here?'

'From bed?'

'Mm-hmm. I could stay here all day.'

You and me both, I think – super unhelpful. I need to get up before I accidentally throw myself at my best friend. Because it turns out that sleep-rumpled and jetlagged Raff is sexy – right down to the gravelly voice.

His phone chimes with an incoming text and he reaches for it, navigating with his thumb. He smiles as he reads.

'Julia,' he says, his eyes transfixed by whatever *Julia* has typed.

He doesn't tell me anything else and although part of me wants to know what level of texting they're at – friendly, flirty, sexy, explicit??? – the rest of me knows better than to torture myself trying to guess.

'I'll be quick,' I say, heading into the bathroom and locking the door.

I gaze at myself in the mirror – unlike Seattle, it isn't pretty. Raff may feel like he's been hit by a train, but I *look* like it.

Still, what's the point of looking good for a guy who is currently texting another woman – a woman who is talented and renowned and (by any measure) really frigging gorgeous?

I open my mouth and silently scream, my hands clenched into fists and my eyes scrunched closed. It feels good to embrace the tension, taking it to the brink and releasing it, but the panacea is temporary and when I step out of the shower, my stomach is tied in knots again.

* * *

'Hello? Anyone home?'

Mom and I are in the living room, sorting through Christmas decorations, and we exchange a look. There's a beat of stillness while recognition dawns.

'That's Issy,' I say, leaping up.

I rush to the entry and Issy is standing next to a huge suitcase, her face red and blotchy. She holds it together for no more than three seconds, then bursts into tears, falling into my arms. Mom comes up behind me and envelops both of us in a hug.

When Issy's sobs subside, Mom and I draw back and glance at each other.

'Isabella, what's going on?' Mom asks gently. She takes Issy by the elbow and leads her into the living room, scooping up a tissue box from an end table as she passes. She sits Issy on the sofa and hands her the tissues.

Issy grabs a handful and wipes her cheeks then noisily blows her nose. Mom and I make wide eyes at each other as we wait for my sister to compose herself. Issy sniffles a few times and does her best to sit up straight.

She looks at Mom, then at me. 'I've left Jon,' she says.

'At home?' I ask.

'Well, yes, but no, I mean I've *left* him. I've left our marriage.'

Inside, I'm rejoicing and I can imagine Mom is too, but Issy is clearly hurting. I figure it'll be a long time before *she's* able to rejoice at no longer being married to the world's biggest douchebag.

'Oh, hun,' says Mom, going to her and wrapping her in another hug. 'Tell me everything.'

Issy glances at me, then bites her lip before burying her face in Mom's arm. I signal that I'll leave them to it and Mom nods over Issy's shoulder. My sister and I are close, but she also knows how I feel about Jon, the one bone of contention between us. I don't blame her for wanting to talk to Mom alone.

I head into the kitchen and find Monica sitting at the counter on a stool, earbuds in and scrolling on her phone. 'Hey,' I say.

She lifts her head and takes out the earbuds. 'Hey.'

'So, heads up: Issy's just arrived. She's left Jon.' I make the 'eek' face.

'Holy shit. *Really*?'

'I hope so.'

'Well, yeah, he's a total dick. He once told Mom she was attractive for a woman her age.'

'*What*?'

'Yep.'

'Ignoring that it's a back-handed compliment, what was he implying by that?'

'Probably something inappropriate – so gross.'

'Yeah,' I reply, shuddering with disgust.

'Oh!' says Monica excitedly. 'Does this mean Issy will be here for the wedding?'

'I guess so. Although, your mom totally lost her shit over Raff coming – and that was with two weeks' notice. This is only five days!'

'Aunt Gina can tell Mom,' she replies matter-of-factly.

I agree it's the most logical solution. *I'm* certainly not going to do it.

'So, do you have much on today?' I ask, wanting to change the subject.

'A facial and a mani-pedi at two, then a hair treatment. Just chilling till then.'

'Enjoying your Mom-free zone,' I say with a grin.

She rolls her eyes, looking more like a teen than a twenty-six-year-old who's about to get married.

'Seriously. You know I love her...' she starts. 'But, Gaby, you have no idea.'

I have some idea but say nothing, letting her unload.

'I've lost count of how many times Brian's asked if we can elope.'

'You still could,' I suggest, my brows raised.

We lock eyes for a beat and burst out laughing.

'Can you imagine? I'd be the only bride in history to have my wedding and my funeral on the same day.' She lowers her voice and looks towards the kitchen door. When she's sure of the all-clear, she says, 'I overheard your mom tell mine that $100,000 was a lot of money to spend on a wedding.'

'Wait, *what*?'

She nods solemnly. 'And you know me – I'd be happy getting married at Bayview Park, looking out at Puget Sound, then having a barbecue in the backyard.'

'Kinda hard to have a barbecue in December,' I say.

'Mm-hmm. I'm sure you'll be shocked to hear that a Christmas wedding was Mom's idea.'

'Oh, I— Actually, I *am* shocked. Isn't Christmas your favourite holiday?'

'Uh-uh. It's Mom's. *My* favourite holiday is Halloween.'

'Ha-ha! Now that would have been a cool wedding theme.'

'Tell me about it. Anyway, I'm beyond caring now. I just want to be married already.'

'Brian's a good guy,' I say – and I mean it. I've only met him a few times but he's a total sweetheart.

'Yeah,' she says with a grin. 'Even Dad likes him – despite the whole Oakland As thing.'

'I warned Raff – I told him if he hears *any* mention of baseball when Uncle Marv's around, he should take cover.'

'I like him,' she says cryptically.

'Your dad? I should hope so if he's paying for a $100,000 wedding.'

'No, you dork – *Raff*. You two are so sweet together.'

'Togeth— We're not a couple, Mon.'

She shakes her head at me, then breaks into a grin. 'Not *yet*.'

'No, I'm serious. Raff's just...' *The man I am falling for more and more each day.* 'We're *friends* – that's *all*.'

'Mm-hmm. That's what I used to say about Brian before I finally admitted I'd fallen in love with him.'

She regards me intently. *How* is she the little girl who used to choreograph dance routines to Beyoncé in her PJs?

I check to make sure Raff hasn't snuck up on us while we've been talking. 'Is it that obvious?' I ask her quietly.

'I wouldn't say *obvious*. I doubt your parents know. They wouldn't have made you bunk together if they knew you had feelings for him. And Raff certainly hasn't cottoned on yet.'

'He *can't* find out, Mon. He's just started seeing someone.'

'I don't get it. If he's dating someone, then how come he's here with you?'

'It's a long story – and he's not here *with* me,' I insist. 'Like I said, we're *friends*.'

'So, what happens when he figures it out?'

'That I have feelings for him? I have no frigging idea. Hopefully, I can keep everything under wraps – at least till we get back to London. Much easier to deal with when we're not sharing a bed.'

'That's not what I meant. I mean, what happens when Raff figures out *he* has feelings for *you*?'

'What?' I shriek, waving away her nonsense with a wry laugh. 'That's nuts. There's no way.'

She looks at me as if *she's* the older wiser cousin and says, 'We'll see,' right as Dad announces that he and Raff are back with the tree.

* * *

'It doesn't *completely* suck,' I say, regarding our lopsided, misshapen Christmas tree, now adorned with every ornament my parents own – even the ugly ones people have gifted them over the years.

Typically, Mom only puts those at the very back of the tree, facing the wall. Or she makes up some feeble excuse about there not being enough room and they stay in the box.

Though, she drew the line at my macaroni masterpieces. I'm either going to have toss them or pack them up and take them back to London.

Issy, who has only just stopped crying, sniggers at my evaluation of our tree. At least I've made her laugh on one of the worst days of her life.

Mom tuts at me. 'Bite your tongue, young lady,' she chides playfully. 'It's a beautiful tree.'

'Is that like when people say all newborns are beautiful when some of them look like those dried-apple dolls?' quips Dad.

Issy, Raff, Monica, and I erupt into laughter and Mom rounds on Dad, wagging a finger at him. 'Roland Gabriel Rivera, all babies *are* beautiful. They are little miracles, each and every one.'

'Come on, Mom,' says Issy, 'you've said more than once that you've delivered an ugly baby.'

Mom stifles laughter. 'That does not leave this house,' she says, narrowing her eyes and pointing at us in turn.

'Understood,' says Dad, setting his phone on the mantle place. 'Okay, time for the family photo in front of the butt-ugly tree.'

'Roland!'

Dad howls with laughter while he shepherds us into place. He puts Raff at the back in the centre and me directly in front of him. Like he's done a hundred times before, Raff drapes one long arm around my shoulders in a half hug. Following Dad's directions, Issy stands next to me on one side and Monica on the other. Monica catches my eye, and a flicker of 'I told you so' crosses her face. I frown at her.

'Gaby, smile!' calls Dad. He presses the button on his phone, then slots into the photo next to Mom. 'Say cheese!' he calls out.

'Cheese!'

'How long do we need to stand here?' asks Mom through her teeth.

Dad rushes over and checks his phone. '*Perfecto*,' he declares.

Raff squeezes my shoulders, momentarily dropping his chin onto the top of my head, then steps away. It's jarring how intensely I feel his absence. Monica surreptitiously flicks me on the leg, and I want to shout at her, 'We're just friends!'

But who would I be trying to convince?

* * *

With Issy showing up unexpectedly, we are now an *extra* full house. She's sharing with Monica, but her old bedroom only has a king single, so she been relegated to the air mattress. Monica offered to take it, but Issy insisted that the bride should have a proper bed for the week.

I'm ignoring that everyone now knows Raff and I are sleeping together.

After dinner – a giant pot of Dad's chili that we'll all be regretting by midnight (me especially, considering my sleeping arrangements) – we move to the living room to play the Christmas edition of Win, Lose or Draw.

My parents *love* games nights, so they have the whole set up – easel, flipchart, and a set of coloured markers. We're playing in pairs and, Raff and I are winning. Monica has accused us of cheating three times.

'We're not cheating!' I insist after a round in which I drew six clues and Raff guessed each one correctly.

'Even these two can't compete with you,' she says, pointing to my parents, 'and they've have been married nearly forty years.'

Issy yelps at the word 'married' and fresh tears spring to her eyes.

'Sorry, Issy,' says Monica, plonking down next to her on the floor. She grabs Issy's hand and squeezes. 'But no crying, okay? We're getting creamed and I need you to focus. I can't lose Win, Lose or Draw – it's my wedding week. *And* it's Christmas.'

I hold my breath. This could go either way. My sister has a decent sense of humour, but even though Monica's joking, is this really the right time for cajoling Issy with humour? She's just walked out on a ten-year marriage.

Issy hiccups, her fingers flying to her mouth. 'Sorry. No crying, got it. But I'm going to need more of this,' she says, reaching for her empty wine glass.

Dad half-stands and tops her up from a bottle of Californian Zin.

Issy drinks a big glug, then gets to her feet. 'Give it,' she says, reaching for the fat black marker I'm holding. I hand it over and Mom gets up with the stack of clues to hold out for Issy to draw.

'Ready?' asks Dad.

'Let's do this!' shouts Issy as if she's about to bungee jump.

Sixty seconds later, she and Monica have added *nine* points to their tally.

'Wowser, brilliant job,' says Raff, clapping.

'Hey! No fraternising with the enemy,' I chide.

'But we're still winning by a country mile, Gabs,' he whispers loud enough for everyone to hear. He adds an open-mouthed exaggerated wink, then grins at me.

And my heartstrings ping as Monica's words echo through my mind.

What happens when Raff figures out he has feelings for you?

Is that what's happening? Because it's starting to feel like it. Or maybe that's just wishful thinking.

23

GABY

After a pretty decent night's sleep, thanks to several glasses of wine and lingering jetlag, I wake up sober and confused. I look over at Raff, who's sleeping with his back to me, and watch the rise and fall of his torso.

What am I doing?

There were countless times yesterday – and last night – when we were just Gabs and Raff, riffing off each other, sharing in-jokes, crushing the others at Win, Lose or Draw and celebrating with a high five...

But then he'd sling an arm around my shoulders and tingles would run down my spine, or he'd say something like, 'Right, Gabs?' and smile at me so intensely, I felt it to my very core.

And since my conversation with Monica, unwanted thoughts keep surfacing like pop-up ads on a free mobile app.

What if we hadn't gone to the Forty Under Forty party? Would I ever have realised how I feel about Raff?

Would Raff want me if Julia wasn't in the picture?

How would he react if I leaned over and kissed him right now?

How would I react if he leaned over and kissed me?

Lying here in the dim dawn light, I'm at war with myself, posing the ultimate question over and over: *should I wake him up and tell him the truth or just suck it up for the rest of the week?*

It's *way* too tempting to poke him awake and spill, so before I do something stupid and derail the most important friendship in my life, I slip out of bed, quickly shower, and get dressed.

I'm right about to head downstairs when I hear Raff's voice through the bathroom door. Hating myself for what I'm about to do, I press my ear against it, straining to hear what he's saying. *He could be talking to CiCi and Devin*, I tell myself.

But then I hear it – clear as a bell. 'So, how's St Moritz?'

My chest tightens and it's suddenly hard to breathe. I could stay and torture myself or...

I opt for self-preservation, slipping out of the bathroom via Issy's bedroom where she's still asleep and Monica is on her phone.

'All yours,' I whisper, indicating the bathroom. She smiles, then throws the covers back and I head downstairs.

'Good morning, sweetheart,' says Dad. 'Coffee?' he offers.

'Yes, please.' I climb onto a stool at the kitchen counter as he pours from the coffee pot. I never drink this stuff in London – it's either a flat white or nothing – but there's something nostalgic about drinking Mom's favourite, hazelnut drip-filter coffee with vanilla creamer, while Dad empties the dishwasher.

'So, a big baking day ahead, I hear?'

'Ah, yep,' I say unenthusiastically. But it's only because I'm worried about spending the whole day with Raff.

'Count yourself lucky – your mom and I are on wedding duties.'

'What wedding duties?'

'Your mom's going with Christine and Monica to pick up the dresses...'

'Dresses? Plural?'

'Uh-huh. You haven't heard about your aunt's mother-of-the-bride dress?'

'Nope.'

'Let's just say that it's a little more *bridal* than it should be.'

'Yikes. Though, that tracks. And I guess there must be bridesmaids' dresses too.'

'I wouldn't know, sweetheart, but probably. Anyway, while they're doing that, Brian, Marv, and I are heading out to Woodinville to collect the wine and beer for the reception. Three different cellar doors and two breweries.'

'Fun! You'd think $100,000 would include delivery fees.'

'You *would* think that, yes,' he says, his lips drawn into a taut line.

'Good morning, hun,' says Mom. She gives me a quick hug from behind and without being asked, Dad pours her a coffee and doctors it with a generous pour of creamer. 'Cin cin,' she says, raising the mug in his direction. She leans against the counter and looks at me over the rim as she drinks her coffee.

'Your dad tell you what's on for today?' she asks.

'Yup. Lots of wedding shit.'

'Gaby,' she chastises. 'Actually, never mind, it is "wedding shit". First dresses, then we're stopping by the florist to check the flower order.'

'Aunt Gina's only coming along to stop me from murdering my mother,' says Monica as she enters the kitchen.

'Or the other way around,' quips Mom. 'And that poor florist. I hope everything's up to Chrissy's standards this time.'

Dad, who has taken on the role of resident barista, pours Monica a coffee.

She thanks him, then turns to me. 'So, what are you up to today?' she asks.

'Morning, all,' Raff says before I can respond. I turn around and his tall frame fills the doorway. He's freshly showered – I can smell his spicy cologne from here – and looking handsome in a rust-coloured sweater and jeans – *fitted* jeans – the new ones. 'Apologies for the late start. I didn't mean to oversleep.'

'No apologies necessary,' Mom and Dad say in unison, like they'd rehearsed it.

'You're on vacation, hun, so sleep as late as you want,' adds Mom. 'Besides, jetlag can be killer.'

'It's hitting me quite hard, I'll admit,' he says. 'And just watch – the moment I adjust to Seattle time, we'll be back on a plane to London.'

His words rip through me like shrapnel. I don't want to imagine the imminent goodbyes with my family. But more so, London is where real life is, where Raff is dating someone and this cosy little bubble I'm starting to settle into doesn't exist.

There's also the little white lie he's just told about oversleeping. Raff has been up nearly as long as I have, only he's been talking to his frigging girlfriend who's frigging skiing in frigging Switzerland.

'Well, we should get going,' says Dad, his voice dragging me back to the kitchen. 'I told Marv we'd be there by eight-thirty.'

He, Mom, and Monica burst into action, gulping down the rest of their coffees, and Monica grabs a granola bar from the pantry. Then Raff and I follow them into the entry, where they all put on outerwear, Dad grabs car keys, and Mom and Monica sling their handbags over their shoulders.

'Bye, sweetheart,' says Dad. 'You two have a good day. And when your sister gets up, try and find something for her to do.'

'Maybe she can help with the baking,' Mom suggests, giving me another quick hug. 'We should be home by three.'

Monica's arms encircle my neck. 'Wish me luck,' she says, and I do.

When we close the door behind them, the house descends into silence – which lasts approximately twenty seconds.

'Morning...' moans Issy from the top of the stairs.

'Hey,' I say brightly. 'How did you sleep?'

'I didn't.' She clomps down the stairs, skulking past us towards the kitchen. 'That frigging air mattress!' she shouts over her shoulder.

I'm sure it played its part, but it's more likely Issy's impending divorce that's the main culprit for her insomnia. And she seemed totally out of it when I snuck past earlier, so hopefully she got *some* sleep.

'Sorry,' I whisper to Raff. He may have signed up for a harried Christmas and the occasional bout of wedding drama, but he didn't agree to play emotional nursemaid to my sister.

He shakes his head, telling me without words that Issy's behaviour isn't a problem. He jerks his head, and we walk in right as Issy holds up an empty coffee pot and bursts into tears.

I look over at Raff – seemingly so confident only moments ago that he was up to the task of looking after Issy – and he seems petrified.

I take charge. 'Here, let me,' I say, taking the coffee pot out of her hand. 'You go sit.' I point to one of the stools and she glumly stumbles around the counter and sits. I put on a new pot of coffee, spilling a mound of grounds on the counter in the process. Just typical Gaby clumsiness, and neither my best friend nor my sister bats an eye.

Once the coffee's brewing, I clean up the mess, then go into the pantry where I scout for Pop-Tarts. My sister may be thirty-six, but she's also a sucker for toaster pastries.

'Strawberry or blueberry?' I ask her, holding up two boxes.

She brightens a smidge and replies, 'Blueberry.'

While they're toasting, I call Raff into the pantry.

'Maybe check what ingredients they have and make a list? I can run you down to Metro Market once I get Issy situated.'

'Sure.'

I go to leave, but he places a hand on my arm, stopping me. He leans in close and I school my reaction. He smells *so* good, like pine and spices and mulled wine – like Christmas personified. 'You're a good sister,' he whispers, his breath on my ear.

Good frigging grief, I need to get out of here.

'Thanks,' I mumble, pushing past him.

Twenty minutes later, I've fed and caffeinated Issy, and corralled her into the shower. She's under strict instructions not to call Douchebag and in case she decides to anyway, I've 'hidden' her phone where she'll never find it: in the enormous tote bag she carries everywhere. She calls it her portable black hole because she can never find anything in it, and I am counting on it doing its job – at least until we get back from the store and I can keep a close eye on her. If there's an emergency, she can call 911 on the landline.

I call out, 'I love you!' and hear a muffled, 'Love you too,' over the stream of water as I close the bathroom door.

Raff's right – I *am* a good sister. Though, Issy would do the same for me if our roles were reversed. As I back Mom's car out of the garage, I'm reminded that she did once – when Eric and I first broke up and he was showing up at mutual friends' parties with Donna on his arm. At least I *think* it was Issy who started the rumour that Eric couldn't get it up.

'Hey,' I say, dismissing thoughts of my 'impotent' asshole of an ex, 'before we go to the store, there's somewhere I want to show you.'

Heading down Queen Anne hill, I turn right onto West Highland Drive. Fortunately, it doesn't appear too busy when we get to Kerry Park, and I find a spot half a block away and parallel park. It takes me several goes because I don't drive in London and it's one of those use-it-or-lose-it skills. But Raff doesn't seem to notice my shoddy parking or how far the car is from the kerb when we get out – he's too engrossed in the view.

'Wowser,' he says, breathless.

He strides ahead, crossing the park to the railing, then scans the entire skyline from downtown, past the Space Needle, along the waterfront with its converted shipping sheds – now mostly hotels and trendy bars – across to the working port, which is like a giant Meccano set, over to West Seattle, then to Puget Sound where the lush, green Orcas Islands are nestled and the ferries running between them and the city look like toys. It's a clear-ish day, meaning it isn't raining but high clouds blanket the sky, hiding Mount Rainier from view.

'You wouldn't know it, but there is a *huge* mountain right there,' I say, pointing in its direction. 'Wait, let me show you.' I take out my phone and search for some pics of the mountain in all its glory to show Raff.

'Wowser,' he says again, looking from my phone to the view and back again. 'It's completely hidden.'

'Yup.' I pocket my phone. 'So, what do you think of my home-town?' I ask. 'And, yes, I am fishing.'

'It's incredible, Gabs,' he says, still staring at the view. 'And I'd say it's probably more so at night. From up here, I mean.'

'Definitely. And look,' I say, pointing at the top of the Space Needle. 'This time of year, they make a Christmas tree out of lights.'

'Can we come back tonight and see it all lit up?' he asks, his eyes meeting mine.

'Yeah, sure,' I reply as casually as I can.

Sure, Raff, let's come back to the romantic lookout after dark and gaze at the city lights. Why the hell not??? If I don't bring it up, maybe he'll forget about it.

'And where would Frasier's flat have been?'

'Huh?'

'You know, from the television show. I know it was shot in a studio, but his view of the city was incredible.'

I can't help it – I crack up laughing, a full-on ha-ha-ha laugh, and poor Raff looks confused. 'Sorry,' I say. 'But it's a running joke here in Seattle – that view doesn't exist. Not unless the building he lived in was right over there.' I point to the middle of Puget Sound where a ferry is crossing to Bainbridge Island.

'You mean, in the middle of the water?' he asks, his eyes narrowed in confusion.

'Uh-huh.'

'But that's...' He chuckles. 'And all this time I had this picture in my head...'

'Don't worry. A lot of people do – apparently, tourists show up all the time wanting to go see the view from Frasier's apartment.'

He shakes his head at himself.

'Come on,' I say. 'Metro is only going to get crazier by the second. Might as well get it over and done with.'

Only I forgot who I was going grocery shopping with.

* * *

'I *love* shopping in a foreign country,' says Raff, unable to tear his eyes away from the assortment of cake sprinkles. 'I mean, some of this stuff you'd only find in a specialty shop back in London.'

'Hashtag America,' I say, making a feeble joke.

'Absolutely,' he replies, missing the joke entirely.

We only have a short list – Mom and Dad have a fully stocked fridge, freezer, *and* pantry – but we've already been here forty-five minutes. Although, that includes the fifteen minutes we spent in the wine section. Despite reminding Raff that my parents have several dozen cases of wine stored under the stairs, he insisted on adding three bottles of French Champagne to our cart.

'No, Gabs! They're a gift from me to your family,' he said when I tried to put them back. 'A thank you for having me. And it's Christmastime – that always calls for Champagne.'

There was a sad, kind-of lonely pleading in his eyes and then it hit me – *hard*. I told him the other night that my parents are his parents, but it's more than that. This Christmas, *we're* his family.

I placed the bottles back into the cart. 'That's super sweet, Raff. Everyone will love it.'

He grinned, the tension from his shoulders falling away as he followed my directions and manoeuvred the cart towards the baking section.

Now, as I watch how entranced he is by sprinkles, I chastise myself.

It's not all about you, Gaby.

I've been so caught up in family drama – first Monica's wedding, now Issy leaving Douchebag – as well as my own stuff, that I haven't once thought about Raff and what he's going through.

His parents brushed him off – at *Christmas* – and the two people he considers his parents are off doing their own thing. And here's me practically drowning in familial love, yet completely up my own ass.

What a shitty, shitty friend I am.

Sometime later, having checked off his entire list – and filled the cart with a lot of items that weren't on it – we stand in line to check out. Like he does most places, Raff stands head and shoulders above almost everyone.

He turns to me, grinning. 'Don't you just love Christmas, Gabs? I'm already having the best time.'

He turns back around and starts decanting our cart onto the conveyor belt.

And that right there – Raff's love of life, his enthusiasm for something as simple as the mayhem of grocery shopping days before Christmas – is why I'm falling for him harder than ever.

I don't know if I'll be able to go back to normal when we get home. I don't want to go back to normal. Because 'normal' means Raff and I are simply best friends and he's dating (frigging) Julia.

As we move up in the line, Raff's takes his phone out of his pocket and taps on the screen with his thumb, smiling gently to himself as he reads. I attempt to get a peek, but all I can see is that his messaging app is open, not what the message says. His head tilts to one side and he starts chuckling.

As he pockets the phone, he looks over his shoulder at me. 'Julia – funny incident on the ski slope,' he says, giving no further explanation.

Of *course* it was her. I probably willed that message into existence just by thinking about her.

And it's not like I need further explanation from Raff. He's super into her and soon we'll be back in London and so will she.

And then what?

24

GABY

'So, how did I do?' I say, holding up the sugar cookie I've decorated. 'Think you'll have a job for me at Baked to Perfection?'

Raff looks up from his perfectly decorated Christmas tree. 'It's, er... *colourful*,' he replies diplomatically. He comes around to my side of the kitchen counter to inspect the other cookies I've decorated. He tried to teach me the proper technique, which involved piping, but I ended up with more frosting on me than on the cookies, so I'm now using a butter knife.

'Is that one supposed to be a reindeer?' he asks.

'Christmas stocking,' I reply.

'Ahh.' He pats me on the shoulder. 'Well, at least they'll taste good.'

'Well, yeah, because you made the dough – *and* the frosting.'

I regard my work; not one cookie looks like it's supposed to.

'It's like we let a bunch of preschoolers in here and gave them a Jackson Pollock painting for inspiration,' I say, selecting the worst of the bunch and biting off what's supposed to be Rudolph's nose.

'It's a good thing you have other talents,' he says with a playful raise of his brows.

In another context, that might have sexual connotations. But I'm so far into the friendzone, I can't even *see* sex or romance or anything non-platonic from here. He's obviously just being nice.

I study him for a moment, the intense concentration on his face, the way he skilfully pipes an intricate row of ornaments on a tiny Christmas tree. He has sexy hands, something that's only occurred to me today. They're large, with long tapered fingers, neat nails, and a smattering of freckles across the backs.

And as I watch their deft, precise movements, I start fantasising about what Raff could do to me with those hands – running them up my naked body, cupping my breasts, reaching between my—

A phone chimes, interrupting the lascivious thoughts about my best friend's hands. Probably a good thing – getting felt up in my parents' kitchen while decorating Christmas cookies would be tacky. And messy.

'Yours or mine?' Raff asks without lifting his head.

'Mine,' I reply, catching sight of the notification on the home screen before it disappears. 'It's an email from Claire,' I say, my stomach clenching in excitement – or is it dread? I wipe my hands down the front of my apron and navigate to the email. Raff abandons his post and reads over my shoulder.

Dear Gaby,

I'm hoping you've done as you were told and haven't checked work emails since you set your OOO message, which is why I'm emailing your personal account. I am thrilled to say that you are our new marketing director, and will start in the role when you return to work early Jan. All the details in your work inbox, including your new salary. Just wanted to give you the news before I signed off for the year.

Huge congrats! I'm really proud of you and I know you'll do brilliantly in the role.

Happy Christmas,
Claire

'I got it,' I say, my voice barely audible. As the news starts to sink in, elation rockets through my body.

'I knew you would!' Raff exclaims, and I turn to him.

'I'm going to be the new marketing director.'

'Yes!'

With my free hand, I grasp his forearm and start jumping up and down. 'I got it. I got it, Raff!' I say through gleeful laughter. Raff grins at me and I stop bouncing. 'What was it you said? About not knowing how much you want something until it's presented to you...'

'Something like that.'

'I mean, yeah, I wanted it but maybe I didn't let myself want it too much, you know – in case I didn't get it, and now that I have...' I look away and exhale slowly, letting the realisation wash over me.

'Gabs.' I meet Raff's smiling eyes. 'Seriously, I am so happy for you – and so proud. Claire's right: you'll absolutely smash it.'

He draws me into a hug, and I sink into the embrace and rest my cheek against his chest, listening to his heartbeat through his sweater and breathing in the scent of his Christmassy cologne.

In the confines of his arms, my head and heart are at war, my head telling me this is just the congratulatory hug of a best friend and my heart longing for more.

So. Much. More.

He draws back slightly, and I look up at his handsome face. How have I never noticed until recently how his crooked smile and the angle of his cheekbones give him a sort-of handsome-elf look – like a red-headed Legolas?

He smiles at me proudly, then leans down and presses a kiss to my cheek, igniting tingles that cover my entire body, giving me goosebumps. Then he releases me and returns to his side of the kitchen counter, leaving a vacuum of want in his wake.

'What's all the noise about?' My sister wanders into the kitchen and heads straight to the coffee pot. I wait for her to pour a mug and doctor it with creamer, and when I know I have her full attention, I answer.

'I went for a promotion at work – actually, it's Raff old role – and I got it.' I grin at her excitedly, not entirely sure how she'll react. Issy's in a miserable place right now, so it's not like I expect her to be elated for me.

She stares at me for a second, then sets down her coffee, her eyes welling with tears. *Uh oh.* Then she crosses the kitchen and hugs me. 'I am so happy for you, sis,' she says.

I return the hug, which conveys so much more than sisterly pride. This is such a shitty time for her and I wish there was more I could do to ease her pain. She sniffles, then steps back, regarding me thoughtfully. 'You always were the smart one,' she says with a devilish smile.

'Me? What about you, Ms 4.0 GPA?'

She lifts a shoulder in a half-hug. 'Okay, so we're both the smart one.'

'And the pretty one,' I add.

'Undeniably.'

We grin at each other, then she swipes at the tears on her cheeks. 'Okay, no more crying!' she declares, going back for her coffee and taking a sip.

'So, you guys are making good progress,' she says, surveying the counter where a rugelach is cooling, fruit mince pies (Raff's favourite) are piled up on a platter, and six dozen cookies are in various stages of being decorated.

'Do you want one?' I ask, indicating the cookies.

'Well, yeah!'

I point to the ones I've done. 'Take one of these. Raff's are too pretty to eat.'

'For sure. Mom will probably save his till next year and decorate the tree with them,' she quips. He chuckles at that, adding another completed Christmas tree to the drying rack.

'Whereas we inherited the Rivera Family can't-so-much-as-draw-a-stick-figure gene,' she tells him.

'I did wonder if the entire family is afflicted,' he retorts with a smirk.

'Hey! Rude,' I reply.

He laughs and Issy sniggers, and I'm glad we've been able to cheer her up – at least for now.

'Right,' says Raff, going to the sink and washing his hands, 'I'll be back in a jiffy – I need a quick loo break.'

He jogs out of the kitchen and up the stairs, and I splatter icing on my last two cookies, then shove the rest of Rudolph in my mouth. I'm munching away – it's *so* good – when I catch Issy staring at me.

'What?' I say through my mouthful.

She leans in and whispers, 'What's going on between you and Raff?'

'Hmm?' I swallow, then brush crumbs from the corner of my mouth. 'What do you mean?'

'I *mean*, I saw you – *hugging* – and you seemed all...' She mimics a dreamy, lovey-dovey look.

I must look like a stunned mullet. I shake my head, breaking my sudden stupor.

'Um...'

'Are you guys into each other?'

'*No.*'

She cocks her head, looking at me disbelievingly, and panic courses through me. God, I'm really running the gamut of emotions today. I look towards the staircase and listen for the sound of Raff coming back – nothing – so I reach for Issy and pull her close. Knowing I have very little time to fill her in, I talk fast.

'Yes, I've fallen for Raff, okay? But he doesn't know. And he's just started dating this woman – Julia – that he met through this match-maker, only he doesn't know he met her through the matchmaker, because he told Freya she could only match him if he didn't know about it. And now he's super into her – Julia – and I have no idea what the fuck I am doing.'

'Seriously? There's a matchmaker involved?'

That's the detail she latches onto?

'Yeah. She and Freya are the only ones who know – about me – and Raff – my feelings, I mean. And now you.'

'But you're sharing a *bed* with him! Holy shit, Gaby. How are you even doing that?'

'I'm a straight-up masochist.'

Her eyes open wider as she looks behind me. 'Yeah, you can totally borrow that dress for the wedding,' she says loudly.

It would *almost* sound convincing if Issy and I didn't wear completely different dress sizes but, thankfully, Raff doesn't seem to think anything of it.

She nudges me in the ribs, then makes a big deal of oohing and ahhing over Raff's cookies.

* * *

We decide we have enough of the preschoolers-on-the-loose cookies – and by 'we' I mean 'Raff' – so he decorates the last two batches. No doubt it's too painful for him watching me decimate cookie after cookie.

I clean up the kitchen around him, occasionally shooing Issy away from the mounting collection of Instagram-ready cookies. For a fleeting moment, I considered posting a few pics to my feed, passing them off as my own, but no one who knows me would believe that, not even for a second.

When the kitchen is clean and Issy and Raff are engaged in an innocuous conversation about his TV appearance, I excuse myself and go into the living room to text Freya about the promotion. She replies right away, even though it must be late in Sweden.

> Yay! I knew you'd get it. So happy for you. How's the other thing?

I double check that I'm on the Freya/Gaby-only chat thread, and not the one we share with Raff. I never want to make that mistake again – especially not now.

> Not great. Harder every day. Sharing a bed out of necessity because my sis is now here. Full house.

> *horrified face emoji*

> Am I a bad person if I hope it doesn't work out with Julia?

> Not a bad person! Just take care of your heart. *heart emoji*

We exchange a few more messages – mostly about how she's been spending her time and her weird aunt, who insists on tucking her in each night. When I get back to London, she and I can compare oddball-aunt stories. She signs off with:

> Hang in there. Love you. *kissing face emoji*

'We're home!' Mom calls from the entry.
'Coming!' calls Issy.

Excited to share my news, I leap off the sofa and go greet the wedding planners, and Issy and Raff come in from the kitchen.

'How'd it go?' I ask as Mom, Dad, and Monica peel off their coats and scarves and hang them up.

Monica flashes me a look that warns, 'Don't ask.'

Mom heads straight for the kitchen, and we all follow. 'Let's just say it's a miracle that I didn't commit sororicide,' she says tersely.

That doesn't sound good. I guess my news can wait.

'Does that mean Aunt Christine's lucky to be alive?' Issy asks.

'Yep,' says Monica, 'and not only because your mom restrained herself. Grrrr.' She bares her teeth, raising her hands as if she's about to strangle someone.

'Can I interest anyone in tea or coffee and some Christmas biscuits?' asks Raff, obviously wanting to be helpful.

'Oh, Raff, you absolute sweetheart,' says Mom. 'Yes to the cookies but I'm gonna need something stronger than coffee. Hun?' She looks at Dad, a pleading look on her face. 'How about you make some of your famous eggnog? Heavy on the brandy.'

'Sure, sweetheart,' he replies with a wink.

Dad busies himself at the stove as Mom fills us in on the highlights (AKA lowlights) from the day, the most enthralling being that Aunt Christine's custom-made, mother-of-the-bride dress is too tight – *way* too tight.

It's her own doing, as she's put on seven pounds in the lead up to the wedding from stress eating. So she's having to wear something from her closet *and* pay the exorbitant cost of the customised dress.

'Holy shit,' says Issy, 'I would *love* to have been a fly on that wall.'

'Uh, no, you wouldn't. Mom's tantrum would put the cast of *Bridezilla vs Momzilla* to shame. I'm lucky we got out of there with my dress and the bridesmaids' dresses. If I were the dressmaker, I'd have told us to go to hell, then kicked us all out.'

'Roland, just pour me a glass of brandy, will you?' Mom asks as she climbs onto a stool. Dad takes a brandy snifter out of an over-head cupboard and serves her a generous pour, then goes back to making eggnog. Mom swigs some brandy, then shakes her head. 'My sister...'

Aunt Christine isn't the only one who's stress eating – Monica's about to eat her third cookie. At least she's taking from the 'Jackson Pollock' pile, but at this rate, Raff may need to make another batch, maybe two.

'Oh, I've just remembered,' Mom tells us, her mood lifting slightly. 'They said on the radio that it's meant to snow tonight.'

'Here?' I ask.

'Yes,' she replies.

'In Seattle?' asks Issy. She and I exchange a look that says, 'Are you sure, Mom?'

'Yes, girls, here in Seattle,' says Mom pointedly. She rolls her eyes, which is very un-Mom-like, but after the day she's had, she must be over everyone and everything.

'Does that mean we might have a white Christmas?' Raff asks hopefully.

'No,' we all say in unison, and Raff looks between us, confused – or it could be disappointment.

'It doesn't stick,' says Mom.

'Well, it rarely sticks but when it does, most of the city shuts down,' says Issy.

'Seattle gets snow so rarely that we don't have the infrastructure to handle it,' explains Dad. 'Not enough snow ploughs, not enough gritters. And the ones they have are used on the highways and to clear streets around hospitals and emergency services.'

'Plus, Seattle is hilly as fuck,' adds Issy. Mom throws her a disapproving look for the profanity.

'Oh dear,' Raff replies, 'I can see how that would be... well, problematic.'

His eyes dart towards Monica and so do mine. She doesn't seem fazed, which is impressive considering how difficult it would be to host a wedding for a hundred and fifty guests if no one can get anywhere. I catch Raff's eye and shrug.

'Well, fingers crossed then,' he says, dropping it.

'Are we drinking this in here or the living room?' Dad asks over his shoulder.

'Living room!' Mom declares. 'I need to relax.'

Dad pours eggnog into mugs and sets them on a tray, and takes them into the living room while Issy forages in one of the cupboards for a small platter, then piles cookies onto it. She picks up a fruit mince pie and sniffs it, then mutters, 'Hmm,' and adds a few to the platter.

'Raff, can you please take this into the other room?' she asks him with a smile.

'I'd be delighted to,' he replies, and I stifle a giggle. Sometimes Raff is so English.

Mom is about to follow Dad and Raff, but Issy grabs her by the arm and pulls her, me, and Monica into a messy huddle.

'What?' I ask her. 'You're being weird.'

'Mom, did you know Gaby has a thing for Raff?' she whispers hurriedly.

'Issy!' I hiss.

'You do?' asks Mom, wide-eyed.

'I knew,' says Monica. 'It's kinda obvious.'

'It is not...' I expel a ragged breath. 'Look,' I say in a hoarse whisper. 'I don't have feelings for Ra—'

'You just told me you did,' says Issy.

I scowl at her. 'You are the worst sister in the world.'

Mom snorts. 'I beg to differ,' she scoffs. 'Chrissy's taken that title.'

'I think Raff feels the same way,' Monica tells Mom, *really* not helping the situation.

Mom gawps at her. 'He does?'

'No,' I insist. 'He doesn't – he's seeing someone – a tall, blonde, curvy goddess,' I add. Surely the contrast between me and Julia will lend weight to my argument.

'But you two would be so great together,' whines Mom, something like pity in her eyes.

Unable to bear it, I break eye contact and glare at Issy. Just because her love life is in shambles doesn't give her the right to charge headlong into mine, stirring up drama.

'Yeah, well, it's not happening,' I say as assertively as I can. I really need to shut this conversation down. 'Now, can we please...' I jerk my head in the direction of the living room.

'Oh!' Mom gasps, grabbing my arm. 'I put you two in the same room! And now you're sharing a *bed*.'

'That's what I said.'

I glare at Issy again. Mom may not be the only one in danger of committing sororicide today.

'It's fine, Mom. I'm fine.'

'But—'

'Are you ladies joining us?'

Dad has paused in the doorway, looking either confused or amused, or a mix of both.

'Sorry, Dad. Mom was telling us what she got you for Christmas,' Issy lies. She shoots me a subtle wink, but her cover story doesn't make up for sparking this shitshow of a conversation in the first place.

'Oh, then I'd better make myself scarce,' says Dad with a grin.

'But don't take too long,' he calls from the hallway. 'Hot eggnog – delicious; lukewarm eggnog – disgusting.'

I wait until I'm positive that Dad's out of earshot. 'Okay, look, you can't say anything. Raff is dating Julia and he's super keen on her and I'm just gonna have to deal, okay? Maybe if they don't work out then— Never mind. I don't even want to go there. So, *please* leave it.'

Mom seems concerned, her lips taut, Monica shakes her head at me, blatantly disbelieving that Raff doesn't reciprocate my feelings, and now Issy won't look at me. It's clear that remorse has kicked in – she's like a dog that destroyed a throw pillow, is covered in feathers, and feels so guilty, it won't make eye contact.

'Come on,' I say.

I lead them out of the kitchen and when we get to the living room, where Mariah is playing softly on the stereo, Raff greets me with a huge smile. 'Are you going to tell them?' he asks.

'Tell them?' I ask, alarmed.

'Yes, your news,' he replies with a laugh.

My news that I've fallen for my best friend? Everyone here knows that except for you and Dad.

Issy nudges me with her elbow and leans close. 'The promotion,' she whispers through barely parted lips.

'Oh, yes! My news!' With everything that's happened since they arrived home, it completely slipped my mind.

I take a seat on the floor next to the coffee table, grab a mug of eggnog from the tray, and tell them about my promotion.

25

GABY

As is the tradition in my family when one of us has good news, we're celebrating my promotion with Dick's – the best burgers, fries, and shakes in Seattle. My parents grew up on Dick's, and so did Issy and I.

Dad, who's old school, runs around with a pad and pen and takes our orders. Even Monica knows what she wants without looking up the menu.

But it's clear that Raff's overwhelmed by the selection of burgers and shakes we're shouting out. Dad must pick up on it too. 'You can come with me and decide what you're having when we get there,' he tells Raff.

And I am all for Dad taking Raff out of the house, so I can deal with the not-so-surreptitious looks my mom keeps giving me.

'Bye!' I say, closing the door behind Dad and Raff. The second they're gone, I beeline back to the living room. 'Mom, you've got to stop that.'

'Stop what?' she asks, and I can't tell if she's being coy or legitimately doesn't know what she's been doing.

'You're acting all weird about Gaby and Raff,' says Issy.

'Yeah, Aunt Gina. It's kind of obvious,' Monica agrees.

Mom looks between Issy and Monica, then at me. 'I'm sorry. I didn't realise I was doing that. I'll...' She lifts both hands, then lowers them as she exhales loudly, indicating she will chill. I fall onto an armchair, relieved but also suddenly exhausted.

'Can I just ask one thing?' says Mom.

'Mom!' chides Issy.

Mom ignores her, fixing me with an intense look. 'How will you know he doesn't reciprocate your feelings if you don't tell him how you feel?'

'I don't. But even if I wanted to, I'm not supposed to tell him.'

'What?' Mom is obviously bamboozled. 'What do you mean, you're not supposed to?'

'Does this have anything to do with the matchmaker?' asks Issy.

'What matchmaker?' asks Mom, her eyes getting even bigger.

'If we weren't having Dick's for dinner, I'd be making popcorn,' quips Monica, her eyes alight with intrigue.

I heave out a sigh and explain about the Ever After Agency and Raff's case, concluding with, 'So, I need to see how it goes with Julia. And that's that,' I add as an afterthought – more for myself than the others.

'That's that?' asks Mom, peeved. 'I don't accept that explanation, Gaby. What if he's secretly been in love with you all this time but he has no idea how you feel, and he ends up with Julia by default?'

'Yes, Mom, that is exactly what is eating me up inside. But I'm in a bind here. Because if he doesn't have feelings for me – hidden or otherwise – then I could fuck up our entire friendship.'

She presses her lips together, a frown settling on her face. But then her expression softens, and she offers a weak smile of concession. 'Okay, Gaby. I'm sure you know what's best. But sharing a room...'

Before we can go down *that* rabbit hole, Issy's phone rings loudly. We all look at her and every muscle in her body tenses.

'That's Jon's ringtone,' she says hoarsely.

'Do you want some privacy?' asks Mom, rising from her chair.

Issy forcefully shakes her head. 'I'm not answering.'

The four of us are silent as we wait out the ringtone and I study Issy's tortured expression the entire time. Today, she's been her old self – joking around, poking her nose into my business, chatting with Raff, but it's all been an act.

She's really hurting. And I didn't see it. Not only have I been a shitty friend to Raff, I'm also a shitty sister.

I go to Issy, kneeling in front of her chair, and enclose her in a tight hug. She starts weeping and the only sound for some time is her sobs. When they diminish, I keep my arms around her, but draw back slightly and look to Mom.

Her lips have disappeared between her teeth and silent tears roll down her face. It must be incredibly painful for her to see Issy like this.

'Sorry,' says Issy through her tears.

'You don't have anything to be sorry for,' I tell her, something echoed by Mom and Monica.

'I was feeling so much better today,' she says, looking up at me with her red-rimmed eyes. 'I told myself, "This is for the best." I mean, it hasn't been good with Jon for *years*, so...' She shrugs.

Years? I think. My sister's been unhappy in her marriage to Douchebag for *years*? God, I never want to end up in that situation.

She wipes under her eyes with her fingertips, and I scout around for tissues. Monica rushes over with a box and I offer it to Issy. She takes three and noisily blows her nose.

'Hun,' says Mom with a sniff, 'we can talk about it some more if you want? Should we go upstairs?'

Issy nods, then bites her lower lip like she used to do when she was a little kid. 'Thanks, Mom.' She wipes her nose again. 'Oh,' she says, as if something's just come to her. 'But what about Dick's? I want Dick's.'

A heavy pause hangs in the air, and I press my hand to my mouth to stop myself laughing. Issy breaks first, and when Dad and Raff arrive home, they're met with four women laughing so hard, we *all* have tears in our eyes.

* * *

'Gabs?' whispers Raff. 'Are you awake?'

Despite Mom's concern about my sleeping arrangements, I deliberately dodged any plans to rearrange them, laying low for the rest of the evening and letting Issy take the lion's share of parental attention.

After dinner, in the kitchen, I overheard Mom filling in Dad in about Douchebag's phone call. A few minutes later, back in the living room, as Issy was listening to Monica tell the gory story of Aunt Christine's bridal shop meltdown, he leant down and silently pressed a kiss to the top of Issy's head. She grabbed his hand, and they exchanged a father–daughter look so steeped in meaning, it brought tears to my eyes.

So many tears tonight – *and* so much laughter. Raff has certainly been exposed to the full spectrum of Rivera Family madness.

But in the darkness, as I stare at the wall across from me where snapshots from high school and college surround the mirror above my old dresser, I debate whether to answer Raff or pretend to be asleep.

Sleep – hah! Impossible when Mom's words keep rolling through my mind on repeat.

What if he's secretly been in love with you all this time...?

Curiosity wins. 'Hmm?' I moan, pretending I've been yanked from the brink of sleep.

'Sorry – I didn't mean to wake you.'

I roll over and face him, scootching backwards so we're not nose to nose. 'It's okay. Can't sleep?'

'No. Monkey brain – can't stop thinking.'

I prop myself up on my elbow, assuming the role of best friend. 'What's on your mind?' It could any number of things, but if he says, 'Julia,' then it's going to be very difficult not to abandon him and go sleep on the sofa.

'It's... Am I doing the right thing?'

That doesn't clarify matters. 'About?' I ask, my voice strained.

He expels a long breath and flops onto his back. 'This is going to sound terrible.'

'Raff – *what*?'

'It's just... Can I preface by saying I really *am* happy for you – and you totally deserve the promotion...'

Ah, right. I get it now.

'But it's made you question whether leaving to work with CiCi is the right thing.'

'Yes.' He turns to me again, and in the dim light of the electronics charging either side of the bed, I can see his eyes are filled with doubt.

'Hey...' Instinctually, I reach for him, grasping his arm and sliding my hand down until it holds his, and he grips it as though his life depends on it. 'It's okay, Raff. But this is your dream, remember? You're going to do amazing at Baked to Perfection. Think of all the joy you'll bring to cake lovers everywhere. And you're going to get *paid* to bake cakes – epic, out-there cakes,' I say, a lilt of laughter in my voice. 'How many people can say that?'

His brows raise momentarily, his expression shifting to one of consideration. 'True.'

'You also get to hire a team, mentor up-and-coming bakers, build out a division – from scratch. And eventually, it will go national. You live for that shit,' I say.

He chuckles softly. 'You're right. I do – as you say – live for that shit.'

'And you're great at it.'

'Thanks.'

We share a smile.

'I suppose it's natural to have doubts,' he says. 'It's a big change.'

'Absolutely. I'd be worried about you if you weren't having doubts. Doubts mean you understand the stakes. And this decision is *high* stakes, so it makes sense that you're scrutinising it from every angle.'

'Really?'

I don't know, Raff. I'm just making this shit up in the moment, I think.

'Of course.'

Then he does something that may be my undoing. He lifts my hand to his lips and kisses it. 'Thanks, Gabs,' he says, his eyes boring into mine. 'You really are the *best* friend.'

Heart: Swoon. Tingles. Kiss me.

Libido: Kiss me everywhere. Then do whatever else you want with me.

Head: He said 'friend', Gaby. Get a grip.

'And, actually, Julia said something similar when I last spoke to her.'

I gasp. I can't help it. The mention of her name – especially in this moment – is like a sucker punch to my gut.

Confusion flickers over his face. 'Are you okay?'

'Mmm-hmm,' I murmur, stretching my mouth into the fakest smile since Melania at the 2017 Inauguration. 'I'm glad Julia agrees.'

He gives me a warm smile, then with a pat on my leg, says,

'Good night, Gabs.' He rolls over and I do the same. This time when the tears come, they're for me.

I am in love with my best friend. And he's falling for someone else.

I know I agreed to the see-how-it-goes-with-the-blonde-bombshell plan, but it's way harder than I expected it to be.

Tomorrow, I'm letting Mom rejig the sleeping arrangements. I can't do this any more.

* * *

After a restless night, I climb out of bed a little before six, leaving Raff to sleep, and go downstairs still in my PJs.

Mom and Dad are in the kitchen, having a hushed conversation over the rims of their coffee mugs, Dad on one side of the kitchen counter and Mom perched on a stool opposite him.

'Good morning, sweetheart,' says Dad. 'Sleep well?'

'Yeah,' I lie.

Mom catches my eye and I can tell she's scrutinising my blood-shot eyes and dark circles. I don't even have to look in a mirror to know they're there. I know exactly what I look like after a shitty night's sleep.

'Coffee?'

Dad pours without waiting for a reply and slides the mug across the counter. I take it gratefully. 'Thanks.'

I sip from the mug, then sit on the stool next to Mom's.

'So, you know that snow we were expecting?' asks Mom with a wry smirk.

'I'd forgotten about that, but yeah.'

'It stuck,' says Dad.

My eyes fly to the kitchen window but it's pre-dawn and all I can see is darkness. I get up and cup my hands against the window, so I can see out. The back yard is blanketed in white, my parents' outdoor furniture forming large white lumps on the deck. I grin, then turn back to them.

'Maybe we will have a white Christmas!'

'You might be missing something,' says Dad.

Then it hits me. 'Oh, shit! The wedding.'

'Mm-hmm,' says Mom.

'Fuck, Aunt Christine is going to freak.'

It's telling that my first thought was of my aunt – and not the bride and groom.

'Yep,' says Mom, adding a weary sigh. She didn't even pick me up for swearing – this is *really* bad.

'Wait – it could melt, though, right? Before tomorrow?' I ask.

'KOMO news says no,' Dad replies. 'There's more snow expected today *and* for the next three days. And Sea-Tac is restricting the number of flights in and out for the foreseeable future. Only one runway is open.'

'So, yes to a white Christmas,' says Mom, 'but it's unlikely this wedding is going ahead.'

'*What?*'

Monica is standing in the kitchen doorway, a stricken look on her face.

'Oh, hun,' says Mom, climbing off her stool. 'I'm so sorry – we were going to find a better way to break it to you than that.'

'Break what? What's happened?'

'Hey, did you guys see outside?' asks Issy, coming up behind Monica.

'Outside?' Monica rushes to the window and like I did a few minutes ago, cups her hands against the window and peers out into the darkness. 'Well, fuck.'

She turns back to us, her jaw slack and her eyes unfocused.

'It could melt,' says Issy, obviously trying to be helpful.

'Ah, no, sweetheart,' says Dad gently. 'More snow's expected.'

'We've just been watching the news and most of the city is shut down,' Mom adds, her eyes locked on Monica.

'But Brian's parents are flying in today – from Kansas,' she says, latching onto one of probably dozens of wedding details flying around her head.

She snaps out of her stupor and looks at my mom. 'Oh my god. Mom is going to *freak*.'

I'm about to tell her I said the exact same thing, but the landline rings – a jarring sound in this age of ubiquitous cell phones.

'That'll be Chrissy,' says Mom, rushing to answer it. 'Hi, Chrissy,' she says, not even glancing at Caller ID.

The sound of my aunt's howling fills the kitchen and Mom takes the handset away from her ear, her face contorted.

'Oh, Chrissy, it'll be okay,' she says, but the howling only pauses long enough for my aunt to wail, 'How?'

Mom turns away from us. 'We'll figure something out... I know, hun. Yep... Mm-hmm... Yeah, it's devastating. I know...'

The rest of us listen to this one-side conversation, exchanging glances. My aunt does know this isn't *her* wedding, right? Shouldn't she have called Monica to see how she's doing instead of calling my mom?

'You need to come over. Does Marv have chains for his truck?' asks Mom. 'Okay, well, you'll have to walk. You've got hiking boots – put them on and get over here... Chris, it's only three blocks... *Because* we've got a full house and it's easier for you two to come here... Okay, see you in a bit.'

Mom ends the call and turns back to us.

'So, that was your mom...' she says to Monica, and I can't tell if she's saying that to be funny. Regardless, Monica starts laughing the maniacal laughter of a bride the day before her wedding in the midst of a Snowpocalypse.

26

GABY

It really puts my situation with Raff into perspective that my cousin's wedding – an event that's been on the calendar for nearly a year – may not go ahead. I've decided to shelve my crap to be dealt with some other time, and switch into professional mode.

On the surface, marketing may not appear to have much alignment with crisis management, but I have *skills*. Raff does too. We've had more than our fair share of campaign-launch disasters caused by factors out of our control – and we've always come through for the client.

I have no doubt that Raff and I can do whatever's possible to ensure Monica and Brian get married tomorrow. We're taking charge!

When he comes downstairs, showered and dressed, I fill him in.

'We're going to fix this,' I say, and his eyes light up.

'If anyone can, it's us. I mean, we're "Raff and Gabs",' he says, igniting tummy flutters from hearing our names said together like that.

'Come on,' I say, ignoring the flutters. 'I've set us up in here.'

I take him into Dad's study, which I've commandeered as our headquarters, and run him through what I've come up with so far.

'Brilliant, Gabs – as always.'

I feel a warm glow inside from his praise, even though he's just being Raff – as in, my supportive champion of a best friend and nothing more. The 'nothing more' part hurts – *and* it comes with a side of longing – but this isn't about me and my misplaced feelings. Today is about Monica and Brian's wedding, and there's no time for dwelling on what will never be.

'So,' I begin brightly, 'Monica's emailed me the guest list, including a breakdown of where everyone lives – who's local, who's supposed to be flying in and so on – plus a list of vendors with contact information, and details about the venue. I've printed everything out, so we can divvy up the work.'

Raff scans the array of pages on the desktop.

'Brian's on his way from Ballard – that's about four miles away – but he's not confident driving in the snow, so he's walking. We shouldn't expect him for at least another hour.'

'How long have you been up?' asks Raff, turning to meet my eyes.

'Since before six.'

He nods, his face contorting.

'Why?'

'I feel bad,' he replies. 'That I overslept again. Meanwhile, look how much ground you've covered already. Sorry, Gabs.'

I shrug, feigning modesty when really I feel sick. Because what if, just like yesterday, Raff didn't oversleep? What if he was snuggled up in *my* bed talking to *her* and that's why he's only just come downstairs?

He crosses to the window and looks out. 'It's hard to comprehend how something so beautiful could cause so much havoc.'

I could say the same thing about you, I think.

I study his profile, the way his eyes narrow as he takes in the blanket of white covering my parents' front yard. It takes all my willpower not to walk over, wrap my arm around his waist, and snuggle into him.

Because despite what's happening between him and Julia, despite the constant alarm bells warning me not to ruin our friendship by confessing my true feelings, I still want him.

'Hello?' Aunt Christine's voice echoes through the entry, and I snap back to the present.

'We're here,' says Uncle Marv. I can hear them stamping their feet, presumably to remove snow from their boots, and I beckon Raff to come say hello. The rest of the family crowds into the entry, and Monica rushes to her mom and falls into her arms.

'Mo-om,' she cries, bursting into tears.

It doesn't matter how much conflict there is between a mother and daughter, sometimes a girl just needs her mom.

'I know, sweetie,' she says, smoothing down Monica's hair.

After witnessing that phone call earlier, it's a huge surprise Aunt Christine is not a complete mess right now and when I catch Issy's eye, I can tell we're thinking the same thing. Maybe Uncle Marv gave her a pep talk on the way over – or a Valium.

Or maybe seeing Monica, who is typically the most chill person I know, *this* upset has activated Aunt Christine's Mama-Bear mode.

The weather is coming for her baby's wedding and she's not gonna let it.

Or I could be completely wrong about that, because amongst all the soothing murmurs, there is not *one* word of assurance that everything will be all right.

'Chrissy, Marv, you haven't met Raff,' says Mom, interrupting a couple of side conversations.

Uncle Marv reaches out to shake Raff's hand. Meanwhile, Aunt Christine releases Monica and looks Raff up and down appraisingly. She flicks her eyes towards me, her chin dropping a quarter inch.

I have approximately 2.4 seconds to school my expression. It's obvious she thinks Raff is my boyfriend – likely because of the last-minute addition of him as my plus one – and the slight incline of her chin is an approving nod.

Geez, Louise.

'Coffee, anyone?' Dad asks loudly, and almost everyone says yes.

Mom herds us into the kitchen and Raff says something about murdering a cup of tea. I push past Uncle Marv and turn on the kettle for Raff's tea while Dad doles out coffee and points to an array of milk and creamer choices.

As I wait for the water to boil, I catch Aunt Christine's hand hovering over the plate of cookies Dad set out. I don't blame her when she goes for one of Raff's rather than mine. It doesn't matter that they taste the same – on day two, mine look about as appetising as lumps of dried-up Play-Doh.

She takes a bite and groans appreciatively. And as she chews – to my horror – the groaning intensifies.

'So, you're the baker,' she asks Raff after she swallows. She may be the first person in history to load the word 'baker' with innuendo.

'Guilty,' Raff replies, smiling modestly.

'Well, cin cin,' she says, raising half a Santa in a pseudo toast.

Her gaze lingers on him a moment longer, then she addresses the room. 'Is it too early for a drink?'

'Chrissy, it's not even nine,' says Mom, her brow furrowed.

'So? My daughter's wedding is supposed to be tomorrow and for all intents and purposes, we're snowed in.' She looks at my dad, then pushes her mug of coffee towards him. 'Roland, better make this an Irish coffee – and a double.'

* * *

'So, now you've met my Aunt Christine,' I say to Raff as soon as we're back in my dad's study.

'Indeed,' he replies with raised brows. 'I didn't know she and your mum are twins. You never said.'

'I didn't?'

He shakes his head.

'To be honest, I tend to forget – probably because they're so different. And not only in appearance,' I say, thinking of my mom's cropped salt-and-pepper hair and makeup-free face and Aunt Christine's honey-blonde bob and full beat. Even today, she's put makeup on.

'I can see why,' he says. 'Right, should we crack on, then?'

Raff picks up his list, his eyes scanning down the page, but before we dive back into work mode, I should probably warn him that Aunt Christine's under the impression we're a couple.

Hah! If only. I bite back a wry smile.

'Um... there's something I need to tell y—' I start, but I'm interrupted by the devil herself.

'I hear this is Wedding Disaster Central,' says Aunt Christine, lingering outside the door. Ninety minutes ago, she was screeching down the phone line, and now she seems as cool as a cucumber. Maybe it's the Valium/whisky combination.

'Hi, Aunt Christine, come on in.'

She wanders in, sipping her doctored coffee, her gaze roving Dad's desktop, which is covered in printouts. She leans against a bookshelf. 'It's all a bust, you know.'

'The wedding?' I ask rhetorically.

'Yep.' She hits the 'P' hard, taking another sip of her coffee. 'A hundred grand...' she says, as if to herself. 'Gone, poof. Just like that.' She snaps her fingers.

'*There* you are, Chrissy.'

Uncle Marv comes into the study, inspecting Aunt Christine the way a parent looks at a teenager when they've arrived home late after a party. 'Maybe slow down on this a bit, huh?' he asks, taking the cup out of her hand. Surprisingly, she lets him. But I probably shouldn't be surprised by anything my aunt does.

'I was just telling these two that it's a bust.' One-handed, she mimes an explosion.

'What is?' he asks her.

'The wedding. A hundred grand. And for what?'

Uncle Marv glances over, clearly uncomfortable to be discussing the cost of the wedding in front of us. 'We don't know that,' he says to her. 'Everyone here is working on a solution.'

'Hah!' she scoffs, giving us the side-eye.

Gee, thanks for the vote of confidence, Aunt Christine.

She may not have intended to insult me, but it wouldn't be the first time she accomplished that without trying. A quick glance at Raff confirms that he's not loving her attitude either.

'Besides,' says Uncle Marv, 'you don't think I'd spend this much on a wedding without taking out insurance, do you?'

Her eyes suddenly expand to the size of saucers. 'You insured the wedding?'

'Of course. I *told* you I did.'

'I must have forgotten. I've had a lot to deal with, Marv,' she whines.

'I know, honey.' With his free arm, he captures her in a hug, rubbing her back as she slumps against him. 'Now, how about we let these two get on with what they're doing?' She nods and he gently leads her out of the room, glancing over his shoulder and mouthing, 'Thank you.'

I salute him – something I've never done before – to *anyone*. It's been a weird morning.

'Wowser...' Raff mumbles under his breath.

'Mm-hmm. Told you. Issy calls her the evil twin.'

He sniggers.

'But not to her face.'

'I guessed as much,' he says with a wink.

'Can I help?' Now Issy's at the door. Have I suddenly developed the ability to summon family members simply by mentioning them?

'Sure, why not?' I reply. 'The more the merrier.' Issy and I are similar that way – we'd both rather help handle someone else's crisis than delve into our own. 'We should probably get the bride in here too – if she's up to it,' I add.

'On it,' she replies.

I go back to my list and am about to call the celebrant when Monica enters, followed by Issy.

'I just heard from Brian,' she says, plopping onto a chair. 'ETA: fifteen minutes.'

'That's good,' I say.

'I love him so much,' she says, a peaceful smile alighting on her face. 'Honestly – I don't care about the flowers or the chocolate fountain or the frigging napkins... I don't care about any of that stuff. I don't care if we have to get married outside in the middle of a snowstorm wearing snowsuits. I just want to marry Brian. I want to be his wife and that's all that matters.'

Which is why I'm going to do everything in my power to make this wedding happen.

'Oh!' Monica claps her hand over her mouth. 'I'm so sorry, Issy.'

Her expression would be comical if it weren't so sweet how concerned she is about Issy's feelings.

'Don't be,' says Issy. 'It's not your fault my marriage is in shambles – please don't give it another thought, okay? This is about you and Brian.' She turns to me and only a sister would recognise the bravado in her eyes. 'Right,' she says. 'What's first?'

I task Issy and Monica with contacting the Seattle-based guests – see who might be able to make it – and Issy suggests they move into the living room.

Raff starts calling vendors, starting with the florist and the caterer, then he'll contact the photographer, and I call the celebrant. If they can't perform the ceremony, everything else is moot. A few minutes later, I grin at Raff. 'We have a celebrant! Her husband has a truck *and* snow chains and she said to keep her updated on the location.'

Now that I know the wedding can legally proceed, I go check on the others, who are making slow but steady progress. The only person without an assignment is Aunt Christine. Mom, who seems as fed up with her attitude and endless sighing as I am, tasks her with making coffee, and she perks up immediately at having a purpose.

I'm back in Dad's study getting an update from Raff when we hear a delighted squeal from Monica.

'Brian must be here,' I say, and we all congregate (again) in the entry as Monica gives him the equivalent of a hero's welcome.

And the guy *seriously* deserves it. He's arrived with a giant backpack strapped to his back and a suit carrier slung over one arm.

'I've packed enough clothes for a few days, and I brought my tux,' he tells us, a little out of breath. And no wonder; he just hiked through a snowstorm.

He's also brought his dog, a huge German Shepherd, who seems unfazed by a four-mile walk through inclement weather.

'And if you haven't met him yet, this is Bear.'

Bear grins at us, his tongue lolling, and Mom calls him into the kitchen, probably to get some water and a dog treat.

Dad relieves Brian of his backpack, making an oof sound as he bears the full weight of it, and Issy takes the tux from him and hangs it in the hall closet. Both Dad and Issy go back to their posts as I give Brian a quick hug and introduce him to Raff.

I tell him that we're on logistics and when he's defrosted, he should help Dad with transport.

'Thanks, Gaby,' he says, gripping my arm. Even though he arrived wearing gloves, his hand is freezing, the poor guy. 'Monica and I appreciate everything you're doing for us,' he says, his hazel eyes boring into mine.

My heart floods with warmth. This man loves my cousin, who I love. He's *family* now.

'It's a team effort,' I say lightly, and he sniggers as if he knows it's a lot more than that.

'Go on. Go help my dad,' I say.

Dad's been on the phone to everyone he knows in the vicinity who has an SUV or a truck, asking if they have snow chains and would be willing to collect Seattle-based guests and take them to the venue.

This is *if* the venue is still able (and willing) to host this wedding. They don't open until late morning, so we won't know for sure until then.

By 11 a.m., we have yeses from thirty-eight guests – *if* they can get to the venue – an affirmative response from the florist, who's based nearby in Uptown, a yes from the caterer but only with an adapted menu, and a maybe from the band. At worst, one of them DJs on the side and has a buddy who can probably get him to the venue, along with his records – actual LPs – and his turntable and mixing desk.

'Well, here goes nothing,' I say to Raff as I dial the venue.

The events manager answers, and I explain who I am and why I'm calling. With a sigh, she tells me she was just about to call to cancel.

'Oh. Are you sure? It looks like we'll only have about forty guests. Is there *any* way you can make that work? A smaller space for instance?' Raff's eyes lock on mine, a deep furrow between his brows, and I hold my breath for the few seconds of silence before she replies.

'I'm really sorry. We just haven't got the staff – not even for a smaller wedding. We're insured for this type of thing, so the couple should be reimbursed for the cost, but it can take time. I'll put everything in an email today and revert in the New Year.'

I wish her happy holidays and end the call.

'Welp... Back to the drawing board.'

27

POPPY

'Hi, darling – *so* sorry I'm late,' says Tristan.

It's not often I get annoyed at Tristan, but this is one of those rare moments, as I've been saving this table and an empty bar stool for twenty minutes, and two days before Christmas, I should be wearing a suit of armour and wielding a sword. If I had a pound for every tut and eye roll in response to 'Sorry, that's taken', I could shout the entire bar a round of drinks.

He leans close and I accept a kiss on the lips, which instantly washes my peevishness away. Tristan's kisses have that kind of power.

'No worries,' I say. 'But if you were any later, I would have got a call from the casting agent for *Gladiators*.'

'Holding a table a bit like running the gauntlet?' he asks.

'You have no idea.'

Just then, he's jostled by a large man in an expensive suit who's boisterously telling a story to a group of similarly suited men. The man doesn't even acknowledge that he's knocked into Tristan, let alone apologise.

'I might have *some* idea,' Tris says to me drily. 'Who chose this place again?'

'Ah, that would be you, babe.'

'Right,' he says with a twinkle in his eye. He checks his watch. 'So, Rav and Jass are due at half-five. Question is, do I wait for them to get here and help you hold the table or head to the bar now?'

I'm about to tell him to go to the bar when I hear, 'We're here, we're here.'

I look to my left, catching sight of Jacinda attempting to push her way between the large man and one of his cronies. 'Excuse me, I'm a pregnant woman and I need to get through.'

The man steps aside instantly. 'My apologies, madam.' Oh, so he *does* have manners.

Or maybe Jacinda just uttered the magic words – she certainly doesn't appear to be pregnant this early on. I file that nugget away for next time I need to save a seat in a bar. 'My pregnant friend is sitting there' obviously carries more weight – so to speak.

'Hi!' she exclaims, kissing me on the cheek, then Tristan. He helps Jass climb onto the stool, as it's high and she's tiny.

'Where's Rav?' he asks.

'Checking our coats – although, in hindsight, probably a stupid idea. It will be New Year's before we get out of here. This place is teeming.'

'I'll head to the bar, then. Wine?' he asks me.

I nod.

'And a mocktail for Mum,' he says to Jass, dipping his head in a pretend bow.

The way the word 'Mum' rolls off his tongue turns my insides to mush. Thoughts of becoming one myself have become almost all-consuming, especially this time of year when we've wound down at work and my sole professional responsibility is waiting on a (likely panicked) call from Gaby.

'So sorry we had to do Christmas drinks out,' says Jass. 'And thanks for coming all the way into Central London.'

'No worries,' I reply with a smile. 'It sounds like your parents achieved the impossible, getting last-minute accommodation like that.'

'Can you believe it? Seventeen of us in one house – though, it's supposed to be *enormous*.'

'Wait, *seventeen*?'

'Yep. Three brothers, three sisters-in-law, seven nephews, Mum and Dad, *and* me and Rav.'

'That's... I mean, I'm the only child in my family – so is Tris – I can't even imagine.'

'It'll be mad but brilliant!' she says with a grin. 'Though, it's so last-minute, I haven't even packed yet, which you know I hate.'

Like me, Jacinda prefers weeks of careful planning and packing in the lead up to a trip.

'The holidays can be really stressful,' I say, grateful for our plan to have a quiet Christmas, just me, Tris, and Saffron. Although, missing my parents is its own kind of stress.

'They are! I feel like I've spent the past month running about, Christmas list in hand, making sure I get the correct LEGO sets. My nephews are so spoilt – one wrong present can cause a tantrum the size of France.'

I chuckle, knowing how much I plan on spoiling Baby Sharma.

'Hiya,' says Ravi, looking harried. 'Total mare at coat check,' he says, kissing my cheek. 'Tris at the bar?' he asks me.

'Yep.'

'Right, back into the fray.' He presses his lips softly to Jacinda's head, then disappears into the crowd. They're so much more affectionate now they're expecting a child.

'Have you heard from Shaz and Lauren?' Jacinda asks. 'I've sent a couple of messages but she's only "hearted" them.'

'Same. But from the pics on Insta, the trip looks like it's going well.'

Shaz and Lauren are in Melbourne over the holidays for Lauren's meet-the-family Christmas. She was incredibly nervous about it until I told her that when I lived in Melbourne and Shaz and I became besties, her family practically adopted me. Any holiday that I didn't go home to Tassie for, they included me in their celebrations. Shaz's mum, Cheryl, even calls me her second daughter. They are going to *love* Lauren – like we all do. I don't even mind if she takes my spot and I'm bumped down to number three.

'Agreed!' says Jacinda. 'Though, I'm so bloody jealous of all those blue-sky, poolside, drinking-chilled-white-wine-on-the-veranda photos. And not just because I can't have wine at the mo.'

I laugh despite feeling a pang of homesickness for Australia. I love Christmas in England – London especially with all the stunning Christmas decorations and window displays – but I still miss hot Christmases, including the food. The mere *thought* of fruit platters and prawns and fat slices of cold ham and six types of salad can get me salivating.

'How about you?' asks Jacinda. 'Today your last day at work?'

'At the office, yes, but my case is still active – well, sort of.'

'This the one with Freya's friend?'

'Yep.'

'So, why is it only sort-of active?'

'Cone of silence?' I ask.

Unlike Shaz and Lauren, Jacinda and Ravi haven't met Raff and Gaby, but they know Freya and I need to maintain a modicum of client confidentiality here.

'Of *course*!' she says, her dark-brown eyes dancing with curiosity. Or is that mischief? 'I live for gossip about your cases – I'd never jeopardise that.'

I fill her in, her mouth stretching into a huge 'O' as the update progresses.

'Blimey. Poor Gaby. So, any update?'

'Actually, no, and I'm not sure if no news is good news or the opposite. And considering that good news for Gaby might mean something else entirely for the case...' I trail off, my mind fixating on how Gaby sought my permission to act on her feelings.

I catch myself staring at the sticky surface of the table, realising that even if Gaby isn't my *actual* client, her HEA is just as important to me as Raff's.

And therein lies the matchmaker's conundrum. Does this mean that if Gaby and Raff don't end up together – and, really, at this point it could go either way – I'm committing to finding Gaby a match?

I shake my head. This is too much to ponder in a crowded bar.

'Pop...'

I lift my gaze and smile at Jass. 'Sorry, just... in my head – about Gaby.'

'Well, send her a message,' says Jass. 'You might be imagining the worst.' She leans closer and says, 'We all do it.' She gives me a knowing smile.

'Yeah, you're right. On both counts.'

She sits back, giving me a self-satisfied look that says, 'Well, obvs!'

I take out my phone and send a casual hey-what's-up? message to Gaby, then slip it back into my handbag.

'Now, back to you,' I say. 'Are you and Ravi telling your family when you see them?'

'Technically, we're supposed to wait a few more weeks – just to, you know, make sure everything's all right – but honestly, I can barely stop myself from shouting about it, even to strangers.'

'Well, you did announce it to them,' I say, pointing at the group of men behind us.

'True,' she says with a laugh. 'I've told Rav I'll do my best, but we'll see how long that lasts. Guaranteed it'll be, "Hello, Mum. Hello, Dad. I'm pregnant."'

I start laughing, then reach for her hand. 'Oh, I'm so happy for you guys.'

'Thanks.' She flashes me an excited grin, then leans in. 'So, when are you and Tris going to start trying?'

I should have seen that coming.

It's the sort of question close friends ask when they're expecting, especially when they know you want to have kids someday.

Only it seems that with all our closest friends moving onto this next phase, 'someday' is feeling a lot closer than it used to.

* * *

Gaby

Around noon, I take a breather to check my inbox, deleting at least a dozen buy-this-thing-you-don't-need emails, then scrolling through all the other non-wedding notifications.

That's when I discover I got a text from Poppy early this morning:

> Just checking in. How are things in Seattle?

As far as texts go, it's completely innocuous, but I've just caught Raff looking at my phone. Thank god she didn't say something like, 'Hey, have you told Raff you're in love with him yet?' or he and I would be having a serious talk right now.

'Sorry,' he says. 'Rude of me, reading over your shoulder like that.'

'It's okay. It's only Poppy – you know, Freya's friend from work.'

'Oh right, yeah. I haven't seen her in ages. I didn't realise you two were friendly.'

'We hung out a couple of times earlier in the month – with Freya.' Fudging the truth a little – well, a lot – but what else am I going to say?

Then it dawns on me; Raff might make the connection.

Me → Poppy → Freya → the Ever After Agency → him giving Freya the go-ahead to match him if he didn't have to go on any dates.

Honestly, I'm surprised he *still* believes that he and Julia met randomly. I mean, *hello*?! For a smart guy, Raff can be pretty dim sometimes. Like now.

'We should organise something,' he says, and I snap back to Dad's study.

'Organise something?' I ask, perplexed. Have I missed a critical detail while I've been in my head? I scan my master list for the umpteenth time.

'Yes, for when we get back to London,' he replies.

'What are you talking about? Organise what?'

'Dinner or drinks – perhaps a games night,' he replies calmly. 'Freya and Freddie, Poppy and Tristan, me and Julia, and you. Doesn't that sound fun?'

Um, no, Raff, that does *not* sound fun. It sounds like the exact opposite of fun. More like Noah's frigging ark with all the people arriving two-by-two and poor, lonely Gaby there all on her lonesome as the seventh wheel.

I'd rather take a dip in the Thames. Naked. In the middle of the day in front of all the tourists.

'Super fun,' I lie with a tight smile. I *cannot* deal with this right now – there's too much to do.

I set my phone down and go back to the list of vendors, assessing where we're at. So far, we've talked to everyone except the woman who's making the most enormous wedding cake known to humanity. I've left a message on her phone, sent an email, and DMed her on both Facebook and Instagram. *Nada*.

Raff's stomach grumbles loudly. Our eyes meet and he flushes with embarrassment.

'Sorry, I haven't had anything this morning, except that cup of tea.'

'Yeah, me neither. Actually, that's a lie. I had a Christmas cookie. Okay, *three* Christmas cookies,' I admit, and he raises his eyebrows at me, his mouth twitching.

Stop being so frigging cute, Rafferty.

I clear my throat so I don't blurt that out.

'Let's take a break,' I say instead.

Like me, Raff likes to leave a clean desk, even if he's just taking a break, and he starts shuffling paper into piles. Now would be a good time to tell him that Aunt Christine thinks we're together, but I can't make myself say the words.

Because what if I jinx it?

Oh, for fuck's sake, Gaby. Jinx it? What are you? Twelve?

But there *is* something I should raise with him. 'Hey, Raff, before we join the others... You understand why I haven't told them about the venue yet, right?'

'Absolutely. You want to wait until we hear from everyone and present the contingency plan all in one go.'

This strategy is something he and I have both employed at Global Reach – individually and together. Launching a campaign can go south for a multitude of reasons. And before going back to the client, it's best to have all the information and a fully formed plan to right the ship. That helps soften the blow and instil confidence.

'Exactly,' I say, glad he gets it.

'I'd do the same thing, Gabs,' he assures me.

'So, you're okay with outright lying if anyone asks?'

'Well, when you put it that way...' he replies, his expression serious.

'Raff! But what if I—'

He laughs. 'Gotcha.' He winks, the left corner of his mouth lifting in a half smile, and it's like a lightning bolt shoots through me, then concentrates between my legs.

Forget 'cute'. Stop being to frigging SEXY, Rafferty.

I'm really out of my depth here.

After lunch, I'll sneak away and text Poppy with an update. Which is that I am dying inside while distracting myself with save-the-wedding duties. Maybe she'll have some keep-my-libido-in-check strategies she can share.

Like not sleeping in the same bed with the person you're lusting after? Or not spending all morning holed up in a small study with him RIGHT THERE?

'Gabs? Are you coming?'

His voice jolts me back to reality.

'Yep!' I reply cheerfully.

Please kill me now.

* * *

Poppy

We're on the sofa watching the *Vicar of Dibley* episode where Geraldine eats four Christmas dinners, and my phone alerts me to an incoming message. It's from Gaby – and it's long.

'Everything all right, darling?' Tristan asks, pausing the TV.

'Umm...' I scan the message, then look at Tristan. 'Not great, actually. It's Gaby. I should call her. Is that okay?'

'Of course.'

I get up and take my phone into our bedroom. As I'm closing the door, Tristan un-pauses the episode, letting out a loud guffaw at Dawn French's priceless facial expression at being served an entire plum pudding to herself.

I climb onto the bed and prop myself against some pillows, then call Gaby. She may not answer – it sounds like there's a house full of people and she's in the thick of handling a wedding fiasco – but she only sent the message a few minutes ago, so fingers crossed.

She answers almost right away. 'Hi, Poppy,' she says, her voice low.

'Hi. Is now a good time to talk? Are you somewhere private?'

'Not at the moment but hold tight.' There's muffled noise as she relocates, but it doesn't take long. 'Okay, I'm in my old bedroom, but there's no lock on the door so I might be interrupted.'

'I considered replying via text, but it might be easier to talk,' I say. 'Sounds like you've got a lot going on.'

'Yeah.' She sighs softly. 'Look, I know what you're going to say.'

I laugh. 'How can you when *I* don't even know what I'm going to say?'

'Really?'

'Yes. Your situation is... ahh... *unique* – and that's before we throw the wedding stuff into the mix.'

'Yeah. It's ripped straight out of a bad romcom,' she says.

'Or a good one. Nothing wrong with the forced-proximity trope,' I reply, thinking of Shaz. It's one of her faves.

Gaby chuckles then exhales noisily. 'Poppy, half the time I feel like I'm on the cusp of saying something. Like I won't be able to hold it in any longer and I'll just blurt out how I feel.'

'I gleaned that from your message. It sounds rough.'

'It is – especially when he does something that's typically Raff, but now I'm seeing it through a new lens and it takes on an entirely different meaning.'

'Such as?' I ask.

'Well, here's one – we hold hands sometimes. We always have – crossing a busy street, if one of us gets bad news – or good news, for that matter. We've always been touchy-feely with each other, but now it has a completely different effect on me. And then I find myself staring at his lips and wanting him to kiss me – but then my brain's like, "Um, Gaby, it's *Raff*."'

'You're confused.'

'I am so fucking confused,' she says.

'Can I ask you something?' I want to broach the topic of Julia, but I need to tread lightly here.

'Ask away,' she replies.

'Does he talk to you about Julia?'

It takes a moment for her to reply. 'Yeah, he does. I can tell he likes her. He even wants to plan a get together when we're back in London. Oh, and get this – you and Tristan are invited!'

That surprises me, but I don't let on. 'Let's cross that bridge if we come to it,' I say instead.

'Isn't the expression *when* we come to it?' she asks dryly.

'Yes, but nothing is set in stone yet. There's so much going on, especially with the wedding. And we can't be sure of Raff's feelings – not in such a heightened environment. But I do have one piece of advice – and you can take it or leave it.'

'You're going to tell me to change the sleeping arrangements,' she states with a tone of resignation.

'Yes. It's one of the few things you can control and it might give you better perspective if you're not sleeping together.' Her breath hitches and I rush to clarify what I meant. 'Sorry – I meant that literally, not well... you know. Sorry – it's been a long day.'

'It's okay. And you don't need to apologise. You're doing me a huge favour by talking to me – especially on Christmas Eve Eve when you should be chilling with your hot husband.'

There are a few seconds of silence, and I can't help smiling. Did she really just say that?

'*And* now you know I think Tristan is hot,' she says, laughing at herself.

'It's okay. There are still times when it hits *me* how good-looking he is.'

'Completely understandable. And on that note... I have a wedding to save, so...'

'Go! That's important work – and I'm speaking as someone in the biz.'

'Thanks, Poppy. I'll let you know how things go – with the other thing, I mean. And if I don't talk to you beforehand, Merry Christmas.'

'Merry Christmas!'

We end the call and I go back into the lounge room and take the remote to pause the TV again. I straddle my hot husband, pressing my lips to his.

'Ms Dean,' he says, giving my bum a squeeze, 'are you trying to seduce me?'

'If you have to ask, I'm not doing a very good job.'

He kisses me again, but a niggling thought raises its head and I gently move away.

'What's wrong?'

'There's nothing wrong, but...'

'Darling?'

He peers up at me with those whisky-coloured eyes. If we have a baby, it will probably have his eye colour, because mine are grey.

'I've been thinking...' I start. 'What if we started trying... for a baby?' I regard him closely to gauge his reaction.

A myriad of emotions dance behind his eyes – joy, excitement, love – and his mouth stretches into a grin.

'I've been thinking about it too.'

'You have?'

'Hard not to when it's all our friends are talking about.'

'I know, right?' I say excitedly.

'It *would* be rather wonderful all of us having children at the same time.'

'Yes!' I slap him playfully on the chest. 'I thought that too.'

He sniggers, then his laughter becomes a questioning smile. 'So, how about we start trying right now?' He lifts his brow inquisitively.

'Are you trying to seduce me, Mr Fellows?'

'I can't be doing a very good job if you have to ask.'

His hand captures the back of my neck and he pulls me into a kiss.

28

GABY

I finally hear back from the cake artist. As she and I talk, Raff's eyes are rivetted to mine, a divot deepening between his brows.

'No, that makes perfect sense,' I say. She apologises again and I reply, 'It's not your fault. We completely understand. Thanks again for getting back to me.'

I end the call and give Raff a resigned smile. 'So, wanna make a wedding cake today?'

He appears to be caught off guard, which surprises me – he was listening to that call, right?

'Yes, of course, I'd be happy to. But there's no way she can get the cake to us?'

'Not unless we rent a helicopter. She's snowed in on the other side of the Snoqualmie Pass – over that way,' I say, waving generally towards the east.

'In that case, I'd be delighted to do my part.'

'Thanks, Raff. It doesn't have to be... you know, *fancy*. I'm sure Monica and Brian would be happy with a Betty Crocker box cake at this point.'

He recoils in mock horror. 'You did *not* just say that to Britain's Best Baker!'

I crack up and he breaks into a (heart melting) smile. 'Is this my life now? You busting out your national title whenever you want to win an argument?'

He shrugs one shoulder.

'Okay...' I say, getting back to replanning this wedding. 'That's the final piece of the puzzle, so now we need to brief everyone.'

'Will your aunt and uncle agree, do you think?'

'They have to. I'm sure Mom and Dad would offer to host it here, but this place is way too small for forty guests,' I reply. 'Actually, forty-two now that Brian's parents have pulled off a miracle.'

'Theirs sounds like the journey from hell – how many stops did it end up being?'

'In the end, six.'

'Blimey, that's dedication.'

'CiCi and Devin would do that for you,' I say without thinking.

Because if I'd thought about it for *one second*, I would *not* have created a hypothetical in which Raff was getting married and CiCi and Devin had to move heaven and earth to attend the wedding. As far as Raff is concerned, his hypothetical bride is anyone but me.

'True,' he says with a smile, and I *so* want to ask him if he's imagining Julia in this scenario, but then again, I don't want to hear him say yes.

I pick up my one-pager where I've written the contingency plan out in full and pretend to read it while the words swim on the page.

'Shall we then?' he asks.

'Yep,' I say, forcing a smile. 'Let's go rally the troops.'

* * *

I run through everything Raff and I have figured out, then look around the living room at my family. 'How does that sound?' I ask them.

Mom beams with pride. 'Sounds great, hun.'

'Yeah, great work, you two,' says Dad, nodding approvingly.

Monica rushes to me and throws her arms around my neck. 'Thank you *so* much,' she says, squeezing me tightly. I return the hug, the one-pager dangling from my fingertips.

Someone clears their throat and Monica releases me.

'Am I really expected to get my home ready to host a wedding in less than twenty-four hours?'

Aunt Christine glowers at me, her hands on her hips, and there's so much to unpack in that one question, I'm not sure where to start.

Fortunately, I don't have to say a thing.

'It's *our* home, honey. And Gaby's right – it's the only viable option.'

'But Marv—' she blusters.

'And everyone here will help us get ready. It won't fall solely on you.'

This seems to appease my aunt – at least partly. 'All right,' she says tersely, her mouth downturned.

'Oh, Mom, it's going to be beautiful.' Monica goes to her and picks up her hand, and Aunt Christine's harsh expression softens a fraction. 'All those flowers, for a start,' Monica continues with a laugh. 'We ordered enough for a *huge* venue... Your home will be so full of flowers, it'll feel like we're at the Chelsea Flower Show.'

Ding, ding, ding, we have a winner, ladies and gentlemen. My aunt *loves* the Chelsea Flower Show – she watches the live stream every year, then gets on a flower-arranging kick that lasts a month or two before she concedes, once again, that she will 'never be a professional'.

Monica jostles her mom, cajoling a smile out of her. 'It *will* be beautiful,' Aunt Christine admits. With her free hand, she cups Monica's face, her eyes tearing up. '*You* will be beautiful, my darling girl. I can't believe my baby's getting married tomorrow.'

She draws Monica into a hug and Mom and I lock eyes across the room. She mouths, 'Great job,' and I modestly dip my head.

'Right, everyone, now that's sorted, we should get back to work. Lots to do,' says Raff, taking charge. And rightly so. Of everything left on the list, baking a wedding cake is up there as the most labour intensive.

As the others spring into action – including Aunt Christine, who starts spouting off everything she and Uncle Marv need to do – Raff takes the bride and groom aside to ask what kind of cake they'd like.

'Gaby, can you come into the kitchen for a sec?' asks Mom.

I follow her out of the room. 'Sure, what's up?'

She looks past me to make sure we have privacy, then leans close. 'So, Monica is staying at Chrissy and Marv's tonight – with Brian.'

'Oh, okay. So, she's not superstitious then.'

'What do you mean?'

'That thing about the bride and groom seeing each other before the ceremony,' I reply.

'Oh, right. Actually, Chrissy mentioned that, and Monica called it "a BS, archaic tradition from the time women were considered chattel".'

'Sounds about right,' I say with a laugh.

Mom regards me closely.

'What?' I reach up and brush around my mouth. 'Do I have mustard on my face?'

'No, hun. It's just that with Monica out of the house, I thought we could make some changes to the sleeping arrangements – put Raff in Issy's old room on the king single and Issy in with you.'

'Ahh...'

How did I not see that coming? And then it hits me: denial – pure, simple denial.

But Mom's right. And so is Poppy. *And* Freya. Sleeping next to Raff has been torture and with these new arrangements, there will be one less thing to obsess over. And, hey, I might actually get some sleep!

'Sure, Mom. Sounds good. I'll go up now and switch out the bedding.'

Mom reaches over and rubs my arm then gives it a squeeze, and the back of my throat prickles, signalling tears are imminent. Now that we've determined how to salvage this wedding, my brain has only one conundrum to chew over – being in love with Raff.

I expel a long sigh, then go upstairs to rummage through the linen closet.

* * *

'I can run you down there,' Dad offers. 'Dave dropped off a set of chains a half-hour ago.'

Raff needs several ingredients for the wedding cake because (of *course*) he offered to make a spiced, white-chocolate mud cake and there is not an ounce of white chocolate in the house – or Aunt Christine and Uncle Marv's. He also needs a few other key items.

Dad says he'll take us down the hill to Metro Market, but I worry about his SUV getting back up the hill – even with chains. Besides, Brian told us people are snowboarding down Queen Anne Avenue, then showed us a guy who's live streaming it to Instagram.

'We can just walk over to Trader Joe's, Dad. It's not that far.'

He frowns at me, then concedes. 'Okay, sweetheart. But if it gets too much out there, call and I'll come get you.'

He makes it sound like a warzone. It's just *snow*. And right now, it's falling gently from the sky. If a blizzard were raging outside, I'd happily let Dad drive us the five blocks there and back.

Raff and I bundle into our warmest clothes and boots, then set out, making fresh footprints in the six-inch blanket of snow. For the first few blocks, we don't talk, which is not unusual for us – neither of us are fill-every-silence type people. And Raff seems content to study each house we pass, his neck craning to see the roofs of the taller houses.

There's an eclectic mix of homes in my parents' neighbour-hood. Many were built more than a hundred years ago, with owners lovingly restoring and maintaining the original style. Quite a few are monuments to modernity, all glass and concrete and acute angles. The one thing most have in common is that they are worth a fortune.

My parents bought theirs soon after they got married when Issy was a baby, in the time she calls 'before you were alive'. I have no doubt they could sell up and retire to the Bahamas on the proceeds of the sale, but my mom loves that house. She once told me that the only way she's leaving is in a body bag. I'd been appalled at the morbid joke, but she'd just laughed.

And here's me, living across the world in a teeny (but cute) apartment, my fourth since living in London. It's hard to imagine getting married and starting a family and living in one house for the rest of my life.

'Penny for your thoughts,' says Raff.

I've been in my head so long, we're already halfway there. But at least I can tell him the truth – most of my thoughts since we arrived in Seattle have been about *him*.

'I'm thinking about how long my parents have lived here – more than thirty-five years now. Since before I was born.'

'Blimey. I don't know many people who have lived in one place for that long. Certainly not my parents. Not even CiCi and Devin.'

'Well, when you make a shit-tonne of money that you've worked your ass off for, you're entitled to move into a mansion.'

The house they live in now is not the one Raff grew up in, which was far more modest – though, just as filled with love, I imagine.

'True,' he says, laughter in his voice. 'But can you imagine buying a house now and still living there when you're seventy?' he asks.

'Nope.'

'Hmm, me neither. I suppose it might be different if you're married, though.'

Okay, I am not letting that comment slide. 'How so?'

'It's part and parcel, isn't it? Building a life together, buying a home.'

'But what if your idea of marriage isn't so traditional? What if you don't want to be tied to a mortgage?'

'Don't you?' he asks, and it's hard to miss the surprise in his voice.

'Not really. I mean, I did – once – when I was with Eric. It's what I was conditioned to believe, how life was supposed to go, right? Fall in love, get married, buy a house, pop out some kids...'

'You don't want children?'

'I didn't say that. It's just... after Eric and I broke up, I re-evaluated, and I discovered that a lot of what I *thought* I wanted wasn't what I wanted at all. I didn't want to spend my entire adult life living in the same neighbourhood where I grew up. I wanted to explore and meet new people and have experiences I couldn't even imagine yet.'

'Is that why you decided to move to London?' he asks.

'I've told you this before, haven't I?'

'Not this part. Only that you had a breakup and moved to London soon after.'

'Oh, well the breakup was the impetus – it sparked several weeks of introspection – but the destination wasn't the point. *Going* was the point. Getting out of Dodge, breaking my routines and habits, getting as far away as possible from *Eric*.'

'So, why London?'

'I considered all the cities where Global Reach had offices, but it came down to *Notting Hill*,' I reply.

'Sorry? Oh, do you mean the film?'

'Mm-hmm. Richard Curtis and his idealistic representation of life in London spoke to me. I was mainlining ice cream and crying my sad little heart out, and Mom put on *Notting Hill*. That night, I went online and looked up flights to London.'

He goes silent and I look up at him.

'What?'

He smiles, his eyes roaming my face, and I look away, unable to bear how much I want him to lean down and kiss me.

'Just that it's lovely how we've known each other for years and are best of friends, yet we still have things to learn about each other.'

I stop myself from howling with ironic laughter.

We still have things to learn about each other.

Indeed, we do, Rafferty. Indeed, we frigging do.

29

GABY

'I think that's everything,' says Raff, checking the contents of the cart.

Through a minor miracle, Trader Joe's is not wall-to-wall people two days before Christmas – must be something about a city-stopping snowstorm – so we've zipped through the aisles in less than thirty minutes.

'Everything in the *store*?' I tease. 'I'd say that's accurate. You do realise we have to lug all this home?'

'Oh, sorry,' he says, being ultra-English – i.e. needlessly apologetic. 'Perhaps we should ask your dad to come and get us.'

I smirk at him. 'I'm *kidding*. It's going to be an incredible cake, Raff. Monica and Brian are going to *love* it. I still can't believe you're making fondant from marshmallows. You've got mad skills, dude.'

'Well, yes, but do we have too much to carry?'

'We'll cope,' I deadpan, then I lose it and grin at him.

'Oh, so you *are* joking.'

'*Yes*.'

'Gaby?'

There's a surreal moment in which the world seems off-kilter and somewhere in the depths of my heart, a hairline fissure painfully cuts through my contentedness. I inhale sharply and the fissure swells – fracturing, gaping, morphing into a chasm. Then I'm sucked backwards, as if I'm being swept into a black hole. Only instead of being consumed by a giant vacuum, I plummet through time, landing eight years ago with a vicious thud.

I turn – seeing the store through a slow-motion lens – and there he is. A thirty-four-year-old version of the only person who has ever broken my heart.

'Eric,' I state, my voice flat and raspy.

'Oh my god, Gaby. It *is* you.'

His face – older now – wears a mask of a smile and his voice cracks on the second syllable of my name like a teenage boy whose voice is breaking.

Beside me, I sense Raff stretch to his full height, a phenomenon so rare, we're bound to see a leprechaun any moment now. Raff's hand finds my waist, and he draws me towards him protectively. I numbly place my hand over his, and our fingers entwine.

'Wow, you look great,' says my ex.

Either his definition of great has dramatically shifted or I'm seriously pulling off this North-Face-meets-the-Michelin-Man vibe.

'Hello. Rafferty Delaney.'

Raff takes a half-step forward, his hand outstretched. As his other hand is cemented to my waist, I'm tugged forward with him.

Visibly shaken, Eric stares at Raff, then his eyes flick towards me. Finally, they land on Raff's outstretched hand. We all know he has no choice but to shake it, and he does.

'Uh... Eric,' he says. 'I'm—'

'Honey, are these the ones?'

Donna appears in the aisle with a toddler in tow, so pregnant she looks like she might give birth any minute now.

Clean up in aisle four, I think.

Eric looks at her as if he's seeing her for the first time, then his gaze drops to the packet of pecans she's holding. 'Uh... yeah.'

Other than uttering his name, I've completely lost the ability to speak.

So, this is Donna. There were *months* when I spent more time on her social media profiles than on my own, but I've never actually met her. She frowns at him, clearly confused at finding her husband in such a state.

'You remember Gaby?' he asks, and when her head swivels in my direction, so many emotions cross her face, I would laugh out loud if this weren't my worst nightmare.

'Hi,' she says. Her mouth hangs open and a deep furrow forms between her eyebrows. Her expression says, 'Fuck. You're her. You're the one I stole him from. And you're here. You're right fucking here.'

Raff's hand squeezes mine and his one-armed embrace tightens, bolstering me.

'Hi,' I say brightly. 'And who's this?'

I wriggle free from Raff's hold and bob down, peering at their toddler, a sweet-looking boy who has no idea that his father cheated on me, then married his mother a few months later.

He ducks behind his mom's leg, gazing at me curiously now that he's 'safe'.

'This is Tyler,' says Eric wanly.

Right, so he gave his kid the name we were going to call our first kid. Fucking fucker. I bet Donna doesn't even know.

'Hello, Tyler. Are you excited about Santa coming?' I ask.

Those are the magic words, and he ventures out from behind his mom's leg. 'Santa's bringing me a little baby brother,' he tells me proudly.

'Wow. Lucky you. You get to be a big brother. That is a *very* important job.'

He beams at me and sticks his chest out. 'And... and if I'm a good boy, I might get a puppy.'

'Puppies are the best,' I say.

'Do you have a puppy?' he asks, his big blue eyes so earnest, my heart may burst.

'I did once. They're amazing.'

He grins at me.

'We should get going,' says Eric. 'But nice to see you, Gaby.'

Really? It's nice to fucking see me, Eric?

Donna says nothing as she guides Tyler back down the aisle the way she came. 'Bye!' Tyler calls, turning around and waving.

'Bye, Tyler,' I reply, waving back.

As I stand, I meet Eric's eye and glare at him, breathing noisily through my nose. I can only imagine what I look like right now – my nostrils flaring, my jaw set, shooting not daggers but *machetes* at him.

So much anger that I didn't know was still in there.

Eric breaks eye contact and follows his wife.

Time stops for I don't know how long and when it starts again, I slump against Raff, tears pricking my eyes. But I will not cry over that asshat. Never again. Because him cheating was the biggest favour he could have done for me.

'Are you all right?' Raff whispers, his voice low. His arm encircles my waist again and he holds me firmly, propping me up as I face my past.

I take in a deep breath through my nose, then exhale slowly.

'I'm okay,' I reply. 'Let's just get out of here.'

* * *

It's a silent walk back to Mom and Dad's and Raff holds my hand the entire time, somehow intuitively knowing that's what I need.

And he's right.

The strength I'm siphoning from him through two pairs of gloves is the only way I make it those five blocks without dropping into the snow and staring up at the grey sky and having a full-blown, rage-filled, teary tantrum.

Do I want Eric?

Fuck no.

But do I want what Eric has with Donna?

That's a harder question to answer, because what hits me as we walk through this winter (fucking) wonderland is that while I may have mourned the loss of Eric – of what we *had* together – I never properly mourned the loss of what I envisioned we *would* have together – our future.

Why doesn't anyone tell you that you also need to process the future that will never come?

Or maybe they do, and I wasn't listening.

I'm listening now.

Tyler – he called his kid Tyler.

My throat closes and tears prick my eyes at the memory of that sweet, little, blue-eyed boy.

I blink back the tears and swallow the lump.

'Nearly there, Gabs,' says Raff softly, squeezing my hand.

I suddenly *love* that Raff calls me 'Gabs' and not 'Gaby'. He's the only person who does and that means it's 'ours', the nickname.

But not 'ours' in the way I want it to be. I bet he'll start calling Julia 'Jules' soon.

When we turn the corner, Mom and Dad's house comes into view and Dad is out front, shovelling the front walk.

'Hey, you two,' he says cheerily. 'Your mom's making hot chocolate.'

I smile at him, feeling an overwhelming sense of 'home'. If I had to be anywhere the day I ran into my ex, at least it's here where I'm surrounded by loved ones.

Safe.

* * *

Busyness has been my salvation through the tumult of this trip and this afternoon is no exception. It's nearly sunset – though, not even 4.30 p.m. – and Raff has me and Issy on sous chef duties. Or is it, sous baker?

So far, there has been a lot of measuring – sorry, *precise* measuring – and stirring and mixing and following instructions to the letter. This isn't a batch of Christmas cookies I can half-ass. This is a wedding cake, and we need to whole-ass every step. When I say that to Issy, she cracks up, earning us a stern look from Raff.

'Sorry,' I mumble.

But I would rather be here, being bossed about by my best friend than unpacking what happened at Trader Joe's.

Even if I wanted to talk it through with Mom, she's otherwise occupied, somehow persuading her friend's college-aged daughter and *her* friends into being waitstaff at the reception – now a buffet with a bar, rather than a sit-down dinner. They're getting paid in wine.

And Dad is back on the phone, confirming pickups with the fleet of volunteer drivers, including locations and guest names. Even though they'll refuse at first – happy to do the favour for my much-loved Dad – they're getting paid in beer.

When a wedding guest list drops from one hundred and fifty to forty, there is a lot of extra booze.

In the kitchen, the three of us work methodically, finding our rhythm, and Issy insists on 'entertaining us' with mortifying stories from my childhood. As in, entertaining Raff, who's guffawing at my embarrassing anecdotes.

'Did she ever tell you about the night she started her period?'

'Issy, *no*.'

Raff's cheeks turn candy pink, and mine have heated up too.

'What? It's funny! You wanted to go to the *hospital*.'

'Issy!'

'She thought she was dying and asked me to call 911,' she tells Raff.

'Oh, er...' Raff mutters.

'He doesn't want to know,' I scold.

'*Fine!* But you'd think the daughter of an OB-GYN would have paid more attention in health class.'

'Issy!'

She shakes her head, still laughing at the memory, and goes back to making fondant snowflakes. If she weren't so good at it, I'd kick her out for breaching the sister code. She's lucky I don't launch into the story of her getting her driver's license. Or *failing* her driver's license – *four times*. She was the only person in her junior class who couldn't legally drive. Though, she did drive *il*legally a handful of times – something I was sworn to secrecy about in exchange for rides to the movies.

My phone rings with an incoming video call. 'It's Freya,' I announce, accepting the call. 'Hey, Frey! Merry Christmas Eve Eve!'

She giggles. 'Hello! Wait, are you wearing an apron?'

'Yep.' I flip the camera so she can see Raff and Issy. 'We're making a wedding cake.'

'You are not,' she says with a laugh. 'Oh,' she says when I direct the phone camera towards the cooling cake tiers. 'You are!'

'Well, *I* am,' says Raff, lifting his gaze from a huge bowl of fondant. 'Gabs has been relegated to clean up.'

'Phew,' Freya replies dramatically.

'Hey!' I cry, pretending to take offence – though we all know I have the culinary skills of a llama.

Freya giggles again. 'Hello, Issy!' she calls out, and Issy waves. They've never met in person, but they've said hello a few times on calls like this one – mostly when Freya's been at my place and Issy has called.

'It's wonderful that you could be there for Christmas,' says Freya. 'What a lovely surprise for your family.'

Issy's eyes meet mine and I mouth, 'Sorry.'

She fakes a smile at the phone, uttering, 'Mm-hmm,' before going back to her snowflakes. Next time I talk to her alone, I'll tell Freya Issy's real reason for showing up unexpectedly.

'So, why are you making a wedding cake?' Freya asks.

'Shall I take this one?' I ask Raff, and he nods.

I flip the camera back around and quickly fill Freya in on the Snowpocalypse wedding.

'Wowser – that's far more exciting that what's happening here.'

'What's happening there?' I ask.

She brings her phone so close to her mouth, I could give her a dental exam. 'I'm *so* bored, Gaby. It's either sit around with my older relatives who drink *glögg* and play Alfabet all day – it's like Scrabble, but it's in Swedish and I am nowhere *near* fluent enough to join in, so I just end up doing the drinking part...'

I snigger. 'Or?'

'Or I go cross country skiing with my cousins – and you know how unfit I am. I went with them on my second day and they practically had to bring me home on a dog sled!'

I'm sure she's exaggerating, especially since her family lives in the outskirts of Stockholm. I doubt there are random dog sleds roaming the 'burbs, looking for unfit Brits who need assistance.

'Doesn't sound super fun,' I commiserate.

'Sorry for the whinge,' she says, finally taking the phone away from her mouth.

'It's okay. That's what second-best friends are for,' I quip.

Raff looks up, a quizzical look on his face, and I scrunch my nose at him. It's a slip-up because if he asks about it, I'll have to make something up.

Freya sighs. 'Anyway, I should go.'

'Yeah, it's late there.' I check the clock, realising that Freya's awake in the middle of the night. 'We miss you, Frey.'

'We miss you!' Raff calls out, and suddenly Freya looks like she's about to cry.

'Love you both!' She gives me a wan smile and ends the call.

I'm putting my phone away, ready to do another round of clean-up, when Raff's phone chimes with an incoming message. He looks over at it and breaks into a smile. 'Oh, lovely. It's Julia.'

He wipes his hands on a dish towel, then collects his phone and leaves the kitchen. Issy meets my eyes again, and this time it's *her* telegraphing sympathy to *me*.

* * *

Right after 7.30 p.m., Dad comes into the kitchen.

'Looks like you're making amazing progress,' he says, looking around.

And we are. All the cake tiers are out of the oven and cooling – two layers each of two different sizes – the frosting is made and most of the decorations are done.

'Thank you. Nearly there,' says Raff. 'Well, for tonight, anyway. It'll be best if I assemble the cake and ice it in the morning, then add the flowers when we get there. Now, I haven't got any doweling,' he adds with shrug, 'so it's a bit of a risk it will sink but—'

'Doweling, as in wooden doweling?' Dad interrupts.

'Yes, it's used to create stability in tiered cakes. It goes in, then you place a cardboard disc on top, then stack the next layer.'

'Well, you're in luck, son. I've got some in the garage – a few different thicknesses too...'

They grin at each other. 'Perfect,' Raff says.

This charming tableau of the two men I love most in the world, punctuated by Dad calling Raff 'son', makes my heart so full, it might burst. Yet, at the same time, it's a reminder that Raff isn't mine and he isn't going to be Dad's son any time soon.

'Well, I've done all I can,' says Mom, joining us. 'Oh, wow,' she says, clocking everything we've accomplished. 'You guys are machines!'

I shove aside my maudlin thoughts and smile at her. 'Don't forget Raff made a much bigger cake in only five hours to win *Britain's Best Baker*. By *himself*.'

'Even so, I couldn't have got this far without your help,' he replies magnanimously. '*Or* amusing stories from Gaby's childhood,' he adds, tossing a conspiratorial glance at Issy.

'Ah-hah!' says Issy, pointing one of Mom's fondant tools at me, a remnant of her cupcake-baking phase. Before today, I had no idea fondant tools were even a thing.

'So, you guys about ready to call it good?' Mom asks. 'I'm starving – how about I do something simple, like grilled cheese?'

I groan with pleasure – *nothing* is better than my mom's grilled cheese sandwiches. She could open a café that just sells those, and it would be a huge success.

'We've finished up for tonight,' says Raff. 'But I'll need some clingfilm.' Mom stares at him blankly.

'Plastic wrap, Mom,' I tell her, being fluent in both American and British vernacular.

'Oh, right.'

Mom gets Raff what he needs, and we pack all the delicate

fondant decorations into containers, being particularly careful, the way Raff showed us.

Then Issy and I switch gears and help Mom make an enormous stack of her famous grilled cheese sandwiches, while Dad goes to 'the cellar' – AKA the space under the stairs where they store wine on IKEA bookshelves – and returns to the kitchen with two bottles of Oregon Pinot, my favourite varietal from my favourite region.

'Two, Roland?' asks Mom from the stove where she's working a loaded griddle.

'There are five of us. That's only two glasses each,' he replies, and Mom shrugs.

When the wine is poured and Mom flips the last sandwich onto the platter, we pull our stools up to the kitchen counter.

On the whole, it's been a satisfying and productive day.

If I completely ignore that I ran into my ex today, getting a painful glimpse into a life I once thought would be mine.

30

GABY

All five of us oversleep.

Of *course* we do. Dad opened a third bottle of wine, then after scoffing at least two sandwiches each, we moved to the living room for brandy, Christmas cookies, and several rowdy rounds of Jenga. Carb overload + alcohol + rigorous smack talk + exhaustion = none of us getting out of bed before 8.30 a.m.

And we're due at Aunt Christine and Uncle Marv's at 10 a.m.

That scene in *Home Alone* the morning the family is flying to Paris – that has *nothing* on the Rivera household this morning. Somehow, amid panicked cries of 'Have you seen my [insert object here]?' and 'I know we put that wedding present somewhere!' and 'Argh! I forgot my shapewear in San Francisco!' we have all showered and are in various stages of getting ready.

While Issy and I put on our makeup – i.e. fight for space in front of the bathroom mirror like we did when we were teenagers – Raff is in the kitchen, hurriedly frosting the cake, and Dad is hunting for doweling in the garage, cursing himself for not doing it last night. I'm pretty sure I heard his bandsaw a few minutes ago.

Mom pokes her head into the bathroom. 'Hi, girls. Can one of you zip me up, please?'

'You look pretty, Mom,' I say, pausing my mascara application while Issy zips her up.

'Thanks, hun. You girls do as well.'

'Well, Gaby does. I look fat,' says Issy, scowling at herself in the mirror.

'Isabel Lee Rivera,' says Mom, noticeably leaving off Issy's married name, 'you are absolutely beautiful and I will not have you talking about yourself like that.'

Issy's lips disappear between her teeth, but she doesn't argue. While I've taken after Mom and Aunt Christine, Issy is a Rivera woman through and through. I've always envied her curvy hips and big boobs, but the grass is always greener, right?

Mom squeezes in between me and Issy, who's dusting on some setting powder.

'Can I borrow some lipstick?' she asks. 'Nothing too dark.'

Issy and I both freeze, our eyes meeting in the mirror. Our mom is an attractive woman, but she almost never wears lipstick – even for special occasions. I've seen her in blush a few times, maybe mascara, but never with colour on her lips.

'Do you want me to do your makeup, Mom?' asks Issy, turning to her. 'I'm nearly finished with mine.'

Mom steps back and waves her hand dismissively. 'Oh, never mind. It's silly. And we don't really have time, anyway.'

'Sure, we do, Mom – it won't take long. Besides, we can be a little late. The wedding doesn't start till two.'

'Yes, but I promised Chrissy we'd be there to help set up and—'

'Mom,' says Issy, taking her gently by the shoulders. 'Sit.'

'You want me to sit on the *toilet*?' she asks, her eyes wide with horror.

'On the *lid*, Mom,' I say. 'Geez.'

Mom starts laughing, clearly pleased with herself that she got me.

'Oh – *hilarious*,' I say dryly.

'So, how are things with you?' she asks me. 'Are you going to tell Raff how you feel?'

'Shh,' I hiss.

I stick my head through the door to Issy's room where Raff is now staying, but it's empty. I listen out and hear movement in the kitchen, meaning the coast is clear. But that doesn't mean I want to talk about Raff.

I turn around and Mom and Issy are watching me, twin frowns of concern etching their faces.

'What?' I look away and take out a small brush to shape my full brows.

'Things seemed a little tense when you got back from the store yesterday,' says Mom. 'Everything all right between you two?'

'Close,' says Issy, and Mom closes her eyes, then Issy starts smoothing taupe eyeshadow over her lids.

This gives me time to decide if I should tell Mom about seeing Eric. It might shift her focus away from me and Raff.

'We ran into Eric at Trader Joe's.'

Mom's eyes fly open and Issy looks at me over her shoulder, her mouth open.

'With Donna and their three-year-old, *Tyler*.'

'Oh, hun, why didn't you say anything?' Mom asks.

'Because when we got home, we were straight into cake making. Besides, I didn't want to talk about it.'

'Was Raff with you?' asks Issy. 'Like, right there with you?'

'Yeah... I'm pretty sure he gave Eric the impression we're a couple. And that he did it on purpose – to protect me.'

Issy faces me, pressing both hands to her heart, one of them still holding the eyeshadow brush. 'I heart Raff so much. What a man to do that for you.'

'Issy's right – that is a stand-up guy, right there.'

My throat closes, just like it did yesterday, and all I can do is nod. Because what is there to say? It's yet another reason why Raff's the perfect man for me – he *literally* stood by me as I faced my past.

No, he didn't just stand by me; he held me up.

I exhale slowly and direct my eyes back to the mirror. I grab a tube of lip gloss and run the wand over my lips, smacking them together. Then I squeeze out a dollop of hair product, rub my palms together, then run my hands over the loose curls I barrel-tonged earlier.

When I look back at Mom and Issy, they're still watching me, empathy practically oozing from their pores.

'*Stop*, I'm fine,' I say emphatically. 'Let's just get over there, do Aunt Christine's bidding, wish the bride and groom a happy life, then get drunk at the reception. Okay?'

I leave before they can answer. In my old room, I pop the lip gloss into my clutch, step into my heels, and head downstairs to see if Raff needs my help.

'Fuck, fuck, fuck, fuck, fuck.'

'Everything okay?' I ask, eyeing Raff sympathetically. It's not that he never swears, but he's almost always unflappable. This is not him being unflappable.

'Fine,' he replies curtly, frowning at a petal-thin fondant snowflake. He places it on the cake and it falls off. 'Fuck.' He tuts at himself, then sighs.

'Any reason you're channelling Hugh Grant in *Four Weddings*?'

'I don't have the equipment I'm used to and unless I make another batch of sugar syrup, I can't get this final snowflake to stick.'

'Give it.'

I hold out my hand and he places the delicate snowflake in my palm. Then I walk over to the trash can and throw it out.

'Gaby!'

'What? You already have dozens of snowflakes – *that are attached*. Fuck the one that wouldn't play ball.'

'But now I have to smooth out the icing where I've made a mess.'

He frowns intently at the cake, then picks up a palette knife. I walk back to him and take it out of his hand.

'Raff,' I say softly. 'The cake is *gorgeous*. And it'll be even more so when we add the flowers, including the one that will go right here.' I point to the spot where the snowflake was supposed to go. 'You weren't this flustered when you were baking on national TV. What's going on?'

He looks into my eyes, his gaze intense.

'I want it to be perfect. It's one thing making a cake that only the crew is going to eat – and honestly, they'll eat practically anything – but this is my first cake for a real occasion. And your family has been *so* wonderful. This is already the best Christmas I've ever had.'

'But what about your Christmases with CiCi and Devin?'

'They're lovely, of course, and they've always gone above and beyond to make me feel wanted – *included*. But they've put so much of their life together on hold for me – it's *their* time now.'

'I get that,' I say – not from personal experience, but from what I know of Raff and his relationship with CiCi and Devin.

'But your family, Gabs... It's what I've always dreamed of.'

'You've always dreamed of complete chaos?' I ask, giving him my best I-don't-buy-it look.

'Are you joking? I love the chaos and the noise and the banter. How you all came together yesterday to solve a crisis. And last night was the *most* fun. I don't even care that I'm slightly hungover. Yours is *exactly* the type of family I wished for when I was a boy. And that's not to disparage CiCi and Devin – not at all – but especially yesterday, with everyone here, I felt like I was part of something... I don't know... *vibrant* and real and messy and...' He holds up his hands as if he's trying to materialise whatever it is from thin air. '*Wonderful.* I'm like the little English waif in a Christmas story, taken in by the boisterous American family and ensconced in familial love.'

'That's... that's how you see us?'

'Absolutely. Even before we came here and you were telling me about them. There's clearly a lot of love between you all – even with your Aunt Christine.'

'Yeah, she's a lot, but she's ours,' I joke, and he sniggers softly.

He turns serious again. 'And *you*, Gabs... seeing you in your element, taking charge like that – how you got everyone on task and handled your aunt and assured Monica and Brian that everything was going to be all right. I seriously doubt this wedding would be going ahead if it weren't for you. *You* were the glue. You brought everyone together, then led them to victory.'

I chuckle, giving him a half-smile and narrowed eyes. 'Victory?'

He shrugs, smirking self-deprecatingly at his own effusive outburst. 'You know what I mean. That's why I want this cake to be the best one I've ever made. For your family. For *you*.'

The way he's looking at me right now, with so much tenderness, I want to throw my arms around his neck and kiss him.

I settle for a hug, which he returns in a brotherly way. 'It's already the best cake you've ever made, Raff, because you made it with love,' I say, my cheek pressed against his chest. I release him and peer up through my lashes. 'Okay, that was so cheesy, Mom could make a sandwich out of it.'

'Don't remind me. They were so delicious, I had four.'

'*Four?* What are you, a teenage boy home from football practice?'

'I'm not sure I understand that one.'

'Yeah, me neither. Never mind. Good thing I have other skills, right?'

'Yes. I doubt you'll be offered a comedy special any time soon,' he quips.

'Yeah, yeah – now who's not funny?'

I survey the cake, which really is gorgeous, but is still in two parts. 'So, I'm guessing you're waiting on Dad with the pieces of doweling? Then what?'

'Then I clean them off, insert them in here' – he points to the bottom tier – 'lay this disc of card down, and place the second tier on top. Without messing up the icing or losing any decorations.'

'Right, so just the most stressful part to go?'

'Mmm.' He frowns, regarding his not-quite-done-masterpiece.

'Here, here,' says Dad, rushing in from the garage. You'd think he was carrying the holy grail with how much reverence he places those little round bits of wood onto the countertop.

'Precisely what I needed. *Thank* you, Roland.'

'You're welcome, son. Now I'd better get dressed for the wedding, or I'll be in the doghouse.' He leaves the kitchen and jogs up the stairs.

I'm not sure why he said that. Mom and Dad don't have the kind of marriage where he 'gets into trouble' with Mom. She isn't the boss of him the way Aunt Christine is with Uncle Marv. I'm also not loving this new thing where he calls Raff 'son'. Too close to home.

'*And* done.'

'What?' I've been in my head again and I missed it.

Sitting on the counter in front of a beaming Raff is an abso-

lutely gorgeous, two-tiered, Christmas-themed wedding cake decorated in white and silver. And when we get to Aunt Christine and
Uncle Marv's, Raff will add two dozen white miniature roses,
completing the design.

'Seriously, how did you do that so quickly? I thought you'd need
help.'

'Not to be rude, Gabs, but having you help with something like
this...?' He shakes his head. 'Besides, it's the most stressful part but
it's quick.'

'One of those if-you-overthink-it-you'll-mess-it-up things?'

'Precisely.'

'Well, bravo, and Monica and Brian are going to love it.'

He beams at me.

'But *please* go and get into that sexy new suit of yours, or we'll be
late.'

Shit, did I just say 'sexy'?

Raff's brows lift and so do the corners of his mouth. 'Why, Ms
Rivera, I didn't know you felt that way,' he teases.

Fuck, fuck, fuck, fuck.

'It's a nice suit,' I reply, my chin lifted. 'Kudos to your stylist.'

Something flickers across his face, but I can't discern what it
means. 'Well, my suit thanks you.' Our eyes lock. 'And you look
beautiful, by the way. I should have told you when you first came
in, but I was too far up my arse fretting about finishing a certain
cake.'

There's that self-deprecation again, but that's not what's making
my jaw hang loose. Raff told me I look beautiful. He's never said
that before – nice, lovely, pretty... But never beautiful.

I remain speechless, rooted to the spot, but Raff either doesn't
notice or decides not to make anything of it.

'And on the subject of the cake...' he says, going to the pantry
and taking out the plastic wrap. I watch, amazed, as he makes a

plastic dome around the cake, the sort of baker's trick you might see on an Instagram reel. Then he flashes me a grin and says, 'Back down in a jiffy wearing my sexy suit.'

Fucking fuckety fuck.

I think Raff and I were just flirting.

31

GABY

The time between arriving at Aunt Christine and Uncle Marv's and the ceremony zips by at the speed of light. Channelling my inner wedding planner, a new-found set of skills I'll be happy to shelve after today, I've barely had time to catch my breath.

Any time I hear, 'You'll need to check with Gaby', I beeline in the direction of the voice and issue a (gentle) command, make a decision, or give praise. Never underestimate how much adults love being told they've done a good job.

At T-minus thirty minutes, I go up to Monica's room to check on the bride. 'It's only me,' I say, knocking on the door as I open it. 'Oh, *Monica*,' I sigh, taking in the sight of my cousin in all her bridal glory.

She's standing by the window, her hair in an elaborate up-do, her makeup flawless, and wearing the most gorgeous bias-cut, fish-tailed, ivory-silk gown I've ever seen.

If she were in a romcom, this shot would be on the poster. She is a *stunning* bride.

'Aww, thank you, Gaby,' she drawls – underneath it all, still *her*.

'Not bad, huh?' says her maid of honour and best friend, Nicole.

I've known Nicole since she was a sassy ten-year-old. Now she's a sassy twenty-six-year-old with a degree in aeronautical engineering who moonlights as a makeup artist.

She circles Monica with a critical eye once more, then flashes me a smile. 'You know, my kit's still out if you'd like a touch-up,' she says, nodding towards the en suite.

'Oh.' My gaze swings to the floor-length mirror by the bed. I don't look *bad*, but it was probably naïve of me to do my makeup and expect it to still be in place hours later. 'If you're sure you have time,' I reply.

'Always time for touch-ups,' she says, directing me into the bathroom where – ironically – she tells me to sit on the toilet, reminding me of Mom.

I'm really going to miss her when we go – *and* Dad. It's now the part of the trip where the reality of departing begins to intrude on the joy of being here.

Issy might be feeling that too – the back-to-real-life feeling. Although, it's unclear when she's planning on going home to face the music. As far as I can tell, Jon is still calling several times a day and she's still avoiding him.

And I can hardly compare my real life with hers. I've got a new role and close friends and a city I love to go back to. She has Douchebag and an impending divorce.

'So, who's that smoking-hot guy you brought as your date?' asks Nicole.

For a split-second, I don't know who she's talking about, but then I do. Raff – who *is* looking particularly sexy today. And it's not just the suit. He's styled his hair the way he was shown and because we had such a frantic morning, he didn't shave today. The stubble makes him look edgier and even more handsome.

I don't answer right away, so Monica does for me. 'That's Raff, Gaby's best friend. They're not-so-secretly in love with each other but pretending not to be. The rest of us are waiting on a Christmas miracle.'

I stare at her, gobsmacked.

'Even Brian said so,' she adds smugly.

'Don't you have something *bridal* to do?' I ask her, my eyes narrowed.

'Nup.' She holds her arms out. 'I'm fully bride-ified. Besides, if I go out there before Dad comes to walk me down the aisle, Mom will...' She flaps her hand. 'You know... be *Mom*.'

'True,' I say, even though there's not really an aisle. They'll be married on the first landing of the staircase while we all look on from the outrageously large foyer.

'So, what's stopping you?' Nicole asks me, recapturing my attention.

'He's met someone,' I reply.

Nicole lifts my chin with her forefinger and scrutinises her work. She picks up another brush and blends along my cheekbones.

'And where's she, the gal he's dating?'

'*She* is in St Moritz, skiing with her rich-as-fuck parents and her hot fuckboy of a brother.'

Nicole blinks at me and steps back, then trades a look with Monica before her eyes land back on me.

'Later, when we're drunk, I want to hear how you know the hot brother is a fuckboy, but for now, I'll say this: she's there and you're here. If he wanted to be with her, he'd be with her. But he's not.'

'Because he's here,' Monica chimes in.

'Did you two rehearse this? Is this a shitty wedding version of *Who's on First*?'

'You're being evasive,' says Monica, her brows arched.

I exhale loudly through my nose and look up at Nicole, then circle my face with a finger. 'How's this? All done?'

'All done,' she says with a self-satisfied smile. She spins me around by my knees to face the mirror. 'Now you're as hot as your non-boyfriend.'

'Hotter,' says the bride.

I'm about to protest, but a laugh tumbles out of my mouth instead. 'Okay, okay,' I say, standing and smoothing out my silk slip dress.

I angle my face in the mirror, checking out Nicole's incredible work. In a matter of minutes, she has evened out my complexion, given me a smoky eye, and made my cheekbones pop. I tousle my hair, zhuzhing it to give it more of a sexy, bed-hair look.

I'll admit it: compared with how I normally look, I *am* hot.

I pull my shoulders back and lift my chin, meeting my own gaze steadily in the mirror. I may not be a tall, buxom heiress but I've got professional-level makeup, a good hair day, and proximity on my side.

Raff had better look out. I may give my family that Christmas miracle after all.

* * *

The ceremony was short and (very) sweet, which made many guests dab at their eyes with tissues and Aunt Christine keen as if she were at a funeral.

Immediately after the bride and groom kissed, I switched back into wedding-planner mode, ably assisted by Issy. Now the formal photos have been taken, the buffet's been served, and enough wine has been poured that the makeshift dancefloor is wall-to-wall people dancing to Maroon 5's 'Moves Like Jagger' – including Dad, who (sadly) dances *exactly* like Mick Jagger. You wouldn't know from his freestyle moves that the man's salsa skills are next level.

I watch the dancefloor for a few more moments, loving seeing everyone enjoying themselves, then seek out Raff. It's been go, go, go since we got here and he and I keep missing each other.

He's in the den chatting with a co-worker of Monica's I met earlier, a plucky, round-faced girl with a lithe dancer's body and a lusty look on her face. She's twirling a lock of her hair with one hand and touching Raff's forearm with the other. Everything about her screams, 'Let's get out of here and get naked.'

Before the night of the Forty Under Forty party, I would never have considered myself a jealous person. Now, envy seems to have made itself at home. I should start charging it rent.

'Hey, guys,' I say – casual, friendly, *breezy*.

Dancer gal, whose name I've forgotten, glowers at me. I'm clearly cutting her grass, but she doesn't know she's third in line behind me.

'Hello, Gabs,' says Raff, leaning down to kiss my cheek. His breath smells like toasted honey, which must be from the sparkling wine – his glass is almost empty. 'I was just telling—' He stops short. 'I'm so sorry, I've forgotten your name.'

Dancer gal does *not* like that. She looks between us, frowning, and says, 'It's Heidi.'

'Sorry, *Heidi*,' continues Raff, seemingly none the wiser that she's calculating how to extricate herself from this conversation. 'Anyway, I was telling Heidi here about how you practically pulled off this entire wedding by yours—'

'Excuse me,' says Heidi, interrupting. 'I need the bathroom.'

She pushes past me, huffing as she leaves.

'That was a bit rude,' says Raff, looking perplexed. He seriously has no idea.

'Come on, you beautiful idiot,' I say, taking his hand. 'I want to dance.'

'All right, but why am I an idiot?' he asks, trailing behind me.

* * *

One dance turns into five – Raff may be sexy, but there's room for improvement on his dancing skills – and then the DJ announces that it's time to cut the cake.

Two of the college-student waiters wheel it in on a butcher's block they appropriated from the kitchen, draped in a white tablecloth.

There's a chorus of ooh from the wedding guests, which isn't surprising. It's *spectacular*, especially now the roses have been added, and with the way the silver glitter and edible paint picks up the light, it looks luminescent.

'Before we cut the cake,' says Brian, stepping forward, Monica's hand resting on the crook of his arm, 'my wife and I' – the ooh turns into an aww and the newlyweds beam at each other – 'would like to thank a few people...'

He mentions his parents, who only made it to Seattle a few hours ago and appear weary but happy, and his brother who arrived late last night from Idaho to be his best man. He also gives a special mention to Bear, who was an admirable stand-in ring bearer. Bear lifts his head at the sound of his name, dropping it back onto his paws when he realises there's no treat on offer, sending a ripple of laughter around the room.

Brian then gives a shout-out to my parents and Issy for their help yesterday and this morning, and profusely thanks Aunt Christine and Uncle Marv for being such wonderful, generous in-laws and for welcoming him into their family.

'Now I can say I have parents in Wichita *and* Seattle.'

'Oh!' Aunt Christine howls. She buries her head into Uncle Marv's shoulder, breaking into another bout of sobbing, and he pats her on the back.

'And my turn,' says Monica. She turns to Nicole and gives a

speech about friendship and how having Nicole as a friend is like having a sister. 'Ditto, queen,' Nicole replies, blotting under her eyes with the pads of her ring fingers.

'And to two very special people,' says Monica, 'one I've known my whole life and one I've only just met but already love... To my cousin, Gaby – we absolutely would *not* be here today if you hadn't taken over and bossed us around and made this wedding happen. You really gave Seattle weather the finger and I love you to death.'

I grin and blow her a kiss as laughter fills the room.

'And to Raff – in just a few days, you've become part of our family. You are such a great guy and, seriously, this cake is *beyond*. It's absolutely gorgeous, and we know it's going to be delicious. We're both *so* grateful.'

I look up at Raff and our eyes meet, both of us swelling with pride, but also basking in the intense love and gratitude coming our way.

But Monica isn't finished.

'We are *so* glad Gaby brought you into our lives,' she says. 'And if everyone could please raise your glasses... To Gaby and Raff.'

'To Gaby and Raff,' forty-five people say together.

Then the room shifts off-kilter and I suddenly feel queasy.

Why did she phrase it like that? That I 'brought Raff into their lives'. That makes it sound like I brought my boyfriend home to meet the family.

It was fine when she and Nicole were teasing me earlier because that was merely joking around, but she made it a toast. In front of *everyone*.

But didn't I start drinking the Kool-Aid too?

Standing in Monica's en suite, hadn't I looked myself in the eye and, bolstered by a smoky eye and assurances that everyone sees it – something between me and Raff – hadn't I told myself I would...

I would what?

What had I *actually* thought I would do?

Confess my love to him over the Dungeness crab cakes? Seduce him with my mediocre dance moves? There are professional dancers at this wedding!

Or did I think I'd slip under the comforter later tonight and wait for him to finish brushing his teeth?

Surprise, Raff! I'm naked, hopped up on wedding cake, and horny!

I am such a frigging idiot.

Well-wishers crowd around, patting me on the back and offering to buy me a drink – 'hilarious' when it's an open bar. I smile and say, 'Thank you,' a dozen times, edging towards the living room door so I can make my escape.

When I make it to the doorway, I take several deep, gulping breaths, then turn and scan the cavernous room. The music has resumed, with half the guests back to boogeying, and the other half spooning cake into their mouths, moaning in ecstasy and wearing oh-my-god-how-good-is-this-cake? expressions.

I spy Raff and – wouldn't you know it – *Heidi* has taken hold of his hand and is dragging him towards the centre of the dancefloor. I'd bet my left arm he still doesn't get that she's into him.

He starts off laughing, protesting weakly, but when she tries to place his hand on her hip, his countenance shifts dramatically. I can tell that he gets it now. He gets it, and Heidi is making him uncomfortable.

He steps away, his polite way of telling her to get lost, but she ignores his protests, tugging on his hand and gyrating like a classically trained exotic dancer.

Raff stands stock still, his eyes darting in all directions, panicked. *He's looking for an out*, I think, which is confirmed when his gaze meets mine and he mouths, 'Help.'

Help is on the way, Rafferty!

I charge back onto the dancefloor, mumbling apologies for jostling other guests as I go, and march right up to Raff.

'Hi, babe! Sorry to leave you all alone while I was in the bathroom,' I say loudly for Heidi's benefit.

She finally stops dancing, but did she just 'hey!' me, as if she has some claim on Raff? Wasn't she there for the part where my cousin made a speech and practically welcomed him to the family?

Well, screw you, Heidi!

I reach up and lock my hands behind Raff's neck and pull his head towards me, landing the kind of kiss that can only be described as a keep-your-hands-off-my-man kiss.

And the most surprising thing is not the eruption of whoops from inebriated wedding guests around us, nor the, 'You go, girl,' Issy shouts across the room, nor the blood rushing in my ears.

The most surprising thing is that Raff kisses me back.

32

GABY

I wake early the next morning – well before dawn, lying on my back as my eyes adjust to the dim light. Issy is snoring softly beside me, which happens when she drinks.

What the actual fuck did I do last night?

I try to catch hold of the moments leading up to me kissing Raff in the middle of the dancefloor – and him kissing me back – but they elude me. All that materialises are some static snapshots and blurry movement, like something out of a Christopher Nolan movie.

I kissed Raff.

And Raff kissed me back.

That is, until he came to his senses and sprang apart from me, staring at me wild-eyed, his mouth working but no sound coming out.

At some point in all that, Heidi left in a huff. Well, the room, not the wedding. By that time, there was a huge line for rides home with the snow chain brigade, which was being managed by Dad's friend, Dave, while he ate three pieces of wedding cake.

Issy snuffles and rolls onto her side, and I return to the here and now. Oh right, it's Christmas.

Merry fucking Christmas, Gaby.

How the hell am I supposed to face him? Or anyone in my family?

Here I am protesting from the mountain tops – well, from the top of Queen Anne hill – that Raff and I are just friends, and then I go and kiss him in front of everyone. At a wedding! At least I didn't catch the bouquet. That was Heidi. Frigging Heidi.

'What?' asks Issy, rolling over and squinting at me in the dim light.

Shit, I must have said that last part out loud.

'Nothing, go back to sleep.'

She props herself up, elbow on the mattress, cheek in her hand. 'I'm awake. Spill.'

With a sigh, I throw one arm over my head, colliding with the bed frame. 'Ow!' I whisper. 'Mother *fucker*.'

'Are you okay?'

I shake out my hand. 'Yeah – it stings though.'

'Yeah, I didn't mean your hand, you dork. I mean are *you* okay? About you and Raff?'

I look over and she's wearing her big-sister face. I miss that face. I miss Issy. Not right at this moment – because she's here – but there is something to be said for sisterly love. It's like bestie love on steroids.

'Shouldn't I be asking you that?' I retort.

'So, we're both a mess.'

I snigger. 'You're the mess. I'm just a little untidy.'

'Yeah, yeah...'

'You can talk to me, you know. All this shit with Raff aside, I'm, like, a real grown-up. I know stuff.'

'Like what stuff?' She gives me a dramatic side-eye, which I'm sure is supposed to make me laugh, but enough joking around.

'Like Jon is not good for you. He's only happy when he's big noting himself or putting you down. And I hate what that does to you, Is. We all do – me, Mom, Dad...'

'Then why didn't you say something?' she asks, her voice small and hoarse.

'Because you love him. And it would have hurt you.'

She sniffs and wipes under her nose with the back of her fingers. 'I get it. But I don't love him any more. I can't remember the last time I felt anything even *resembling* love towards that man.'

Referring to Jon as 'that man'... Even someone like me, without a long romantic history to point to, knows it's a marital death knell.

'You know why he didn't want to come up for Monica's wedding or have Christmas with Mom and Dad this year?'

I shake my head.

'One of his clients offered him the use of their condo in the Bahamas over the holidays and for him, that was a no-brainer. Why would we come to dreary old Seattle with my boring family when we could "vacay in paradise"?'

'Did he really say "vacay"?'

'What do you think?'

'And we're not boring! That Jenga tournament was intense.'

This teases out a weak smile that vanishes almost instantly.

'You're right, you know,' she continues. 'He does put me down – *constantly*. I'm boring and I never want to go anywhere. I'm stupid because I don't understand crypto, even though he doesn't either – not really. Oh, and I'm fat and unfashionable, which means I don't fit in with his real estate buddies or their perfect, Californian wiv—'

Her words give way to sobs and I reach for her, enfolding her in a tight embrace, and rocking her gently as I whisper that it will be okay.

Inside, I'm seething. If I ever see that man again, every ounce of hate I have for him for making my sister feel worthless – my beautiful, funny, kind, smart sister – will manifest in violence.

I can't say how long we stay like that, but eventually Issy stops crying and gets out of bed. 'I need to pee,' she says, disappearing into the bathroom. I hear the toilet flush, then the sink run.

If I know Issy, she's splashing water on her face, then looking in the mirror and telling herself to get a grip. She always was hard on herself, but when you add a verbally abusive husband into the mix, it must be impossible not to see yourself as 'less than'.

I sit up, tucking my knees into my chest, waiting for her to come back. Then something occurs to me.

She scuttles across the bedroom floor – it's chilly out from under the covers – and jumps back into bed, pulling the comforter up around her chin. I wait for her to snuggle in before telling her my idea.

'Hey, so you know Dad's friend, Dave?'

'Dave who drove us to Aunt Christine's and Uncle Marv's? Yeah. I mean, a little.'

'He's a divorce attorney – one of the most respected in Washington.'

'The guy in who looks like Dave Grohl, who ran the underground Uber network for the wedding?'

'Yeah. Don't get hung up on how he looks... He's a *divorce* attorney.'

Finally, she gets it. 'Oh. *Oh.* I don't know that... And I'm not saying I want...' Her eyes have gone wide – *and* wild.

'Issy, you've been the big sister all my life. Let me be the big sister now.'

'What do you mean?'

'I *mean* you left Jon days before Christmas, you're not taking his calls... You know you're not going back to him, so isn't a divorce the next logical step?'

'No, you're right. It's just... *divorce* – that word.' She shudders.

'Yeah. But you've got me and you've got Mom and Dad. We're here for you.'

'Thanks, sis. I'll think about it.'

Letting Issy 'think about' divorcing Douchebag is allowing her the space to recognise that it's what she already wants – *and* needs. Besides, there is no way my parents are going to let her go back to Jon without her knowing her options. I'm crossing all my digits that she'll be divorced by her birthday in October.

We're quiet for a moment, each in our own thoughts, then she nudges me with her knee.

'Wanna go see what Santa brought us?' she asks, taking me back to every Christmas in our childhood when Issy would come into my room and wake me up.

'Fuck yeah.'

* * *

Our Christmas stockings, including the latest addition with 'RAFF' embroidered on the collar, are stuffed to the gills, something 'Santa' would have done after we got home from the wedding and Issy, Raff, and I went to bed.

'How long do you think Mom and Dad are going to stay up late and play Santa for us?' asks Issy, her mouth filled with chocolate.

'Forever. Or at least until we give them grandchildren,' I reply as I unwrap a candy cane. 'Then they'll do it for our kids.'

'I thought I heard voices.'

Raff enters, sleep-rumpled and wearing PJs with reindeer on

them. I spent several nights in the same bed as him and he wasn't wearing those.

'Merry Christmas,' says Issy. 'And nice pyjamas.'

He looks down as if he's surprised by what he's wearing. 'Oh my god! Father Christmas must have brought them.'

'You dork,' I say.

He meets my eyes with a grin, making my heart flood with warmth. And that's not the only part of me that heats up, because that crooked smile and those green eyes watching me with an impish expression... they do things to me.

Issy goes to the fireplace and takes down Raff's stocking. 'Here,' she says, holding it out.

He comes further into the room, a look of astonished delight on his face. 'Oh, I hadn't expected...' he says to her. He looks to me and I nod at him encouragingly. 'Well, how lovely.'

He accepts the stocking with a grin, then brings it over to the sofa, sitting on the opposite end to me.

Right as he's about to dip his hand inside, he stops. 'Sorry, should we be waiting for your mum and dad?' he asks, looking between us.

'They won't be up for ages,' I reply.

'They always stay up really late,' Issy adds. 'It's their thing – stay up late on Christmas Eve, stuff the stockings, drink brandy...'

'Now we're older,' I say, 'they do this thing where they reminisce about each Christmas from our childhood, including which big present "Santa" brought us.'

'Remember the year of the Barbie Dream House?' asks Issy with a smirk.

'Ha-ha-ha!' I turn to Raff. 'You have never seen two little girls more excited about anything ever in the history of the world. What were we?' I ask Issy. 'Five and seven?'

'Yeah, that sounds about right. I'm pretty sure our squeals were so high, all the dogs in the neighbourhood went berserk.'

'We were pretty cute,' I say to Issy.

'Wait – so they still do that, stay up late on Christmas Eve?' Raff asks disbelievingly. 'Even after last night?'

Issy and I share a look.

'For sure,' says Issy. 'Why do you think Dad rounded us up at quarter to eleven? It was his exit strategy. Even if the wedding had gone ahead exactly as planned, I can guarantee he and Mom planned to be back here by eleven, then send us to bed, so they could have their traditional Christmas Eve, just the two of them.'

'It's their Christmas Eve date night,' I add, feeling a surge of love for my parents.

'Wowser,' he mutters to himself. 'My parents barely *speak* to each other. Talk about couple goals.'

Couple goals.

Like supporting each other through life changes and awkward situations? Like championing your partner's successes and being there to pick up the pieces when it all goes to shit? Like sharing in-jokes and having entire conversations simply by exchanging a look?

Like us, Raff?

'You still haven't looked in your stocking,' Issy says, gently admonishing him.

Issy bites the head off another chocolate Santa to punctuate her point, and I shake my head, dislodging my futile thoughts. I go back to my stocking, taking out trinkets and candy, and laughing at a magnet that says, 'In Seattle, we have two seasons: rainy and August.'

I look over at Raff, who's now delving into his stocking, each item he takes out making him smile with delight.

I love this man and last night, he kissed me back.

Now what?

* * *

Hours later, we're all in the living room wearing our ugliest Christmas sweaters – although, I'm still not sure Raff knows we're wearing ours ironically – surrounded by discarded Christmas wrapping. 'White Christmas' is (aptly) playing on the stereo and we're munching on rugelach, mince pies, and Christmas cookies, even though none of us can possibly be hungry after Dad's traditional Christmas brunch.

Actually, I may never be hungry again after that. Eggs, sausage, bacon, hashbrowns, grilled tomatoes – Dad's plate drowning in the hot sauce he gets sent in from Texas.

Right before we sat down to eat, Raff cracked a bottle of Champagne and when Mom had a sip, she declared it was too nice to make Mimosas from, so we had our juice on the side.

We're on the third bottle now and there are only two presents left under the tree – mine for Raff and his for me.

'I'm going next,' I say, getting up from the floor. I stamp my feet, which are seconds away from getting pins and needles, then retrieve a large, flat, gift-wrapped box and hand it to Raff. He accepts it with a curious smile, and I go back to my spot on the floor by the coffee table.

As we have with every gift – oohing and ahhing as the wrapping is peeled away – we all watch him remove the paper, then lift the lid on the box. The gift inside is wrapped in tissue paper with a gold sticker holding it in place, and he slides his finger underneath the sticker to release it. When he parts the tissue paper, revealing the gift, he gasps.

'Oh, Gabs,' he says in a whisper.

'What is it?' asks Issy.

I flick at glance at Mom, who helped me with the gift-wrapping, and she raises her eyebrows, giving me an excited smile.

Raff takes out a crisp, white jacket and holds it up in front of him.

'It's monogrammed chef's whites,' he says, his voice filled with wonder.

He sets it back in his lap, his long fingers running over the embroidered Baked to Perfection logo, under which is 'Rafferty Delaney'.

'The hat's in there too,' I say.

'Oh, really?' He digs deeper into the box and takes out a toque. 'Wowser.' He looks over at me. '*Thank* you.'

'Put it on!' says Issy.

'All right.' He stands and slips on the jacket and does up the buttons, then positions the hat on his head. I don't love a chef's hat, to be honest, but CiCi said they're not really worn while working – they're more for show. He'll wear the jacket, though, and he'll need four more – one for each workday – but I wanted to give him his first.

'How do I look?' he asks us, stretching his arms out and doing a slow turn.

'Like a pro,' says Dad.

'Like a pastry chef,' Mom replies.

'You look hot,' says Issy, and my head swivels sharply in her direction. She pretends not to notice that I'm glaring at her.

Raff laughs it off. 'Well, I'm not sure about that, but it certainly makes it feel real,' he says with a nervous laugh. He turns to me, suddenly earnest. 'Really, Gabs, thank you. It's brilliant.'

'You're welcome,' I say, ignoring the tummy flutters that penetrating look induces.

'Right, and now my gift for you...' He rushes over to the tree, still in his chef's whites, and comes back with a smallish box about the size a mobile phone comes in. I look up at him, confused. Did Raff buy me a new phone?

'Well, open it,' he says, still standing there.

Unlike he did, I tear the paper, revealing a white box without any branding. So not a phone then. I eye him curiously and he nods, prompting me to lift the lid. I do.

Inside are tightly packed cards and I use a nail to prise one free. It's a Global Reach business card and under my name is 'Marketing Director'.

Now I know how Raff felt a few minutes ago, seeing his name on his chef's jacket. It *does* make it feel real. But wait...

'You must have had these made before I landed the role.'

'Yes.'

'But...'

'I *knew* you'd get it, Gabs,' he says, his belief in me emanating from his eyes. 'All I had to hope for was that Claire would break the news before Christmas.'

'Wow, that's... *Thank* you, Raff.'

'That is so sweet,' says Issy. 'Your gifts to each other – they're, like, the same.'

Raff and I look at her, then back to each other, and share a grin. Because Issy's right. These gifts both say, 'I believe in you.'

'Hold on... what if didn't get the job? Or what if Claire hadn't told me before Christmas? What would you have given me then?'

'A rather boring cashmere jumper.'

'Is it here?' I ask.

'In Seattle? Yes.'

I raise my brows and blink at him slowly, making him laugh. 'How about I give it to you on your birthday?'

'Her birthday's in June,' interjects Issy.

'All right, yes, fair point. I'll go up and get i—' Raff's phone chimes with a text notification. 'Hang on, this could be Aunt CiCi and Uncle Devin.'

He slips his phone out of his pocket to check, and I look down at my new business card.

Gabriela Rivera
Marketing Director
Luxury Brands Division
Global Reach

It's kind of an old-school gift – well, it would be if we worked in Seattle – but people in London still exchange business cards. And even if they didn't, it's the gesture that counts – a manifestation of Raff's belief in me.

'Um... would you please excuse me?' says Raff. 'I should...'

When I glance up at him, he suddenly seems very uncomfortable.

'Is everything all right?' Mom asks.

'Yes,' he says with a fake smile. He waves his phone. 'It's not them but...'

'Oh, is it your parents?' I ask, concerned.

I wouldn't put it past them, doing their 'parental duty' of wishing their only child a Merry Christmas, not realising – or caring – the impact the intrusion will have. Raff has gone from elated to deflated in mere seconds.

'No. Umm... it's Jules.' He fake smiles again. 'I won't be long,' he says.

When he leaves the room, unease snakes through my veins, making me shiver.

Not only was he uncomfortable when that message came in, but he called her 'Jules'. He's given her a nickname. A Raff nickname.

GABY

Ignoring the concerned looks from my family – especially Mom and Issy, who know how I feel about Raff – I get up and go into the entry, where I put on my boots, coat, and gloves. Issy is hot on my heels.

'Are you going somewhere?'

'I need to... be somewhere else – anywhere else.'

'I'll come with you.'

'No, it's okay, Is. I want to be alone.'

'It might not mean anything,' she says. 'It's just a text message. And he kissed you back last night. I saw it. We *all* saw it. He's probably telling her it's over.'

'He called her "Jules", Issy. Raff only gives his girlfriends a nickname when he's serious about them. When Winnie became "Wins", that's when Freya and I knew for sure that she was sticking around.'

'That doesn't mean anything,' she says dismissively. 'He calls you "Gabs".'

'Exactly.'

She frowns, confused. 'I don't get it.'

'It doesn't matter,' I say, not wanting to explain something so frigging obvious. 'I'm going for a walk. I need to clear my head.'

'Okay, fine, but here.' She thrusts a beanie at me and I tug it on, then leave.

At first, I don't know where I'm going but then it comes to me, and I head towards West Highland Drive. It stopped snowing overnight, but everything is still blanketed – roofs, lawns, shrubs and bushes, cars... The snow is melting on the street itself, now a translucent, milky white, but the sidewalks are covered in white, a few sets of footprints, including children's, the only indication that people have been out.

Ahead, outside a blue and white house, a father makes a valiant effort at helping his child ride their new bike on the shovelled driveway. He lifts his hand and says, 'Merry Christmas.'

'Merry Christmas,' his child echoes, only they're missing their front teeth, so it comes out as 'Cwrithmath'. *Cute.*

I stop at the end of their driveway. 'Merry Christmas,' I say. 'Did Santa bring you a bike?'

They nod at me, wide-eyed and flashing that toothless grin.

'Well, you must have been *very* good this year.'

'I was! Wasn't I, Daddy?'

Daddy concurs, sending me a knowing smile.

'Were you good this year?' the child asks me.

'Mostly.'

'What did Santa bring you?'

Santa brought me my dream job and precious time with my family and freedom for my sister from a bad marriage and the realisation that I may have the best friend in the world, but that's all he will ever be to me.

'A sweater,' I reply, and they scrunch up their nose at what is clearly a lame present. 'Well, I'll let you get back to riding your bike. You're already *really* good at it,' I say, and they puff out their chest with pride.

'Thanks,' says their dad with a wave.

I keep walking as a question goes around my mind on a loop: how can Raff and I remain best friends when I'm in love with him and he wants someone else?

By the time I get to Kerry Park, there's a break in the clouds and actual sun shines down on me. An older couple is sitting on one of the benches, and there's a guy with a Shih Tzu that's wandering around off lead while he scrolls on his phone.

I cross to the wall and dust off some snow so I can sit, swinging my legs over the edge and looking out at my beautiful hometown.

And that's the crucial distinction. Seattle is my hometown, but London is home.

Not too long ago, I wondered what it would be like to move back here, but I now know it's not what I want. Sure, I'll feel home-sick from time to time, but after this past week, I can't imagine moving back. Because my life is there now. And I have so much to be excited about.

My thoughts return to Raff... Not so excited about how that's going to play out. But whatever happens, I'm not running back here. I'm not the same Gaby I was eight years ago, the girl who packed up her life to put as much distance as possible between her and the man who broke her heart.

Broke her heart...

Am I *really* heartbroken over Raff? Is that what this is? Can you feel the loss of something that was never yours to begin with?

'All right if I join you?'

Raff.

Of course it is. Not only can I manifest family members with my mind, but Raff as well. What a shitty superpower.

'Sure,' I reply, and he repeats my actions from a few minutes ago, sitting six inches away.

'I came downstairs and you'd left.'

'Just wanted some fresh air.'

'Right.' I can tell he's trying to figure out how to say something and it takes him two false starts to get there. 'Gabs, about last night—'

'Yeah, sorry about that,' I say, laughing it off.

'Sorry?' He isn't apologising; he's asking for further explanation.

Sure, Raff – happy to explain why I kissed you in front of everyone.

'It's just... She just seemed hell-bent on getting you onto the dancefloor, so... you know...'

I glance at him and he's clearly baffled, but I am *not* spelling it out for him – this is torture enough.

I expel a long sigh. 'So, how's Julia?' I ask, mentally slapping myself. I don't want to talk about the kiss, so I bring up his girl-friend? What the fuck is wrong with me?

'Er... good. She's good.'

'Good – *great.*'

He angles his body towards mine. 'Can I... Last night...'

I meet his eye. 'You know what, Raff? I really don't want to talk about it, okay? That girl wouldn't leave you alone and you needed my help and I'd had a couple of glasses of wine, so I kissed you. No big deal.'

I'm hurting him, I can tell from his wounded expression, but I can't see how any of what I've said is hurtful. I'm letting him off the hook.

'Right,' he says again – his go-to when something is anything but.

And I can tell he's not only hurt, he's also still confused. I make a split-second decision to spell it out.

'Seriously, Raff, you don't need to worry about me. *Yes*, I recently discovered that I have feelings for you, but I promise I'm content just to be your friend – your *best* friend. And I'm happy for you – *really*. I'm glad you've found someone, that Freya's plan worked.'

I recognise the instant the words are out of my mouth that I've gone too far, Raff's sharp inhale of breath proving me right.

'Look—'

'What do you mean Freya's plan worked? Wait, are you talking about *Julia*?'

'Don't you mean *Jules*?'

It's a ridiculous and unnecessary dig and it does nothing to make me feel better about how I'm handling this.

He huffs out another sigh, his jaw set with anger now. '*What?*'

I can't sit here any longer, so I swing my legs back over the wall and stand, then stare out at the view. In a feat of curious timing, the clouds have cleared enough to see the base of Mount Rainier.

'You called her "Jules",' I say, resigned that I'm in a nightmare of my own making – I may as well see it through. 'Back there at the house.'

'She asked me to – that's what her friends call her.'

Well, that was unexpected. 'Oh,' I say, nothing else coming to mind.

'Oh? A moment ago, that name seemed to carry a bit more weight than "oh".'

'Never mind,' I tell him. 'It doesn't matter.' Especially now it's moot.

'I will mind, thank you very much,' he says, getting up and rounding on me. I've only ever seen Raff this angry when he confronted CiCi about entering him in *Britain's Best Bakers* without his consent. It's unnerving having his anger directed at me, even if I deserve it.

'And what the bloody hell has Julia – or Jules or whatever you want to call her – got to do with Freya?'

Seriously? He still doesn't get it?

'You know, for someone so smart, you can be really dumb.' It's mean, but now *I'm* getting pissed off.

'I beg your pardon.'

'Yep – *dumb*. Julia was a set-up, Raff. That party – the one you were invited to last minute – that was so you could meet her. You'd already passed on Jane and Ava, so Julia was Plan C.'

'Who the hell are Jane and Ava?' he asks, throwing up his hands.

'The talkative one from the food safety course and the gal at the day spa. Those were set-ups.'

'They were not. They couldn't have been. *How?*'

'Come on, *seriously*? You know Freya. Did you *really* think you could give her the okay to match you' – he tries to interrupt me, but I continue – 'what she *perceived* as the okay to match you, and she wasn't going to run with it? And you told her "no dates", remember, so we had to get creative.'

'We?'

'Oh, yeah. The second we left CiCi and Devin's that day, she roped me into her little scheme, and it was full steam a-fucking-head.'

It finally seems to be sinking in, and he stares hard at the ground, then sits heavily on the wall.

'And so, Julia...' He lifts his head and looks at me questioningly.

'Julia was "third try lucky". All we had to do was get you to the party, then she would come over and introduce herself.'

'So, *she* was in on it?' he asks, unravelling yet another layer of deception.

I nod.

'I see,' he says – his other go-to understatement when everything's gone to shit. His gaze goes back to the ground, several emotions traversing his face in mere seconds.

'I suppose that explains a few things,' he says, but it's unclear if he's speaking to me or himself.

'Like what?' I ask softly, the fight ebbing out of me.

I go to his side and sit, taking his hand. He places his other hand on mine, letting me in. He must have run out of steam too.

'Oh, you know... certain things she'd say. Slip-ups, I suppose. It doesn't matter, though. It was never going to work, anyway.'

'What?' Now it's my turn to be surprised.

'We're too different. We want different things. She's old money and privilege and... too much like my parents' set, if I'm honest.'

His thumb moves slowly against the back of my hand, as 'whys' whiz through my mind.

Why did he keep dating her?

Why all the texts and video calls since we arrived in Seattle?

Why did he suggest we all get together for a frigging games night when we're back in London?

But that's where the line between 'best friend' and 'wannabe girlfriend' gets blurry.

Which Gaby wants answers the most?

I admit to myself that it's the latter, which is why I keep quiet. Raff needs his best friend right now – and if that's all I'll ever be to him, then so be it.

I don't want to lose him. I *can't* lose him.

'On reflection, I only went out with her because I was flattered that someone like Julia would be interested in me. I'm not proud to say this, but it was an ego boost of sorts.'

Ahh – someone like Julia. A tall, buxom, beautiful blonde with a fuck-tonne of money. The opposite of me.

And then out pops the question of a wannabe girlfriend. 'What do you mean by "someone like Julia"?'

'Flashy. Larger-than-life. *Famous* – and proper famous, not like I was for about fifteen minutes, but world-renowned. It was an intoxicating mix to begin with, but it's been wearing off.'

'So, why keep dating her then?' Another question I probably shouldn't be asking.

'You make it sound like she was my girlfriend,' he says with a dry laugh. 'We only went out a couple of times – I haven't even kissed her.'

He hasn't kissed her?! My heart starts thumping even harder as the realisation hits. Raff hasn't kissed Julia, but he *has* kissed me.

'And, yes, she was fun enough to talk to, and she's a very interesting person in some respects, but she's not right for me – as a girlfriend, I mean.'

'She isn't?' I ask, my eyes fixed on his face.

'Well, no. And I decided that when I got back to London, I'd tell her we could only be friends. Only after this morning, I didn't want to wait. When she messaged just now, I called her and told her it wasn't going to work out.'

'You did?'

'Course,' he replies with a gentle smile. 'She's not who I want.'

'So, who do you want?' I ask, my voice barely above a whisper. Hope perches on one shoulder cheering me on, while dread plonks itself on the other telling me not to be ridiculous.

He angles towards me, his grasp on my hand tightening.

'I want to be with someone who shares my view on life – that family, including those we *choose* as our family, are *the* most important people – that "home" is a feeling, rather than a place – that being there for our loved ones when they need us fills us up inside.'

He shifts closer, our thighs now pressed together.

'And I want someone who understands that to make a dream come true, you have to work hard at it – not have it handed to you, like...'

His voice fades away, but I can tell he's referring to Julia.

'Anyway,' he continues, 'I know I really can't talk as I'm about to work for my aunt—'

'Hey, you *earned* that. You've worked extremely hard to become the baker you are – *you're* an artist, Raff. You're talented, yes, but talent means nothing if you don't apply yourself to develop and hone it.'

'And that right there...' He gazes deep into my eyes, his eyes creased at the corners and glossing with tears. 'I want to be with someone who knows precisely what to get me for Christmas – a gift that tells me they see me, they believe in me, they can imagine my future and that it's brighter than I could ever, *ever* have dreamt.'

I gulp, not trusting my voice and transfixed by those beautiful green eyes.

He lifts his hand and lightly trails his fingertips down my cheek. If this isn't a scene right out of a Hallmark movie...

'I'm sorry it took me so long to see it – and I promise it *had* occurred to me before you kissed me on the dance floor last night – right after we ran into your ex, as a matter of fact – but never mind all that...'

He shakes his head, then meets my eyes again, drawing in a slow breath. 'It's you I want, Gabs. I want you.'

He wants me. Raff wants *me*.

My breath hitches. This feels like one of those surreal scenes in a movie where the camera tracks out while the focus zooms in.

'And just to backtrack a few moments...' he says, his mouth quirking. 'You mentioned you recently had a similar realisation?'

'I kept trying to talk myself out of it,' I say, finally finding my voice. 'I told myself that you were with Julia now and I needed to see how that played out. At least that's the advice I got from Freya.'

There's a flicker of something in his eyes – shock? – then it turns to something harder – irritation maybe. 'She is quite the little puppet master, isn't she?'

'Please don't be mad at Freya. She only wanted you to be happy – *wants* you to be happy.'

'Right. Only, it's a lot to process right now.'

'I get it. You have no idea how many times I wanted to tell you and—'

He leans close, stopping my words with a kiss.

It begins softly, his lips pressed against mine in a 'shh' of a kiss, and before I can draw back, his lips capture mine possessively. I succumb, melting into him, drowning in sensations.

With my free hand, I grasp the back of his neck and our mouths move together, hungry, curious, excited, yet with an undercurrent of familiarity. He tastes of vanilla and cinnamon and nutmeg, of the dry toastiness of the Champagne. His hand finds the nape of my neck, his fingers tangling in my hair as the kiss deepens, the tip of his tongue sending an electrical current coursing through me, heating me up from the inside out.

I can't say how much time passes. Or at what point the kiss slows. Or who draws back first. But eventually, we pause, our lips almost touching, and when I open my eyes, he's regarding me with wonder.

He leans his forehead against mine, and our eyes lock as our breaths mingle in the air between us.

This is Raff – the funny, affable, thoughtful guy, my closest friend and ally, my champion, my *person*. And I'm overcome with how much I love him – all of him, who he is and who he will be. Who we will be together.

I sigh contentedly.

'Gabs?' he says, his voice raspy.

'Mmm?'

'Can we go back now? My bum is frozen to this wall.'

'You dork. Way to ruin the moment.'

He grins, drawing me in for a quick kiss. 'I love it when you call me that. It's so sexy.'

I get up. 'Come on, dork. There are people at home who will be *dying* to hear our news. And Freya. *And* Poppy.'

He stands, placing a guiding hand on my lower back, but stops. 'Wait – Poppy?' It's laughable watching him make the connection, the one I was worried about only a couple of days ago. 'Ahh, so Poppy was my matchmaker.'

'Yep.'

'Well, she wasn't very good at it,' he quips.

'Please never tell her that – I like Poppy. Besides, she's better than you think.'

'How so?'

'Because she had me pegged from the get-go. And I'm only just realising this now,' I say as more pieces of the puzzle slot into place, 'but I'm pretty sure she had a hand in us getting together.'

'I'm not following.'

'It's a story for another time, Rafferty. Let's go home. I'm also freezing my butt off.'

'Come here first.'

He gathers me into an embrace and I wrap my arms around his waist, pressing my cheek to his chest, eyes closed and listening to his muffled heartbeat through his coat. Dreamily, I inhale deeply and open my eyes.

'Raff! Oh my god, look!' I say, springing apart from him.

He follows my gaze and there it is, Mount Rainier, snow-covered and majestic against a wintry, pale-blue sky.

'Fuck me, that *is* big.'

I laugh, and so does the guy with the dog.

'Come on.' I tug at his hand, and we begin the walk back to my parents' house.

EPILOGUE

SEPTEMBER THE FOLLOWING YEAR

'Do you see them?' I ask Raff. I'm standing on my tiptoes, peering around other people, but the crowd is too dense. I can't see who's coming through the doors at Arrivals.

'Not yet.' He tightens his grip on my shoulder.

'They landed an hour ago,' I say, impatient.

'I know. It's so bloody annoying how long it takes, especially for Americans.'

I look up at him and he's smirking at me. 'Are you teasing me?'

'I wouldn't dare.' He smacks a kiss on my head.

'And now you're patronising me,' I say, pretending to be annoyed.

'I would say *placating*, rather than— That's them! They're here.'

'Where? Where?'

'Come on.'

He takes my hand, leading me through the crowd, offering polite apologies as we go – typical Raff. When we reach the end of the walkway, there they are – Mom, Dad, and a newly divorced Issy.

'You're here!' I shout, my arms out wide.

Issy squeals and throws her arms around me, and I squeeze her back. I cannot *believe* my sister is moving to London!

'Great to see you, sweetheart,' says Dad. 'But we should...' He motions that we should get out of everyone's way.

'Good call, Dad,' I say, because everyone else is here for the exact same reason – to welcome loved ones.

Dad pushes the cart loaded with luggage – mostly Issy's, I'd say – and we find a small clearing thirty yards away, then go back to our reunion, Dad hugging Raff while Issy looks on, and Mom giving me a tight hug. She draws back, regarding me with tears in her eyes. 'You look beautiful.'

'Thanks, Mom. You too.'

'Liar. But give me a decent night's sleep, *then* tell me.' I snigger, and she leans closer. 'And you and Raff together...' she says, looking at him over my shoulder. 'I'm so happy for you, hun. It sounds like you two are making quite the life together.'

'I love it, Mom. I love *him*. I never realised it could be like this.'

She squeezes her eyes shut for a second, a huge smile on her face, as if she can't believe her luck. That makes two of us.

'Hi again, sweetheart,' says Dad.

'Hi, Dad. I missed you.'

'I missed you too.' He hugs me close, and my arms wrap around his middle. He kisses the side of my head before releasing me. 'It's gonna be hard with both you girls over here.'

'I know, but it's one plane ride now – not two – so you get to see both of us at once. And Issy needed this – a fresh start.'

'Well, that's true.'

'Plus, CiCi gets to add a communications whiz to the team.'

He smiles, but it's bittersweet and we both know it.

'Your mom and I are really proud – of both of you.'

'Thanks, Dad.'

Issy reaches for my hand, and I turn to her. 'So, you ready to see our new apartment?' I ask her.

'So ready.'

'You're going love it,' says Raff. 'It's even closer to mine than Gabs' old flat – lovely building, new kitchen and bathroom, leafy aspect...'

'Aren't you taking the baking world by storm? You sound like a real estate agent,' Issy teases.

'One should always have a back-up plan,' he says with a wink. 'Right, the car's this way, everyone,' he says, taking over the cart and leading the way.

As we walk out of the terminal towards CiCi's borrowed car, I look around me. I am so fortunate to have this much love in my life, to be here with my favourite people in the world. Mom and Dad are only staying for ten days to help Issy get settled and to visit me and Raff, but we are going to squeeze every precious moment out of that time.

And once Issy is settled, both in our apartment and her new role, I've promised to introduce her to Poppy. Because Issy deserves a happily ever after too.

ACKNOWLEDGEMENTS

When I met my partner, Ben, eighteen years ago on a sailing trip around the Greek Isles, he told me he wanted to live a bigger life. This resonated with me. I was feeling 'stuck', unable to pinpoint the reason for the constant yearning I felt.

We both knew it was impossible for us to be together – the ten-year age gap and the 15,000 kilometres between our hometowns were insurmountable hurdles. Until they weren't. Until we decided to make a life together – a bigger life – and I left Sydney to join him in Seattle.

Ah, Seattle...

We called it home for four years and it is a *beautiful* city. But even more beautiful than the city and surrounds are the people. We made lifelong friends while living there and when this book comes out, we will be there again – revisiting favourite haunts, basking in the wondrous natural beauty, but most importantly, reconnecting with loved ones. In many ways, this book is a love letter to Seattle – and to those people who made our time there so special.

But it's also about facing fears and living the bigger life, no matter what that might mean for those who read it. Which means it's primarily a love letter to Ben. Thank you, babe, for riding the highs and lows of writerly life with me, and for making publication days and all the mini milestones in between so special. And thank you for the bigger life we've created that lets me have the best job in the world.

Speaking of the best job in the world... This is my fourth book with Boldwood Books – my fourth!

As always, I'd like to thank my wonderful editor, Emily Yau, who has been a champion of this series – and its steward – from the start. And to Megan Haslam, thank you for your brilliant insight and for your clever ideas to really elevate this story.

Thank you also to the rest of the Boldwood team for your ongoing support and the care you take with publishing my books, especially Marcela Torres for being a marketing superstar, and Emily Reader and Jennifer Davies for lending your formidable editorial chops to *Someone Like You*.

Lina Langlee – my brilliant agent – can you believe this is our twelfth book together? As always, I greatly appreciate your unwavering support and guidance (and all those times when you indulge my writerly angst and show me a clear path forward). I am so excited for what's to come for us, and so grateful to have you in my corner!

To my author friends – so many of whom I've got to meet this year! – it is an honour and a privilege to be amongst you. Your work inspires me, it fills my heart, and it brings me joy. You are generous to a fault and so, so encouraging. Thank you for bolstering me when I've needed it. I love being part of this community.

To Nina, Andie, and Fi, my fellow Renegades, by the time this book comes out, I will have met you all in person! How brilliant is that? And there is so much to thank you for, these acknowledgements could easily be pages long. Just know that I love you, I admire you, and I wouldn't want to do this without you.

I am so fortunate to have the unwavering support of my beautiful family and dear friends. Thank you for believing in me – it makes my successes all the sweeter and my challenges easier to bear.

A big thank you to all the booklovers who have embraced my

stories. It thrills me to know that you love my books, and it makes me want to write many, many more.

I hope you enjoyed *Someone Like You*. See you soon for Book Five in the Ever After Agency series...

Sandy xxx

ABOUT THE AUTHOR

Sandy Barker is a bestselling romance author. She's lived in the UK, the US and Australia. She has travelled extensively across six continents, with many of her travel adventures finding homes in her books.

Sign up to Sandy Barker's mailing list for news, competitions and updates on future books.

Visit Sandy's website: www.sandybarker.com

Follow Sandy on social media here:

- facebook.com/sandybarkerauthor
- x.com/sandybarker
- instagram.com/sandybarkerauthor
- bookbub.com/profile/sandy-barker

ALSO BY SANDY BARKER

The Ever After Agency Series

Match Me If You Can

Shout Out to My Ex

The One That I Want

Someone Like You

LOVE NOTES

LOVE IN EVERY CHAPTER

WHERE ALL YOUR ROMANCE
DREAMS COME TRUE!

THE HOME OF BESTSELLING
ROMANCE AND WOMEN'S
FICTION

 WARNING:
MAY CONTAIN SPICE

SIGN UP TO OUR
NEWSLETTER

https://bit.ly/Lovenotesnews

Boldwood

Boldwood Books is an award-winning fiction publishing company seeking out the best stories from around the world.

Find out more at www.boldwoodbooks.com

Join our reader community for brilliant books, competitions and offers!

Follow us
@BoldwoodBooks
@TheBoldBookClub

Sign up to our weekly
deals newsletter

https://bit.ly/BoldwoodBNewsletter